W9-DJH-519

McGRAW-HILL's

CONQUERING SAT CRITICAL READING

McGRAW-HILL's

CONQUERING SAT CRITICAL READING

Second Edition

Nicholas Falletta

New York / Chicago / San Francisco / Lisbon / London / Madrid / Mexico City
Milan / New Delhi / San Juan / Seoul / Singapore / Sydney / Toronto

The McGraw·Hill Companies

McGRAW-HILL's Conquering SAT Critical Reading

Copyright © 2011 by The McGraw-Hill Companies, Inc. All rights reserved. Printed in the United States of America. Except as permitted under the United States Copyright Act of 1976, no part of this publication may be reproduced or distributed in any form or by any means, or stored in a database or retrieval system, without the prior written permission of the publisher.

1 2 3 4 5 6 7 8 9 10 11 12 13 14 15 QDB/QDB 1 9 8 7 6 5 4 3 2 1 0

ISBN 978-0-07-174878-0
MHID 0-07-174878-4

LIBRARY OF CONGRESS CONTROL NUMBER: 2010933210

Printed and bound by Quad/Graphics.

McGraw-Hill books are available at special quantity discounts to use as premiums and sales promotions or for use in corporate training programs. To contact a representative, please e-mail us at bulksales@mcgraw-hill.com.

SAT is a registered trademark of the College Entrance Examination Board, which was not involved in the production of, and does not endorse, this product.

CONTENTS

CHAPTER 1

ALL ABOUT TAKING THE SAT

Here are some frequently asked questions about the current SAT along with answers that are essential for your success when taking the test. This information and additional facts about the SAT test appear on the official College Board website at www.collegeboard.com.

WHAT IS THE SAT?

The Scholastic Assessment Test, or SAT, is a test of reading, writing, and mathematical skills that is required for admission to many colleges and universities. More than two million students have taken the SAT in a single year. The test, which takes 3 hours and 45 minutes, is divided into ten sections, as follows:

- Two Math sections of 25 minutes each
- One Math section of 20 minutes
- Two Critical Reading sections of 25 minutes each
- One Critical Reading section of 20 minutes
- One Multiple-Choice Writing section of 25 minutes
- One Multiple-Choice Writing section of 10 minutes
- One Essay section of 25 minutes
- One Critical Reading, Writing, or Math section of 25 minutes, consisting of experimental questions that will not be counted in your score

The table below gives an overview of the SAT.

Critical Reading	67 Questions 19 Sentence Completion 48 Passage-Based Reading	70 minutes 2 25-minute sections 1 20-minute section
Writing	49 Questions + Essay 18 Identifying Sentence Errors 25 Improving Sentences 6 Improving Paragraphs 1 Essay	60 minutes 2 25-minute sections 1 10-minute section
Math	54 Questions 44 Multiple-Choice 10 Grid-Ins	70 minutes 2 25-minute sections 1 20-minute section

DO I REALLY NEED TO TAKE THE SAT?

All 4-year colleges and universities evaluate student candidates based on several criteria. They all look at your past academic accomplishments—in other words, your high school grades. They also consider letters of recommendation, admission essays, and extracurricular activities. In addition, four out of every five institutions of higher learning also consider scores on a standardized test, and the SAT is the most frequently required test. So, the answer to this question is simple and essentially unchanged for decades. Your SAT score is a very important factor in gaining admission to many colleges and universities in the United States and throughout the world.

HOW IS THE SAT SCORED?

SAT scores are reported on a scale of 200–800 for each section of the test. About a month to 6 weeks after you take the test, you and the colleges you have applied to will receive a report that shows a separate score for Writing (W 200–800), Mathematics (M 200–800), and Critical Reading (CR 200–800). The total maximum score is 2,400.

The scores you receive are scaled scores. They are not the same as the number of questions you answered correctly on each test. Scaled scores are calculated by finding the number of questions you answered correctly, subtracting a fraction of the number you answered incorrectly, and then converting the resulting number to a number on a scale that takes into account how well you did compared to others who took the same test.

WHEN SHOULD I TAKE THE SAT?

The SAT is given on weekend dates spread throughout the academic year. To find out the test dates, visit the College Board website at www.collegeboard.com. If you are planning to apply for Early Decision, you should take the SAT at the end of your junior year in high school. If you plan to apply for regular admission, you should take the SAT in the fall of your senior year.

HOW DO I REGISTER TO TAKE THE SAT?

You can register to take the SAT at the College Board website; however, you will need to use a credit card to register online. Alternatively, you can register by mail using the form in the SAT Registration Bulletin, which is available in most high school guidance offices. After you register, you will receive an admission ticket. When you get the ticket, be sure to put in a safe place until test day.

WHAT SHOULD I BRING WITH ME ON TEST DAY?

The following items are essential to bring with you to the SAT testing site on the day of the examination.

- your SAT admission ticket
- a photo identification of some kind—for example, your school ID card or your driver's license
- several new and sharpened number 2 pencils
- a watch or small desk clock
- a calculator and some extra batteries
- bottled water or fruit juice
- a healthful snack for one of your breaks—for example, a protein bar or a box of raisins
- eyeglasses or contact lenses, as needed

WHAT DO THE SAT CRITICAL READING SECTIONS MEASURE?

The Critical Reading sections consist of Sentence Completion questions and passage-based reading questions. The Sentence Completion questions measure your knowledge of word meanings and your ability to understand the logical structure of a sentence. Passage-based reading questions test your ability to read and understand long and short reading stand-alone passages and paired passages from a variety of fields.

WHAT CAN I DO TO RAISE MY CRITICAL READING SCORE?

This book can help you raise your Critical Reading score. It will familiarize you with each type of question you will face on your test and provide detailed step-by-step instructions and strategies for answering each one. It will help you diagnose your weaknesses and then show you how to eliminate them. It provides just the insurance you need to guarantee that you will be prepared for whatever the SAT Critical Reading test may have in store for you. Be sure to use or adapt the SAT Fitness Plan presented in the next chapter. This plan presents many essential suggestions and helpful tips that will help you achieve your best on the SAT.

CHAPTER 2
PLANNING YOUR SAT TRAINING PROGRAM

This chapter will give you . . .

- tips for planning your SAT study program
- test-taking strategies to help you get higher scores
- hints for doing your best on the day of the test
- sample SAT study plans

When you take the SAT, you'll want to do everything you can to make sure you achieve your best and receive your best possible score. That means studying correctly and learning good test-taking strategies. Here are some tips to help you do your best.

STUDYING CORRECTLY

1. Study Every Day.

Contrary to what you may have heard, you can improve your SAT scores with study and practice. If possible, start your preparation at least 1 month before your exam. If you plan to use the 4-week SAT study plan, set aside 30 minutes 5 days a week for SAT practice. If you plan to use the 2-week study plan, you'll need to set aside 1 hour 5 days a week for SAT practice. Use the SAT Fitness Plans at the end of this chapter to help you identify what to study each day.

2. Study Without Distractions.

Clean off your desk or find yourself another clean, uncluttered spot to study. Turn off your radio, television, CD, and MP3 player. You'll find that you can think better without outside interference.

3. Get to Know the Format of the Test.

Use the practice tests in this book to familiarize yourself with the format of the Critical Reading test. That way you'll know exactly what to expect when you take the actual test, and you won't be faced with unexpected surprises on SAT day.

4. Get to Know the Test Directions.

If you are familiar with the test directions ahead of time, you won't have to waste precious test time reading them and trying to understand what is required of you. The directions used in the practice exams in this book are modeled on those you'll see on the actual Critical Reading Test. Learn them now, and reap the benefits later.

5. Learn to Pace Yourself.

Get used to the idea of moving quickly but carefully through each test. Use a timer to get a feel for just how long it takes you to complete each section. Work to get up to speed so you can answer as many questions as possible in the time allowed.

■ USING GOOD TEST-TAKING STRATEGIES

1. Answer All the Easy Questions First, Then Tackle the Harder Ones.

The Critical Reading Test consists of two question types: Sentence Completion Questions and Passage-Based Reading Questions. Because sentence completion questions involve a single sentence, they take much less time than reading questions. For this reason, you should always answer all the sentence completion questions first.

2. Use the Process of Elimination.

Remember that on any multiple-choice test, the answer is right in front of you. Try eliminating answer choices you know are incorrect. Often this will help you to select the correct answer.

3. Work Quickly and Steadily.

Recognize that you may not be able to answer every question on the test. When you realize that you are not making progress on a particular question, leave it and move on. DO NOT obsess over any question you cannot answer. If you have time at the end of a section, you can return to questions you skipped over and try to make an educated guess at the answer. However, you should know that you do not have to answer every question to get a good score on the SAT.

4. Make Educated Guesses.

Your score on the multiple-choice questions is based on the number of questions you answer correctly minus a percentage for incorrect answers. For every correct answer you get 1 point. For each incorrect answer one-quarter of a point is subtracted from your total. Blanks do not count at all. In other words, simply filling in answers will probably not earn you a better score. However, you can improve your score by making educated guesses. An educated guess is a guess you make after you have eliminated one or more answer choices as definitely incorrect. Each time you eliminate an answer choice, your chance of guessing correctly from the remaining choices goes up.

5. Pay Attention to the Answer Sheet.

Remember that the answer sheet is scored by a machine, so you have to mark it carefully. Fill in the answer ovals completely, erase thoroughly if you change your mind, and do not make any stray marks anywhere on the sheet. Also make sure that the answer space you are marking matches the number of the question you are answering. If you skip a question, make sure that you skip the corresponding space on the answer sheet. Check yourself every five to ten questions to make sure you are marking the right spot.

PREPARING YOURSELF FOR TEST DAY

Even when your studying is completed, there are still a few things you can do to make sure that all goes well on test day.

1. The Night Before

- Set out your clothes, pencils, watch, calculator, test admission ticket, picture ID, and any drinks or snacks you want to take with you. That way, you won't have to run around in the morning trying to collect all the things you need.
- Get to bed at a reasonable hour and try to get 8 hours of sleep. Believe it or not, a good night's sleep will probably do more for your score than a late-night study session the night before your test.

2. On Test Day

- Eat a good breakfast. You might want to consider having eggs or some other protein source that will stay with you longer than a doughnut or toast.
- Make sure you're awake. If you are not a "morning person," allow a few extra minutes for a short workout or jog to get your body moving at its full potential.
- Leave yourself plenty of time to get to the test center. Figure out in advance exactly how much time you need to get to the test center. Then add 20 minutes as a safety cushion. That way you can be sure to arrive on time and in control, instead of breathless and flustered.

CHOOSING YOUR SAT STUDY PLAN

Depending on how much time you have before you take the SAT exam, use either the "4-Week SAT Fitness Plan" or the "2-Week SAT Fitness Plan." Both plans involve the same amount of time spread out over different time periods.

4-Week SAT Fitness Plan

Week 1	Day 1	Read Chapters 1 and 2
	Day 2	Take Diagnostic Exam (Chapter 3)
	Day 3	Score Your Test
	Day 4	Analyze Results to Determine Strengths and Weaknesses
	Day 5	Study Explanations
Week 2	Day 1	Study Chapter 4
	Day 2	Take Practice Exam 1 (Chapter 6)
	Day 3	Score Your Test
	Day 4	Analyze Results
	Day 5	Study Explanations

Week 3	Day 1	Study Chapter 5
	Day 2	Take Practice Exam 2 (Chapter 7)
	Day 3	Score Your Test
	Day 4	Analyze Results
	Day 5	Study Explanations
Week 4	Day 1	Take Practice Exam 3 (Chapter 8)
	Day 2	Score Your Test Analyze Results Study Explanations
	Day 3	Take Practice Exam 4 (Chapter 9)
	Day 4	Score Your Test Analyze Results Study Explanations
	Day 5	Review Previous Exams

2-Week SAT Fitness Plan

Week 1	Day 1	Read Chapters 1 and 2 Take Diagnostic Exam (Chapter 3)
	Day 2	Score Your Test Analyze Results Study Explanations
	Day 3	Study Chapters 4 and 5
	Day 4	Take Practice Exam 1 (Chapter 6)
	Day 5	Score Your Test Analyze Results Study Explanations
Week 2	Day 1	Take Practice Exam 2 (Chapter 7)
	Day 2	Score Your Test Analyze Results Study Explanations
	Day 3	Take Practice Exam 3 or 4 (Chapter 8 or 9)
	Day 4	Score Your Test Analyze Results Study Explanations
	Day 5	Review Previous Exams

CHAPTER 3

DIAGNOSTIC SAT CRITICAL READING EXAM

The following pages present four full-length practice Critical Reading sections that will give you a very good idea of what the actual SAT is like. You will see samples of every type of Critical Reading question, and you will get to know what kinds of reading and language skills you'll need to get your best score.

Try to take this Diagnostic Exam under actual test conditions. Find a quiet place to work and set aside a period of approximately 1 hour and 10 minutes when you will not be disturbed. Work on only one section at a time, and use your watch or a timer to keep track of the time limits for each section. Mark your answers on the Answer Sheet, just as you will when you take the real exam.

At the end of the test you'll find an Answer Key and explanations for every question. After you check your answers against the Key, review the explanations, paying particular attention to the ones for the questions that you answered incorrectly.

Once you have worked your way through this practice exam, you will know how ready you are right now for actual SAT Critical Reading questions. You will also find out whether you are able to work fast enough to finish Critical Reading test sections within the time allowed, or whether you need to improve your test-taking speed. With the knowledge you gain, you'll be able to plan a preparation program that fits your needs.

ANSWER SHEET

Directions

- Remove this Answer Sheet from the book and use it to record your answers to this test.
- This test will require 1 hour and 10 minutes to complete. Take this test in one sitting.
- The times for each section are indicated at the start of the section. Sections 1 and 2 are each 25 minutes long, and Section 3 is 20 minutes long.
- Work on only one section at a time. If you finish a section before time has run out, check your work on that section only.

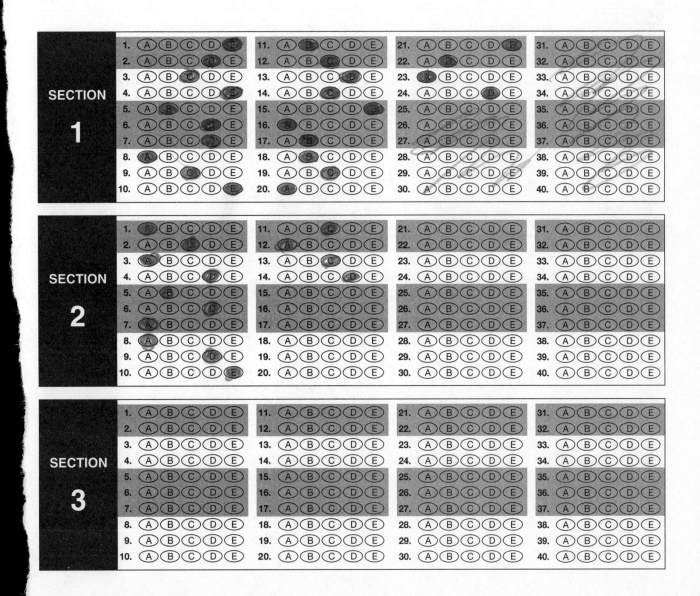

■ SECTION 1 QUESTIONS

Time—25 Minutes

24 Questions

Directions: This section consists of sentence completion questions and questions based on reading passages. For each question, select the answer you think is best and record your choice by filling in the corresponding oval on the answer sheet.

Directions: Each sentence below has one or two blanks. Each blank indicates that something is missing. Following each sentence are five words or sets of words labeled A, B, C, D, and E. You are to select the word or set of words that, when inserted in the sentence, best fits the meaning of the sentence as a whole.

EXAMPLE:

1. Despite our best efforts to protect the environment and keep it safe, until the problems of pollution are _____, the future of our environment seems, at best, _____.

    (A) created . . . gloomy
    (B) revoked . . . secure
    (C) solved . . . uncertain
    (D) replaced . . . revered
    (E) increased . . . unknown

    Correct Answer: C

1. After waiting patiently for an extraordinarily long period of time, the crowd was infuriated by the extreme _____ of the concise announcement that said simply, "Tonight's concert is cancelled."

    (A) coarseness
    (B) affluence
    (C) brevity
    (D) congruity
    (E) denial

2. Although she had a modest upbringing, the entrepreneur now lives in the most _____ building in the city.

    (A) spartan
    (B) factious
    (C) salubrious
    (D) opulent
    (E) exiguous

3. Unfortunately, the campers encountered unexpectedly _____ weather, making them wish they had brought outerwear that was more _____.

    (A) propitious . . . conspicuous
    (B) arctic . . . chromatic
    (C) frigid . . . substantial
    (D) gelid . . . delicate
    (E) temperate . . . durable

4. Either _____ or _____, every story the dinner guest told was crude or dull.

    (A) lascivious . . . vapid
    (B) ribald . . . succinct
    (C) lubricious . . . vibrant
    (D) salacious . . . provocative
    (E) capricious . . . vacuous

5. The supervisor forced his subordinates to _____ with his every whim, lest they find themselves _____ from his good graces.

    (A) accord . . . garnered
    (B) comply . . . banished
    (C) assent . . . abetted
    (D) concur . . . sanctioned
    (E) contend . . . exiled

6. After missing the bus, Mitch was saved from a 3-mile trudge to school by the _____ appearance of his next-door neighbor's car heading into town.

    (A) luxurious
    (B) serene
    (C) requisite
    (D) fortuitous
    (E) commodious

GO ON TO THE NEXT PAGE

7. Once the pizza parlor opened down the street, a strong, _____ scent of garlic _____ the neighborhood.

   (A) palatable . . . saturated
   (B) acrid . . . abdicated
   (C) benign . . . infiltrated
   (D) pungent . . . permeated
   (E) inconspicuous . . . pervaded

8. Although the management's relationship with the union had never turned adversarial it had always been _____ at best.

   (A) convivial
   (B) apathetic
   (C) tempestuous
   (D) oblique
   (E) copasetic

Directions: The passages below are followed by questions based on their content. Questions that follow a pair of related passages may also ask about the relationship between the paired passages. Answer each question on the basis of what is stated or implied in the passages and any introductory material provided.

Questions 9–12 are based on the following passages.

Passage 1.

Organic fruits and vegetables are produced without synthetic chemicals, such as fertilizers, pesticides, and antibiotics, and do not contain any genetically modified organisms (GMOs). Relative to conven-
5 tionally produced fruits and vegetables, organics are typically raised on small-scale, independent operations such as family farms and sold at slightly higher prices. Currently, organics account for about 1–2% of total food sales in the U.S. and are available in
10 over 73% of supermarkets throughout the country.

Since the early 1990s, the retail market for organics in developed economies has been growing by about 20% annually because of increasing consumer demand. Concern for the quality and safety
15 of food and the potential for environmental damage from conventional agriculture are apparently responsible for this trend. And, as proponents are fond of pointing out, "organics just taste better."

Passage 2.

The first commercially grown, genetically modified
20 food crop was a tomato created by the biotechnology company Calgene. Known as the "FlavrSavr," Calgene submitted the product to the Food and Drug Administration in 1992, and after the agency determined that it was, in fact, a tomato and did not
25 constitute a health hazard, it went on sale in 1994. The FlavrSavr was produced with a special set of technologies that alter the genetic makeup of the tomato by manipulating its DNA molecules. It bruises less easily and ripens at a slower rate than a
30 conventionally grown tomato; therefore, prolonging its shelf life.

In the U.S., most genetically modified fruits and vegetables have not been given final approval for public consumption. Surprisingly, the few that have
35 been approved are not required to be labeled as genetically modified.

9. Passage 2 is primarily concerned with

   (A) the safety of genetically modified fruits and vegetables
   (B) the origins of a specific genetically modified product
   (C) the process by which the FlavrSavr was developed and marketed
   (D) comparisons between the FlavrSavr and conventionally grown tomatoes
   (E) the advantages of genetically modified fruits and vegetables

10. Which of the following conclusions is supported by both Passage 1 and Passage 2?

   (A) Confidence in food safety and quality is a valid concern.
   (B) Eating fruits and vegetables is an important aspect of a balanced diet.
   (C) Demand for fresh produce is on the rise in much of the world.
   (D) Innovations are enhancing growth in the fruit and vegetable economies.
   (E) Environmental concerns shape the decisions farmers and consumers make.

GO ON TO THE NEXT PAGE

11. The main difference between Passage 1 and Passage 2 is that

   (A) Passage 1 provides concrete data on organic foods, whereas Passage 2 relies on personal opinion when discussing genetically modified foods

   (B) Passage 1 focuses on the price of organic foods, whereas Passage 2 focuses on technological advances in genetically modified foods

   (C) the primary concern of Passage 1 is market growth, whereas the primary concern of Passage 2 is government intervention

   (D) Passage 1 seems supportive of organically produced foods, while Passage 2 seems somewhat skeptical of genetically modified foods

   (E) Passage 1 provides an historical overview of organically grown foods, whereas Passage 2 focuses on one product

12. Which statement would both authors most likely agree with?

   (A) It is important to know how the fruits and vegetables you eat were produced.

   (B) The markets for both genetically modified and organically grown fruits and vegetables are likely to increase in the years ahead.

   (C) Longer shelf lives for fruits and vegetables benefit producers.

   (D) Fruits and vegetables that have been genetically modified pose no health risks to consumers.

   (E) Supporting small-scale family farms is worth the slightly higher price you will pay for the fruits and vegetables grown on them.

Questions 13–24 are based on the following passage.

In 1933 American educator, literary critic, and author William Lyon Phelps retired after more than thirty years as a professor of English at Yale University. He delivered this speech during a radio broadcast on April 6, 1933.

The habit of reading is one of the greatest resources of mankind; and we enjoy reading books
Line that belong to us much more than if they are borrowed. A borrowed book is like a guest in the house;
5 it must be treated with punctiliousness, with a certain considerate formality. You must see that it sustains no damage; it must not suffer while under your roof. You cannot leave it carelessly, you cannot mark it, you cannot turn down the pages, you
10 cannot use it familiarly. And then, some day, although this is seldom done, you really ought to return it.

But your own books belong to you; you treat them with that affectionate intimacy that annihilates
15 formality. Books are for use, not for show; you should own no book that you are afraid to mark up, or afraid to place on the table, wide open and face down. A good reason for marking favorite passages in books is that this practice enables you to remem-
20 ber more easily the significant sayings, to refer to them quickly, and then in later years, it is like visiting a forest where you once blazed a trail. You have the pleasure of going over the old ground, and recalling both the intellectual scenery and your own
25 earlier self.

Everyone should begin collecting a private library in youth; the instinct of private property, which is fundamental in human beings, can here be cultivated with every advantage and no evils. One
30 should have one's own bookshelves, which should not have doors, glass windows, or keys; they should be free and accessible to the hand as well as to the eye. The best of mural decorations is books; they are more varied in color and appearance than any wall-
35 paper, they are more attractive in design, and they have the prime advantage of being separate personalities, so that if you sit alone in the room in the firelight, you are surrounded with intimate friends. The knowledge that they are there in plain view is both
40 stimulating and refreshing. You do not have to read them all. Most of my indoor life is spent in a room containing six thousand books; and I have a stock answer to the invariable question that comes from strangers. "Have you read all of these books?"
45 "Some of them twice." This reply is both true and unexpected.

There are of course no friends like living, breathing, corporeal men and women; my devotion to reading has never made me a recluse. How could it?
50 Books are of the people, by the people, for the people. Literature is the immortal part of history; it is the best and most enduring part of personality. But book-friends have this advantage over living friends; you can enjoy the most truly aristocratic society in
55 the world whenever you want it. The great dead are beyond our physical reach, and the great living are usually almost as inaccessible; as for our personal friends and acquaintances, we cannot always see them. Perchance they are asleep, or away on a jour-
60 ney. But in a private library, you can at any moment converse with Socrates or Shakespeare or Carlyle or Dumas or Dickens or Shaw or Barrie or Galsworthy. And there is no doubt that in these books you see

GO ON TO THE NEXT PAGE

these men at their best. They wrote for *you*. They
65 "laid themselves out," they did their ultimate best to
entertain you, to make a favorable impression. You
are as necessary to them as an audience is to an
actor; only instead of seeing them masked, you look
into their innermost heart of hearts.

13. A borrowed book is most like

  (A) a long-lost friend
  (B) a suspicious stranger
  (C) an honored guest
  (D) a comfortable companion
  (E) a welcome distraction

14. The author suggests that in contrast to a borrowed
book, a book you own should be

  (A) handled with courteous respect
  (B) treated with affectionate abandon
  (C) protected from all harm
  (D) shared with friends
  (E) hidden away for safekeeping

15. As used in line 7 "sustain" most nearly means

  (A) nourish
  (B) confirm
  (C) withstand
  (D) comfort
  (E) support

16. The statement in lines 22–25, "You have the pleasure of going over old ground, and recalling both the
intellectual scenery and your earlier self," primarily
suggests that revisiting a book

  (A) brings back memories you might otherwise not
recall
  (B) gives you insight to facilitate personal growth
  (C) helps you recall places you have traveled to
  (D) gives you a collection of memories to draw
upon for the future
  (E) provides you with the intellectual capacity to
shape the present

17. In lines 21–22, the metaphor describing returning to
a marked-up book suggests that the markings

  (A) show which passages you read
  (B) make a trail through the book
  (C) point out misleading ideas
  (D) evoke a sense of wrongdoing
  (E) recall an earlier version of yourself

18. The advantage of book friends over living friends is
that book friends

  (A) are all members of the aristocracy
  (B) are always at your beck and call
  (C) are already dead
  (D) have more personality
  (E) are beyond your physical reach

19. The passage supports which of the following statements?

  (A) Devotion to reading makes one a recluse.
  (B) Literature makes history everlasting.
  (C) Good friends are never inaccessible.
  (D) Book friends replace living friends.
  (E) Reading is a lonely pursuit.

20. The passage serves mainly to

  (A) explain why books are an important resource
  (B) encourage the teaching of great literature
  (C) discuss the advantages of owning books
  (D) stimulate interest in public libraries
  (E) explore the author's literary preferences

21. The speaker implies that authors and actors are alike
in all of the following EXCEPT:

  (A) wanting to impress you
  (B) seeking to entertain you
  (C) needing an audience
  (D) revealing their innermost feelings
  (E) trying their best

22. The last paragraph suggests that the author

  (A) primarily prefers books to people
  (B) believes a great book can outlive its author
  (C) thinks it is best to own a book rather than bor-
row a book
  (D) has been an avid reader for more than 30 years
  (E) prefers classic literature over contemporary
literature

GO ON TO THE NEXT PAGE ➤

23. All of the following can be explicitly answered by the passage EXCEPT:
    (A) Why does the author think books should be read twice?
    (B) When should a person begin building a private library?
    (C) Why does the author feel it is a good idea to mark up books?
    (D) How does the author consider the habit of reading?
    (E) What advantage do books have over living friends?

24. With which of these statements is the author most likely to agree?
    (A) Most people enjoy collecting things.
    (B) Children should get in the habit of buying books.
    (C) Books are the best gifts for children.
    (D) Children should be encouraged to collect things from an early age.
    (E) Some books are intended only for show.

END OF SECTION

IF YOU FINISH BEFORE TIME IS UP, CHECK YOUR WORK ON THIS SECTION ONLY.

SECTION 2 QUESTIONS

Time—25 Minutes

24 Questions

Directions: This section consists of sentence completion questions and questions based on reading passages. For each question, select the answer you think is best and record your choice by filling in the corresponding oval on the answer sheet.

Directions: Each sentence below has one or two blanks. Each blank indicates that something is missing. Following each sentence are five words or sets of words labeled A, B, C, D, and E. You are to select the word or set of words that, when inserted in the sentence, best fits the meaning of the sentence as a whole.

EXAMPLE:

1. Despite our best efforts to protect the environment and keep it safe, until the problems of pollution are _____, the future of our environment seems, at best, _____.

   (A) created . . . gloomy
   (B) revoked . . . secure
   (C) solved . . . uncertain
   (D) replaced . . . revered
   (E) increased . . . unknown

   Correct Answer: C

---

1. _____ even from a distance, Mount Everest is the highest mountain in the world, and certainly one of nature's wonders.

   (A) Prodigious
   (B) Deceptive
   (C) Resplendent
   (D) Gilded
   (E) Exquisite

2. A talented _____, she had a wide array of stories and loved to get the crowd laughing with one of her hilarious anecdotes.

   (A) pundit
   (B) raconteur
   (C) sybarite
   (D) pugilist
   (E) thespian

3. Miles Davis, the _____ jazz trumpeter, was renowned as much for his enigmatic style as his _____ playing.

   (A) legendary . . . pedestrian
   (B) obscure . . . exceptional
   (C) arcane . . . transcendent
   (D) ubiquitous . . . plebeian
   (E) acclaimed . . . virtuosic

4. Despite the _____ tone of the play, the subject matter was rather _____.

   (A) grave . . . pensive
   (B) ominous . . . morbid
   (C) effervescent . . . jocund
   (D) sober . . . farcical
   (E) solemn . . . bleak

5. Even though he lost, the results were so close that the candidate was _____ about his chances of winning the next election.

   (A) felicitous
   (B) sanguine
   (C) peripatetic
   (D) precipitous
   (E) virulent

GO ON TO THE NEXT PAGE

Directions: The passages below are followed by questions based on their content. Answer each question on the basis of what is stated or implied in the passages and any introductory material provided.

Questions 6 and 7 are based on the following passage.

A slavish bondage to parents cramps every faculty of the mind; and Mr. Locke very judiciously ob-
Line serves, that 'if the mind be curbed and humbled too much in children; if their spirits be abased and bro-
5 ken much by too strict a hand over them; they lose all their vigor and industry.' This strict hand may in some degree account for the weakness of women; for girls, from various causes, are more kept down by their parents, in every sense of the word, than
10 boys. The duty expected from them is, like all the duties arbitrarily imposed on women, more from a sense of propriety, more out of respect for decorum than reason.

6. The author seems to view the way children are raised with

   (A) unbridled contempt
   (B) somber resignation
   (C) intellectual disdain
   (D) pacified ambivalence
   (E) amicable objectivity

7. The author would most likely agree that the will imposed by parents over their children, in the end would

   (A) enrich the children's development and temper the evolutionary process of free thinking
   (B) hasten the oppression of the individual desires for the greater good of a free society
   (C) fortify children with faith in not only their parents but also the society in which they live
   (D) undermine the children's individuality and compromise their ability to question devotion
   (E) strengthen familial faith by allowing children to embrace the wisdom of their parents

Questions 8 and 9 are based on the following passage.

The indictment, handed down Thursday by Fifth-Circuit Judge Lani Tavares, alleges that the devel-
Line opers had willfully misled the city with deceptive calculations used to determine the amount of school-
5 tax they would be responsible for paying the district. Under the original agreement, the land used to develop the condominiums could only be rezoned based on an assessment of two children per unit. This would have created a tax-based income suit-
10 able for the district to add an additional 160 children to school rosters. However, the developers, Five Star Housing Inc., later re-calculated their payment based only on the 43 children whose families had actually moved into the complex.

8. Phrases such as "willfully mislead" and "deceptive calculations" are used to best characterize the developers actions as

   (A) criminal
   (B) unlawful
   (C) negligent
   (D) suspect
   (E) scrupulous

9. Which of the following situations is most analogous to the impropriety the developers are accused of?

   (A) A landscape company charging a homeowner for tree-trimming work that the company never performed.
   (B) A mechanic charging a car owner for repairs that went beyond those approved by the vehicle's owner.
   (C) A group of eight diners agreeing to a restaurant's policy of a mandatory 20% tip on parties of six or more and then leaving a 10% tip.
   (D) A catering company billing a wedding couple for 150 guests who attended a reception rather than the 100 guests it had contracted for.
   (E) A parent inquiring about a babysitter's rate to care for two children for 3 hours then dropping off three children for 4 hours.

GO ON TO THE NEXT PAGE

Questions 10–17 are based on the following passage.

This passage is from *The Moccasin Maker,* a collection of stories by E. Pauline Johnson. The daughter of a Mohawk Chief and an Englishwoman, Johnson was born at Six Nation Indian Reserve in Canada. As a young woman, Johnson's mother Lydia had lived with her sister and brother-in-law at an Indian Mission in the Canadian wilderness. There she met a handsome young Mohawk boy who worked as an interpreter at the church. In this excerpt, Johnson tells the story of how her father came to marry her mother.

Perhaps it was this grey shadow stealing on the forest mission, the thought of the day when that
Line beautiful mothering sister would leave his little
friend Lydia alone with a bereft man and four small
5   children, or perhaps it was a yet more personal note in his life that brought George Mansion to the realization of what this girl had grown to be to him.

Indian-wise, his parents had arranged a suitable marriage for him, selecting a girl of his own tribe,
10 of the correct clan to mate with his own, so that the line of blood heritage would be intact, and the sons of the next generation would be of the "Blood Royal," qualified by rightful lineage to inherit the title of chief.
15 This Mohawk girl was attractive, young, and had a partial English education. Her parents were fairly prosperous, owners of many acres, and much forest and timber country. The arrangement was regarded as an ideal one—the young people as per-
20 fectly and diplomatically mated as it was possible to be; but when his parents approached the young chief with the proposition, he met it with instant refusal.

"My father, my mother," he begged, "I ask you to forgive me this one disobedience. I ask you to
25 forgive that I have, amid my fight and struggle for English education, forgotten a single custom of my people. I have tried to honor all the ancient rules and usages of my forefathers, but I forgot this one thing, and I cannot, cannot do it! My wife I must
30 choose for myself."

"You will marry—whom, then?" asked the old chief.

"I have given no thought to it—yet," he faltered.

"Yes," said his mother, urged by the knowing
35 heart of a woman, "yes, George, you have thought of it."

"Only this hour," he answered, looking directly into his mother's eyes. "Only now that I see you want me to give my life to someone else. But my
40 life belongs to the white girl, Mrs. Evans' sister, if she will take it. I shall offer it to her to-morrow—to-day."

His mother's face took on the shadow of age. "You would marry a *white* girl?" she exclaimed, in-
45 credulously.

"Yes," came the reply, briefly, decidedly.

"But your children, your sons and hers—they could never hold the title, never be chief," she said, rising to her feet.
50 He winced. "I know it. I had not thought of it before—but I know it. Still, I would marry her."

"But there would be no more chiefs of the Grand Mansion name," cut in his father. "The title would go to your aunt's sons. She is a Grand Man-
55 sion no longer; she, being married, is merely a Straight-Shot, her husband's name. The Straight-Shots never had noble blood, never wore a title. Shall our family title go to a *Straight-Shot*?" and the elder chief mouthed the name contemptuously.
60 Again the boy winced. The hurt of it all was sinking in—he hated the Straight-Shots, he loved his own blood and bone. With lightning rapidity he weighed it all mentally, then spoke: "Perhaps the white girl will not marry me," he said slowly, and
65 the thought of it drove the dark red from his cheeks, drove his finger-nails into his palms.

"Then, then you will marry Dawendine, our choice?" cried his mother, hopefully.

"I shall marry no one but the white girl," he an-
70 swered, with set lips. "If she will not marry me, I shall never marry, so the Straight-Shots will have our title, anyway."

The door closed behind him. It was as if it had shut forever between him and his own.
75 But even with this threatened calamity looming before her, the old Indian mother's hurt heart swelled with a certain pride in his wilful actions.

"What bravery!" she exclaimed. "What courage to hold to his own choice! What a *man!*"

10. In the context of this passage, a "grey shadow" is stealing up on the mission because

(A) Lydia is afraid of her brother-in-law
(B) Lydia's sister is dying
(C) Lydia's sister has four small children
(D) George Mansion fears he might lose his job
(E) not enough sunlight can penetrate the thick forest

GO ON TO THE NEXT PAGE ▶

11. As used in line 4, "bereft" most nearly means

    (A) baffled
    (B) overbearing
    (C) benevolent
    (D) bereaved
    (E) improvident

12. The main reason George Mansion refuses to accept his parents' choice for a bride is that he

    (A) does not respect his parents
    (B) does not like the woman they have chosen
    (C) is in love with someone else
    (D) wants to hurt his parents
    (E) no longer honors any of the customs of his people

13. The passage indicates that at the time marriages within the tribe could best be described as

    (A) traditionally arranged by parents
    (B) dependent upon exchanges of money or land
    (C) completely up to the young people involved
    (D) required at a certain age
    (E) valid only if sanctioned by the tribal council

14. George Mansion's biggest regret in choosing to marry Lydia is that

    (A) he would no longer be a member of the Mohawk nation
    (B) he was not following the traditions of his forefathers
    (C) his parents would no longer speak to him
    (D) the family title would go to people he hated
    (E) he would not be able to have children

15. The initial attitude of George Mansion's parents toward his decision to marry a white girl is primarily one of

    (A) worried puzzlement
    (B) outraged embarrassment
    (C) sincere sympathy
    (D) shocked disbelief
    (E) resigned acceptance

16. All of the following are mentioned as reasons for George to marry the woman his parents have chosen for him EXCEPT:

    (A) his children
    (B) the family title
    (C) tradition
    (D) blood lines
    (E) bravery

17. In the context of the passage, the mother's words "What a man!" (line 79) indicate that she

    (A) was angry at her son for defying her wishes
    (B) was proud of her son for standing up for what he wanted
    (C) was not likely to forgive her son
    (D) would not accept her grandchildren
    (E) did not like her sister's sons

Questions 18–24 are based on the following passage.

In this passage, Dana Gioia, chairman of the National Endowment for the Arts, discusses a recently released survey of reading in America.

For the first time in modern history, less than half of the U.S. adult population now reads literature, according to a comprehensive survey recently released by the National Endowment for the Arts.
5   *Reading at Risk: A Survey of Literary Reading in America* presents a detailed but bleak assessment of the decline of reading's role in the nation's culture and is not a report that the National Endowment for the Arts is happy to issue.
10   Anyone who loves literature or values the cultural, intellectual, and political importance of active and engaged literacy in American society will respond to this report with grave concern.
    Reading at Risk is not a collection of anecdotes,
15   theories, or opinions. It is a descriptive survey of national trends in adult literary reading. Based on an enormous sample size of more than 17,000 adults, it covers most major demographic groups—providing statistical measurements by age, gender, educa-
20   tion, income, region, race, and ethnicity. Conducted by the U.S. Bureau of the Census and spanning 20 years of polling, the Survey of Public Participation in the Arts, the data source for *Reading at Risk,* is as reliable and objective as any such survey can be.
25   While not every measurement of reading was built into the study, the report provides so much data in such detail that it constitutes a comprehensive factual basis for any informed discussion of current American reading habits.
30   The key results of the survey are condensed in the "Executive Summary," but the report can be further summarized in a single sentence: literary reading in America is not only declining rapidly among all groups, but the rate of decline has accelerated,
35   especially among the young. The concerned citizen

in search of good news about American literary culture will study the pages of this report in vain.

Although the news in the report is dire, I doubt that any careful observer of contemporary Ameri-
40 can society will be greatly surprised—except perhaps by the sheer magnitude of decline. *Reading at Risk* merely documents and quantifies a huge cultural transformation that most Americans have already noted—our society's massive shift toward
45 electronic media for entertainment and information.

Reading a book requires a degree of active attention and engagement. Indeed, reading itself is a progressive skill that depends on years of education and practice. By contrast, most electronic media
50 such as television, recordings, and radio make fewer demands on their audiences, and indeed often require no more than passive participation. Even interactive electronic media, such as video games and the Internet, foster shorter attention spans and ac-
55 celerated gratification.

While oral culture has a rich immediacy that is not to be dismissed, and electronic media offer the considerable advantages of diversity and access, print culture affords irreplaceable forms of focused
60 attention and contemplation that make complex communications and insights possible. To lose such intellectual capability—and the many sorts of human continuity it allows—would constitute a vast cultural impoverishment.

65 More than reading is at stake. As this report unambiguously demonstrates, readers play a more active and involved role in their communities. The decline in reading, therefore, parallels a larger retreat from participation in civic and cultural life.
70 The long-term implications of this study, therefore, not only affect literature but all the arts—as well as social activities such as volunteerism, philanthropy, and even political engagement.

What is to be done? There is surely no single so-
75 lution to the present dilemma, just as there is no single cause. Each concerned group—writers, teachers, publishers, journalists, librarians, and legislators—will legitimately view the situation from a different perspective, and each will offer its own recommen-
80 dations. The important thing now is to understand that America can no longer take active and engaged literacy for granted.

Reading is not a timeless, universal capability. Advanced literacy is a specific intellectual skill and
85 social habit that depends on a great many educational, cultural, and economic factors. As more Americans lose this capability, our nation becomes less informed, active, and independent minded. These are not qualities that a free, innovative, or
90 productive society can afford to lose.

18. The data source for *Reading at Risk*

(A) includes readers of all ages
(B) consists primarily of young, affluent readers
(C) is lacking in the details necessary for an informed discussion
(D) is too diverse to support statistically significant conclusions
(E) is considered objective and reliable

19. Lines 38–41 ("Although . . . decline.") suggest that the author views the results of the study with

(A) surprise
(B) caution
(C) alarm
(D) skepticism
(E) ambiguity

20. The "cultural transformation" mentioned in lines 42–43 is best described as

(A) the increased availability of Internet access in homes and schools
(B) the change from reading to electronic media as the primary source of entertainment and information
(C) the change in preference from reading literary works of the past to reading current nonfiction
(D) the rapid decline in the number of students enrolled in literature classes in recent years
(E) the decline in volunteerism and participation in political activity

21. Which best captures the meaning of the word "engagement" in line 47?

(A) contemplation
(B) involvement
(C) focus
(D) commitment
(E) conviction

22. The contrast between reading and electronic media is best described by which terms?

(A) active versus passive
(B) written versus spoken
(C) immediate versus long-term
(D) social versus political
(E) entertaining versus informational

GO ON TO THE NEXT PAGE

23. The main purpose of the passage is to
    (A) criticize a study
    (B) justify an expenditure
    (C) support one side in a debate
    (D) report the results of a study
    (E) suggest a solution for a problem

24. The author is most likely to agree with which of the following?
    (A) As reading declines, computer literacy increases.
    (B) Literary reading is not important in a technologically advanced society.
    (C) Advanced literacy is the basis for a free, innovative, and productive society.
    (D) *Reading at Risk* provides good news about the state of American literary culture.
    (E) Reading is a timeless, universal capability common to all Americans.

END OF SECTION

IF YOU FINISH BEFORE TIME IS UP, CHECK YOUR WORK ON THIS SECTION ONLY.

SECTION 3 QUESTIONS

Time—20 Minutes

19 Questions

Directions: This section consists of sentence completion questions and questions based on reading passages. For each question, select the answer you think is best and record your choice by filling in the corresponding oval on the answer sheet.

Directions: Each sentence below has one or two blanks. Each blank indicates that something is missing. Following each sentence are five words or sets of words labeled A, B, C, D, and E. You are to select the word or set of words that, when inserted in the sentence, best fits the meaning of the sentence as a whole.

EXAMPLE:

1. Despite our best efforts to protect the environment and keep it safe, until the problems of pollution are _____, the future of our environment seems, at best, _____.

   (A) created . . . gloomy
   (B) revoked . . . secure
   (C) solved . . . uncertain
   (D) replaced . . . revered
   (E) increased . . . unknown

   Correct Answer: C

1. Even after two weeks in the Caribbean sun, Denise still had the _____ of a researcher accustomed to spending her days in the dim recesses of the science library.

   (A) countenance
   (B) repose
   (C) comportment
   (D) gait
   (E) pallor

2. Luis twisted his ankle Wednesday afternoon, but it was not until Thursday morning that he noticed the ankle had become _____ and uncomfortable to walk on.

   (A) desiccated
   (B) tumescent
   (C) bilious
   (D) trenchant
   (E) sullied

3. Boxing legend Muhammad Ali was often described as _____ and _____, because his ability to land a knockout punch inspired fear and commanded respect.

   (A) formidable . . . redoubtable
   (B) petulant . . . intimidating
   (C) menacing . . . facile
   (D) tactical . . . stupefying
   (E) fierce . . . exacting

4. Reports of the senator's _____ displays of wealth have done little to _____ her standing among working-class families or help her bid for re-election.

   (A) flagrant . . . undermine
   (B) ostentatious . . . promote
   (C) unobtrusive . . . solidify
   (D) garish . . . curtail
   (E) strident . . . truncate

5. One would think that the _____ bear, fresh from months of hibernation would eat everything in sight, but he is surprisingly picky.

   (A) hirsute
   (B) servile
   (C) ravenous
   (D) insatiable
   (E) omnivorous

6. According to the editorial, the most _____ error the governor made was _____ the public's trust in him by trying to cover up the scandal.

   (A) grievous . . . appeasing
   (B) deplorable . . . gleaning
   (C) abhorrent . . . placating
   (D) defenseless . . . effectuating
   (E) egregious . . . breaching

GO ON TO THE NEXT PAGE

> Directions: The passages below are followed by questions based on their content. Questions that follow a pair of related passages may also ask about the relationship between the paired passages. Answer each question on the basis of what is stated or implied in the passages and any introductory material provided.

The word "volcano" comes from the little island of Vulcano in the Mediterranean Sea off Sicily. Centuries ago, the people living in this area believed that Vulcano was the chimney of the forge of Vulcan—the blacksmith of the Roman gods. Today we know that volcanic eruptions are not supernatural but can be studied and interpreted by scientists.

Questions 7–19 are based on the following passages.

Passage 1.

Volcanoes are mountains, but they are very different from other mountains; they are not formed by
Line folding and crumpling or by uplift and erosion. Instead, volcanoes are built by the accumulation of
5   their own eruptive products—lava, bombs (crusted over lava blobs), ashflows, and tephra (airborne ash and dust). A *volcano* is most commonly a conical hill or mountain built around a vent that connects with reservoirs of molten rock below the surface of
10 the Earth. The term volcano also refers to the opening or vent through which the molten rock and associated gases are expelled.

Deep within the Earth it is so hot that some rocks slowly melt and become a thick flowing sub-
15 stance called *magma*. Because it is lighter than the solid rock around it, magma rises and collects in magma chambers. Eventually some of the magma pushes through vents and fissures in the Earth's surface, and a volcanic eruption occurs. Magma
20 that has erupted is called *lava*.

Some volcanic eruptions are explosive, and others are not. How explosive an eruption is depends on how runny or sticky the magma is. If magma is thin and runny, gases can escape easily from it.
25 When this type of magma erupts, it flows out of the volcano. Lava flows rarely kill people because they move slowly enough for people to get out of their way. Lava flows, however, can cause considerable destruction to buildings in their path. If magma is
30 thick and sticky, gases cannot escape easily. Pressure builds up until the gases escape violently and explode. In this type of eruption, the magma blasts into the air and breaks apart into pieces called *tephra*. Tephra can range in size from tiny particles
35 of ash to house-size boulders.

Explosive volcanic eruptions can be dangerous and deadly. They can blast out clouds of hot tephra from the side or top of a volcano. These fiery clouds race down mountainsides destroying almost every-
40 thing in their path. Ash erupted into the sky falls back to Earth like powdery snow, but snow that won't melt. If thick enough, blankets of ash can suffocate plants, animals, and humans. When hot volcanic materials mix with water from streams or
45 melted snow and ice, mudflows form. Mudflows have buried entire communities located near erupting volcanoes. Because there may be hundreds or thousands of years between volcanic eruptions, people may not be aware of a volcano's dangers.

Passage 2.

50 On March 20, 1980, a series of small earthquakes signaled the awakening of Mount St. Helens from a 123-year slumber. Over the next two months more than 10,000 earthquakes followed as magma moved into the volcano, wedging the volcano apart at a rate
55 of 5 feet per day. Heat from a rising plume of volcanic ash melted glacial ice creating cement-like slurries of rock and ash called mudflows. Superheated avalanches of hot gas, magma caused a visible swelling of the volcano's north flank creating a
60 feature that scientists called "the bulge."

Many geologists weren't surprised by Mount St. Helens' awakening. In the 1950s, geologists had begun an extensive study of the deposits around Mount St. Helens. In 1975, they published a report
65 predicting that Mount St. Helens was the volcano in the lower 48 states most likely to erupt by the end of the century.

On the morning of May 18, 1980, a magnitude 5.1 earthquake triggered the collapse of the summit
70 and north flank of Mount St. Helens and formed the largest landslide in recorded history. Gas-rich magma and super-heated groundwater trapped inside the volcano were suddenly released in a powerful lateral blast. In less than 3 minutes, 230 square
75 miles of forest lay flattened. The hot gas and magma melted the snow and ice that covered the volcano. The resulting floodwater mixed with the rock and debris to create concrete-like mudflows that scoured river valleys surrounding the mountain.

80 A plume of volcanic ash and pumice billowed out of the volcano reaching a height of 15 miles and

GO ON TO THE NEXT PAGE ➡

transformed day into night across eastern Washington. Avalanches of super-heated gas and pumice, called pyroclastic flows, swept down the flanks of
85   the volcano. While the landslide and lateral blast were over within minutes, the eruption column, mudflows, and pyroclastic flows continued throughout the day and following night. By the following morning, major eruptive activity had ceased, and
90   the landscape appeared to be a gray wasteland.

7. According to Passage 1, a primary difference between volcanoes and other mountains is in

    (A) their height
    (B) their ruggedness
    (C) their age
    (D) where they are located
    (E) how they are formed

8. A volcanic eruption is likely to be most explosive if magma

    (A) is thin and runny
    (B) is thick and sticky
    (C) rises and collects in magma chambers
    (D) pushes out through fissures in the Earth's surface
    (E) becomes lava

9. People may not be aware of just how dangerous a volcano can be primarily because

    (A) some eruptions are not explosive
    (B) centuries may pass between eruptions
    (C) volcanoes are just like mountains
    (D) lava flows rarely kill people
    (E) volcanic ash looks like powdery snow

10. The author of Passage 1 uses italics primarily to

    (A) emphasize words that are used in an unusual way
    (B) indicate words that are difficult to pronounce
    (C) point out foreign words
    (D) highlight important terms that are defined in the text
    (E) indicate words that are not necessary to understanding the passage

11. All of the following can be explicitly answered by Passage 1 EXCEPT:

    (A) What factors contribute to hot temperatures deep inside the Earth?
    (B) Why are some volcanic eruptions explosive, while others are not?
    (C) As dangerous as eruptions can be, why do lava flows rarely kill people?
    (D) Why does magma rise and collect in chambers?
    (E) Why does pressure build up in magma that is thick and sticky?

12. The first sentence of Passage 2 ("On. . . . slumber.") implies that

    (A) Mount St. Helens had never before erupted
    (B) Mount St. Helens erupts every 123 years
    (C) Mount St. Helens last erupted in 1857
    (D) no records exist for eruptions that occurred more than 123 years ago
    (E) no one suspected that Mount St. Helens could erupt

13. As used in Passage 2, line 55, "rising" most nearly means

    (A) growing
    (B) maturing
    (C) approaching
    (D) ascending
    (E) advancing

14. The statement in Passage 2 that "Many geologists weren't surprised by Mount St. Helens' awakening," (lines 61–62) primarily suggests that

    (A) geologists were able to predict when Mount St. Helens would erupt
    (B) the assumptions geologists had made about Mount St. Helens were being proved
    (C) the longer a volcano remains dormant, the more likely it is to become active
    (D) nothing is surprising to geologists
    (E) the heat rising from the volcanic ash had provided an important clue to the geologists

15. The author of Passage 2 describes the events of May 18, 1980, mainly by means of

    (A) scientific analysis
    (B) detached and impartial observation
    (C) vivid language and dramatic images
    (D) presentation of facts in chronological order
    (E) presentation of details in spatial order

GO ON TO THE NEXT PAGE ➡

16. By calling the landscape in Passage 2 "a gray waste-land" (line 90), the author implies that

    (A) the landscape was covered with a blanket of dirty snow
    (B) the landscape was littered with garbage and other waste matter
    (C) the trees were all covered with gray ash
    (D) the sun could not penetrate the forest
    (E) the landscape had been stripped bare and covered in volcanic ash

17. Which of the following best describes the relationship between the two passages?

    (A) Passage 1 explains a scientific principle that is refuted in Passage 2.
    (B) Passage 1 presents a scientific theory that is tested in Passage 2.
    (C) Passage 1 argues against a position that is supported by Passage 2.
    (D) Passage 2 provides an example of a phenomenon that is explained in Passage 1.
    (E) Passage 2 offers a solution to a problem presented in Passage 1.

18. Unlike the author of Passage 1, the author of Passage 2 does which of the following?

    (A) offers general information
    (B) describes a specific situation
    (C) offers specific advice
    (D) provides historical background
    (E) appeals for action to protect the environment

19. Both passages serve to show that

    (A) an explosive volcanic eruption can be deadly
    (B) some volcanic eruptions are not explosive
    (C) lava flows are slow moving
    (D) there is a specific timetable to volcanic eruptions
    (E) an earthquake can trigger a volcanic eruption

END OF SECTION

IF YOU FINISH BEFORE TIME IS UP, CHECK YOUR WORK ON THIS SECTION ONLY.

ANSWER KEY

Section 1

1. C	7. D	13. C	19. B
2. D	8. C	14. B	20. C
3. C	9. B	15. C	21. D
4. A	10. A	16. A	22. B
5. B	11. D	17. E	23. A
6. D	12. C	18. B	24. B

Section 2

1. A	7. D	13. A	19. C
2. B	8. D	14. D	20. B
3. E	9. C	15. D	21. B
4. D	10. B	16. E	22. A
5. B	11. D	17. B	23. D
6. C	12. C	18. E	24. C

Section 3

1. E	6. E	11. A	16. E
2. B	7. E	12. C	17. D
3. A	8. B	13. D	18. B
4. B	9. B	14. B	19. A
5. C	10. D	15. C	

ANSWERS AND EXPLANATIONS

Section 1

1. **C is correct.** This vocabulary-in-context question offers the clue "concise" to help you arrive at the correct answer. Almost immediately, you are able to discount *denial* (E), as the announcement is not a denial, but rather a brief statement of the fact that the concert is canceled. (B) is incorrect because *affluence,* which means "abundance" or "wealth," cannot describe a four-word announcement. Similarly (D) is incorrect because *congruity* means "agreement" or "appropriateness," and the angry crowd is not likely to consider the announcement appropriate. *Coarseness* (A) fits the context of the sentence, however *brevity* (C), meaning "shortness" or "terseness," is the best description of the four-word announcement.

2. **D is correct.** The "although" construction used in this sentence signals that whatever type of building the entrepreneur now lives in, it is likely to contrast with her "modest upbringing." *Spartan* (A), meaning "simple" or "frugal," and *exiguous* (E), meaning "scant or meager" are incorrect as both can be used synonymously with "modest" in the context of the sentence. *Factious* (B), meaning "given to or promoting internal dissension," is also incorrect, as is *salubrious* (C), which means "conducive or favorable to health or well-being." *Opulent* (D), meaning "possessing or exhibiting great wealth or affluence," is the correct answer.

3. **C is correct.** *Unfortunately* is a clue that the weather the campers encountered was not favorable; therefore, you can eliminate both *propitious* (A), which means "favorable," and *temperate* (E), which means "moderate." If the weather were *arctic* (very cold) the campers are not likely to wish for *chromatic* (highly colorful) outerwear, so you can eliminate (B). Likewise if the weather were *gelid* (cold or frozen), the campers would not wish for *delicate* (dainty) outerwear, so you can eliminate (D). The correct answer as dictated by the logic of the sentence is that the

unexpectedly *frigid* (cold) weather made the campers wish they had brought outerwear that was more *substantial* (sturdy or durable).

4. **A is correct.** This type of vocabulary-in-context question asks for you to look for two words that describe the dinner guest's stories. The first word will mean "crude," and the second word will mean "dull." After examining the choices for the first blank, you will see that a case can be made for every answer choice except (E), which you can eliminate because *capricious* (meaning "impulsive" or "unpredictable") has nothing to do with "crude." However, upon turning your attention to the second blank, you will see that only *vapid* (A) is synonymous with "dull." (B) is wrong because *succinct* means "concise," not dull. (C) and (D) are wrong because *vibrant* (meaning "sparkling" or "radiant") and *provocative* (meaning "exciting" or "stimulating") are both opposites for "dull."

5. **B is correct.** This is a fairly straightforward logic-based question. The words "supervisor" and "whim" along with the phrase "good graces" all provide helpful clues, although you will still need to know the definitions of the choices to make an informed decision. Looking at the first blank, you will notice that nearly all of the answer choices seem to work except *contend* (E), which means "to contest or dispute." However, when you shift your focus to the second blank, you will notice that *banished* (B) offers the best fit of the remaining answer choices. (A) and (C) are wrong because *garnered* (meaning "gathered" or "amassed") and *abetted* (meaning "encouraged" or "supported") make no sense in relation to the supervisor's good graces. *Sanctioned* (D) may seem possible because *sanctioned* can mean "penalized." However, people are not sanctioned from someone's good graces. Clearly (B) is the best answer. Subordinates are forced to *comply* with (conform or agree to) the supervisor's whims or they will be *banished* (exiled or dismissed) from his good graces.

6. **D is correct.** *Luxurious, serene,* and *commodious* (meaning "spacious" or "roomy") all describe how the car may have looked, but none of these choices describe how Mitch "was saved from his 3-mile trudge to school." Moreover, the answers are indistinguishable from each other: no one of them is a better answer than the others. A *requisite* (C) appearance would be one that was "required or essential," which does not make sense in the context of this sentence. There is no reason to assume that the neighbor was obliged to drive Mitch to school because he missed the bus. It was the *fortuitous* (meaning "accidental" or "chance") appearance of the neighbor's car that saved Mitch from having to walk to school, making (D) the best answer.

7. **D is correct.** This vocabulary-in-context question offers the clue "strong" to describe the scent of garlic in the first blank. What should you do with this clue? You should look for a first-blank choice that can be used synonymously with "strong." *Palatable* (A) means "acceptable to taste," or "agreeable to the mind or sensibilities," and is not a good match with "strong." Choices (C) and (E) can be eliminated because *benign* (meaning "kind and gentle") and *inconspicuous* (meaning "not readily noticeable") do not fit with "strong." Choice (B), *acrid,* and Choice (D), *pungent,* can be used interchangeably in this context, as both mean "unpleasantly sharp." However, turning your attention to the second blank, you will see that *acrid* is paired with *abdicated* (meaning "relinquished" or "gave up") and does not make sense when used with the noun "aroma." Choice (D) is best. A strong, *pungent* (sharp or acrid) scent of garlic *permeated* (pervaded or penetrated) the neighborhood.

8. **C is correct.** Despite the fact that an "although" construction often signals that you will have two answers that contrast with one another, this sentence offers a one-blank question with a twist. The twist is the word "adversarial" in the first clause of the sentence coupled with the phrase "at best" in the second clause of the sentence. By adding the phrase "at best" to the sentence, you are provided with a clue that the answer you are looking for is close in meaning to the word "adversarial" and will complement it, rather than contrast with it. *Convivial* (A), meaning "sociable" and "merry or festive" is an antonym of the word you are looking for, as is *copasetic* (E), which means "very satisfactory or acceptable." Neither fits well alongside the phrase "at best" in the context of the sentence. *Apathetic* (B), meaning "feeling or showing a lack of interest or concern" is not the best answer, and *oblique* (D), meaning "having a slanting or sloping direction," makes no sense. *Tempestuous* (C), meaning "tumultuous or stormy," is closest in meaning to "adversarial," and it is the correct answer.

9. **B is correct.** Passage 2 describes how and by whom the FlavrSavr tomato was developed; it also tells of its review by the FDA and mentions attributes this tomato is said to have.

(A) is wrong because although Passage 2 discusses the FDA's review, it includes the agency's conclusion that the FlavrSavr "does not constitute a health hazard."

(C) is wrong because the article does not mention how the FlavrSavr was marketed, only how it was developed.

(D) is wrong because the statement that the FlavrSavr "bruises less easily and ripens at a slower rate than a conventionally grown tomato," is only one aspect in the presentation of the FlavrSavr's origins, not the primary focus.

(E) is wrong because the article mentions the prolonged shelf-life of only the FlavrSavr tomato. It does not give any details describing the attributes that other genetically modified fruits and vegetables are said to have.

10. **A is correct.** Passage 1 tells how concerns about food safety and quality are two of the aspects leading to an increased demand for organic foods, and Passage 2 describes how Calgene had to submit FlavrSavr to the FDA for approval before it could be marketed. Only after the FDA determined that the FlavrSavr "was, in fact, a tomato and did not constitute a health

hazard" could the product be sold to the public.

(B) is wrong because there is no mention of fruits and vegetables as being part of a balanced diet in either passage.

(C) is wrong because only Passage 1 provides statistics about growth in the market for organic foods. Passage 2 does not provide any such information.

(D) is wrong because Passage 1 discusses growth in the market for organic foods but does not describe any innovations in production. Passage 2, on the other hand, discusses innovations in the production of tomatoes but makes no mention of economic growth for genetically modified produce.

(E) is wrong because only Passage 1 discusses concerns about the environment. There is no mention of such concerns in Passage 2.

11. **D is correct.** Passage 1 offers a quote from proponents of organically produced foods that "organics just taste better," while Passage 2 mentions the fact that the FDA had to determine that the FlavrSavr was "in fact, a tomato." As well, by including the statement that genetically modified foods are "Surprisingly . . . not required to be labeled," the author seems to be implying that he thinks they should be.

(A) is wrong because although Passage 1 provides statistical data on organic food sales in the U.S., Passage 2 provides factual data, rather than personal opinion, when discussing the development, technology, and government review of the FlavrSavr tomato.

(B) is wrong because Passage 1 provides an overview of organic fruits and vegetables and mentions only that they are priced "slightly higher" than conventionally raised produce. Moreover, Passage 2 provides a history of the first commercially available, genetically modified product; it does not discuss advances made since the introduction of this product.

(C) is wrong because although it could be argued that the focus of Passage 1 is the market growth for organically produced foods, the focus of Passage 2 is not government intervention. In fact, one could also argue that the author of Passage 2 believes there ought to be a bit more government intervention in the development of genetically modified foods.

(E) is wrong because although Passage 1 includes an overview of the organic foods market, it is not an "historical" overview. Indeed, the only date mentioned in Passage 1 is "the early 1990s."

12. **C is correct.** Although it is clear that companies producing genetically modified foods seek to develop products with longer shelf lives, there is no reason to believe that extending the shelf life for organically grown fruits and vegetables would not be of benefit to their producers as well. It is logical to conclude that an organic farmer would be just as satisfied growing a tomato with an extended shelf life as a company such as Calgene would be in producing one.

(A) is wrong because the last sentence of Passage 2 states that genetically modified fruits and vegetables "are not required to be labeled." If the growers of these products felt it was important for the consumer to know how the fruits and vegetables were produced, they would likely label them accordingly.

(B) is wrong because although Passage 1 states that the retail market for organics "has been growing about 20% annually," there is no mention made of market growth for genetically modified fruits and vegetables. Moreover, it is unlikely that the author of Passage 1 would concede market growth to the type of products mentioned in Passage 2.

(D) is wrong because it is not a forgone conclusion that the author of Passage 1 would agree with this statement.

(E) is wrong because there is no way of knowing whether or not the author of Passage 2 believes that supporting small-scale, family farms is worth the extra cost consumers pay to do so.

13. **C is correct.** As stated in lines 4–6, "A borrowed book is like a guest in the house; it must be treated with punctiliousness, with a certain considerate formality."

(A) is wrong because a long-lost friend is not likely to be treated with "considerate formality."

(B) is wrong because borrowed books are to be treated as guests in the house, with careful attention to detail and formality, not with suspicion.

(D) is wrong because a comfortable companion is not likely to be treated with formality.

(E) is wrong because there is nothing to support the idea of a borrowed book as a welcome distraction.

14. **B is correct.** As stated in lines 14–15, you treat your own books "with that affectionate intimacy that annihilates formality." You should not be afraid to mark up your books or to place them on the table "wide open and face down." This affectionate informality is best described by answer choice (B).

(A) is wrong because borrowed books, not the ones you own, are to be treated with great respect.

(C) is wrong because the author says that books "are for use, not for show." He encourages you to mark up your books and to leave them wide open and face down on the table. These acts are not consistent with protecting books from all harm.

(D) is wrong because the author says nothing about sharing books with friends.

(E) is wrong because this is contrary to the author's suggestions to use books, to mark them up and to leave them face down on the table.

15. **C is correct.** The word *sustain* is used in the following sentence: "You must see that it sustains no damage; it must not suffer while under your roof." All of the answer choices

are meanings of the word *sustain;* however, in this sentence choice (C) fits best.

16. **A is correct.** The statement is made when the author is discussing how readers should mark up their favorite passages in books so that they can be easily referenced in the future. In doing so, he refers to going back to favorite passages as being akin to "visiting a forest where you once blazed a trail." However, he makes the point that in order to recall the forest and the trail you once blazed, you must revisit the book. Thus, particular memories of earlier times can only be recalled by revisiting the book and passage that helped create the memories.

(B) is wrong because the author is making the point that revisiting a marked passage in a book helps you recall the point in your life when you first marked the passage, as well as why it was important to you in the first place. Nothing in the statement, or the surrounding text, indicates he is speaking of personal growth. Rather, he is discussing how revisiting marked passages takes you back in time.

(C) is wrong because when the author writes of revisiting "a forest where you once blazed a trail," he is speaking of traveling metaphorically, not physically.

(D) is wrong because the author is clearly writing of revisiting your past. No mention is made of drawing upon your memories for the future.

(E) is wrong because there is no support in the passage for the statement that the author believes revisiting your past helps you shape the present. Rather, the point the author is making is that revisiting marked passages in books takes you back to the time when you first marked the passage.

17. **E is correct.** Returning to a marked up book in later years is "like visiting a forest where you once blazed a trail. You have the pleasure of going over the old ground, and recalling both the intellectual scenery and your own earlier self." In other words, the

markings make you think about what was important to you in that earlier time when you first read the book.

(A) is wrong because the passage assumes you have read the whole book, not just the underlined passages.

(B) is wrong because the metaphor speaks of blazing a trail in the forest, not of making a trail through the book.

(C) is wrong because there is nothing to support the idea that one would mark misleading ideas.

(D) is wrong because the author says there is nothing wrong with marking up a book. So, reviewing the markings should not evoke a sense of wrongdoing.

18. **B is correct.** As stated in lines 53–55, "book-friends have this advantage over living friends; you can enjoy the most truly aristocratic society in the world whenever you want it." You cannot always see your personal friends. They may be asleep or away on a journey. "But in a private library, you can at any moment converse with Socrates or Shakespeare or Carlyle or Dumas or Dickens or Shaw or Barrie or Galsworthy."

(A) is wrong because saying that with book friends "you can enjoy the most truly aristocratic society" is not the same as saying book friends are all members of the aristocracy.

(C) is wrong because not all book friends are necessarily dead and even if they were this is not their advantage over living friends.

(D) is wrong because the author says nothing about book friends having more personality.

(E) is wrong because being beyond your reach is not what makes book friends appealing.

19. **B is correct.** As stated in line 52, "Literature is the immortal part of history. . . ." In other words, through literature history lives on.

(A) is wrong because the author states just the opposite when he says, ". . . my devotion to reading has never made me a recluse."

(C) is wrong because the author says that we cannot always see our good friends. "Perchance they are asleep, or away on a journey."

(D) is wrong because the author implies the opposite when he says, "There are of course no friends like living, breathing, corporeal men and women."

(E) is wrong because the author says that sitting alone in a room full of books "you are surrounded with intimate friends."

20. **C is correct.** The main idea of the passage is to show why it is so much better to own books than it is to merely borrow them.

(A) is wrong because the idea that books are an important resource is only one idea covered in the passage. It is not the main idea of the whole passage.

(B) is wrong because although the author was a teacher of literature, in this passage he is speaking of reading, not teaching.

(D) is wrong because the main idea of the passage is to own books, not to borrow them from a public library.

(E) is wrong because the author says nothing about his own literary preferences.

21. **D is correct.** As stated in lines 64–69, "They wrote for *you*. They 'laid themselves out,' they did their ultimate best to entertain you, to make a favorable impression. You are as necessary to them as an audience is to an actor; only instead of seeing them masked, you look into their innermost heart of hearts." In other words, only authors reveal their innermost feelings.

(A) is wrong because both actors and authors want to impress you.

(B) is wrong because both actors and authors seek to entertain you.

(C) is wrong because both need an audience for their work.

(E) is wrong because it is likely that both are trying their best.

22. **B is correct.** In the last paragraph, the author speaks of "conversing" with such great writers as Socrates, Shakespeare, Dickens, and many others. Moreover, he implies that his means of "conversing" with these writers is by reading their works. The fact that all of the writers are dead leads to the conclusion that the author believes their works are good enough to endure and still merit his time and consideration. Thus, the author believes that great literature will be around long after its author has passed.

(A) is wrong because the author states that "There are of course no friends like living, breathing, corporeal men and women; my devotion to reading has never made me a recluse."

(C) is wrong because this statement is discussed in the second paragraph, not the last paragraph.

(D) is wrong because although the introduction mentions that the author was a professor of English for more than 30 years, it offers no specific evidence to support the statement that the author has been an avid reader for more than 30 years.

(E) is wrong because the passage makes no mention of whether the author has a preference for classic literature over contemporary literature. The author includes the names of several dead writers to convey the point that even when great writers die, you can still know them through their works.

23. **A is correct.** The author states that when strangers ask him if he has read all of his books, he replies that he has read many of them twice; however, he never addresses the question as to why he thinks books should be read twice.

(B) is wrong because it is answered in lines 26–27.

(C) is wrong because it is answered in lines 18–22.

(D) is wrong because it is answered in line 1.

(E) is wrong because it is answered in lines 53–55.

24. **B is correct.** According to the author, "Everyone should begin collecting a private library in youth; the instinct of private property, which is fundamental in human beings, can here be cultivated with every advantage and no evils."

(A) is wrong because although the author might agree that people enjoy collecting things, his point is that the thing they should collect is books.

(C) is wrong because the author never says that books are the best gifts for children, but merely that collecting books should be encouraged.

(D) is wrong because the author is suggesting that children be encouraged to collect books, not things.

(E) is wrong because it is directly contradicted in the passage when the author says, "Books are for use, not for show."

Section 2

1. **A is correct.** Although more than one answer may seem correct for this question, you are looking for the choice that best fits the context of the sentence; that is, the word that offers the best restatement of the description of Mount Everest as being the "highest mountain in the world." *Prodigious*, which means "enormous" or "impressively great in size or extent," is the best answer. Both *resplendent* (C) and *exquisite* (E) could be used to describe Mount Everest; however, because these words are synonyms, neither one can be the best answer. (B) is wrong because it makes no sense to say that "Mount Everest looks *deceptive* (meaning "false" or "misleading") even from a distance," and (D) is wrong because *gilded* means "covered in a thin layer of gold" or "deceptively attractive."

2. **B is correct.** A person "who tells stories and anecdotes with skill and wit" is a *raconteur* (B). A *pundit* (A) is a "critic," or "learned person," and a *sybarite* (C) is a person "devoted to pleasure or luxury." A

pugilist (D) is a boxer, and a *thespian* (E) is an actor.

3. **E is correct.** The fact that Miles Davis was "renowned" is a clue that you can discount both (B) and (C) as possibly correct first-blank answers because *obscure* means "of undistinguished reputation," and *arcane* means "known or understood by only a few." Focusing on the second blank, it is difficult to imagine that a jazz trumpeter whose playing was *pedestrian* (meaning "undistinguished or ordinary") would be considered *legendary*, so you can eliminate (A). It is doubtful that a *ubiquitous* (meaning "seeming to be everywhere at the same time") trumpeter would be "renowned" for his *plebeian* (meaning "common" or "ordinary") playing, so you can eliminate (D). That leaves only (E), which is correct. Davis was an *acclaimed* (meaning "celebrated") trumpeter renowned for his *virtuosic* (meaning "masterful" or "skillful") playing.

4. **D is correct.** This logic-based question includes the clue "despite," which should tell you that the missing word in the first clause will contrast with the missing word in the second clause. That is, despite the tone of the play being *one thing*, the subject matter was *the opposite*. Only choice (D) provides a pair of words with the proper contrast. The tone was *sober* (meaning "serious" or "solemn") but the subject matter was *farcical* (meaning "ridiculously clumsy," "ludicrous," or "absurd").

5. **B is correct.** The logic of the sentence requires a feeling opposite to the way one would normally feel after having lost an election. Try filling in the blank on your own. You might come up with something like this: Even thought he lost, the race was so close that the candidate was hopeful that next time he would win. Thus, you are looking for a word that means something like *hopeful*. The best choice is *sanguine*, which means "optimistic" or "cheerful and confident." (A) and (C) are wrong because *felicitous* means "appropriate" and *peripatetic* means "itinerant" or "wandering," and neither word makes sense in this context. Likewise (D) and (E) are wrong because

precipitous (meaning "impetuous" or "abrupt") and *virulent* (meaning "violent" or "venomous") have nothing to do with a hopeful outlook for the future.

6. **C is correct.** "Slavish bondage" and "kept down by their parents" are clues that the author despises traditional child-rearing methods.

(A) is wrong because the tone of the passage is hardly unrestrained or uncontrolled.

(B) is wrong because the author is not resigned, but rather seems to be advocating change.

(D) is wrong because the author seems to have strong feelings on the subject.

(E) is wrong because there is nothing friendly in the author's tone.

7. **D is correct.** This statement reflects the author's assertions that children's spirits become "abased" and "they lose all vigor and industry" when too much parental control is exercised over them.

(A) and (E) are wrong because each is almost the exact opposite of the point of view the author presents.

(B) and (C) are wrong because society is never mentioned in the passage.

8. **D is correct.** Although the developers' actions are, at best, questionable, the passage provides only enough information to discern that they are viewed with suspicion, making their actions *suspect*.

(A) and (B) can be discounted because there is no perceptible distinction between *criminal* and *unlawful* behavior, and indeed the developers have only been *indicted* and not *convicted*.

(C) is wrong because it implies that the developers were merely careless, and does not fit the context of "willfully mislead" and "deceptive calculations."

(E) is wrong because if the developers had initially been *scrupulous* (meaning "careful" and "upright"), they likely would not have been indicted.

9. **C is correct.** It presents the most analogous situation in which the diners agreed to a condition with the restaurant and then changed the terms of the agreement: unbeknownst to the restaurant.

(A) is wrong because the analogy is inverted and focuses on the landscape company rather than the homeowner.

(B) and (D) are similar to one another in that both situations require the payment of more money than had been called for in the original agreement, though neither provides a comparable parallel to the situation with the developers.

(E) is wrong because the parent merely *inquired* to the babysitter about the price for two children, while never *agreeing* on a price for three.

10. **B is correct.** The grey shadow is defined in the first sentence of the excerpt: "Perhaps it was this grey shadow stealing on the forest mission, the thought of the day when that beautiful mothering sister would leave his little friend Lydia alone with a bereft man and four small children . . ." Lydia would be left alone with a bereft man only if her sister should die.

(A) is wrong because there is nothing to suggest that Lydia is afraid of her brother-in-law.

(C) is wrong because the children are not responsible for the shadow of gloom upon the house.

(D) is wrong because there is nothing to suggest that George fears for his job.

(E) is wrong because there is nothing to suggest that the shadow has anything to do with a lack of sunlight.

11. **D is correct.** *Bereft* means "saddened by loss" or "bereaved." If Lydia's sister died, her husband would be a sad and lonely man.

(A) is wrong because *baffled* means "puzzled" or "confused."

(B) is wrong because *overbearing* means "arrogant" or "domineering."

(C) is wrong because *benevolent* means "kindly" or "charitable."

(E) is wrong because *improvident* means "careless."

12. **C is correct.** George tells his mother that his life "belongs to the white girl, Mrs. Evans' sister." Later he says, "I shall marry no one but the white girl . . . If she will not marry me, I shall never marry." Clearly George is in love with someone else.

(A) is wrong because George begs his parents to forgive him for "this one disobedience." If he did not love and respect his parents, he would not care whether they forgave him or not.

(B) is wrong because there is no indication that George even knew this woman. She may have been known only to his parents.

(D) is wrong because his words and actions indicate that George both loves and respects his parents and, therefore, it is unlikely that he would set out to hurt them.

(E) is wrong because George says "I have tried to honor all the ancient rules and usages of my forefathers, but I forgot this one thing."

13. **A is correct.** As stated in line 5, "Indianwise, his parents had arranged a suitable marriage for him . . ." In other words, the way of the Indians was for parents to arrange marriages for their children.

(B) is wrong because although it is mentioned that the Mohawk girl's parents were fairly prosperous, there is no indication of any exchange of money or land in connection with the marriage.

(C) is wrong because the custom is for parents to arrange marriages for their children.

(D) is wrong because there is no mention of a specific age at which members of the Mohawk tribe must marry.

(E) is wrong because there is no mention of the need for the approval of the tribal council.

14. **D is correct.** George realizes that he is not honoring the traditions of his fore-fathers, but still he wishes to marry Lydia. Once his father mentions that the family title will go to the Straight-Shots, George winced. "The hurt of it all was sinking in—he hated the Straight-Shots, he loved his own blood and bone." This seems to be George Mansion's biggest regret.

(A) is wrong because there is no mention that George will no longer be a Mohawk, just that his children will not carry his family title.

(B) is wrong because George seems to have already accepted this fact.

(C) is wrong because although his parents are angry and hurt, still his mother's last remarks indicate that she is proud of her son and will probably accept his decision.

(E) is wrong because there is nothing in the passage to support this choice.

15. **D is correct.** When George told his parents of his desire to marry Lydia, his mother's face "took on the shadow of age" and she exclaimed incredulously, "You would marry a *white* girl?" Her reaction shows both shock and disbelief.

(A) is wrong because the parents are more than puzzled by George's decision.

(B) is wrong because while their reaction may be described as outraged, the parents do not display embarrassment.

(C) is wrong because the parents do not sympathize with their son's decision.

(E) is wrong because the parents express shock and anger, not resignation and acceptance of George's decision.

16. **E is correct.** The bravery mentioned in the last two lines of the passage refers to George's courage in holding to his own choice for a bride. It has nothing to do with marrying the woman his parents have chosen for him.

(A) is wrong because George's mother points out that if he marries Lydia his children "could never hold the title, never be chief."

(B) is wrong because his father says that if George married Lydia the family title would go to "your aunt's sons."

(C) is wrong because the passage states that the tradition is for parents to arrange a suitable marriage for their sons.

(D) is wrong because the parents have chosen a girl "of the correct clan to mate with his own so that the line of blood heritage would be intact" and the sons of the next generation would be qualified to inherit the title of chief.

17. **B is correct.** Her words indicate that the mother is proud of her son for showing such courage.

(A) is wrong because this exclamation does not indicate anger.

(C) is wrong because being proud of her son, she would probably forgive him in the future.

(D) is wrong because she does not say that she will not accept her grandchildren, only that they cannot take on the family title.

(E) is wrong because this remark is not addressed to her sister's sons, but to her own son.

18. **E is correct.** As stated in lines 23–24, the data source for *Reading at Risk* is "as reliable and objective as any such survey can be."

(A) is wrong because the survey is based on a sample of adult readers.

(B) is wrong because the sample covers most major demographic groups, "providing statistical measurements by age, gender, education, income, region, race, and ethnicity."

(C) is wrong because the survey provides "so much data in such detail that it constitutes a comprehensive factual basis for any informed discussion of current American reading habits."

(D) is wrong because it contradicts the information given in the passage.

19. **C is correct.** The author says that "the news in the report is dire." He is clearly alarmed at the seriousness of the decline in reading literature detailed by the report.

(A) is wrong because the author says he doubts "that any careful observer of contemporary American society will be greatly surprised" by the results of the study.

(B) is wrong because there is nothing in the passage to suggest that the author is cautious in his interpretation of the results of the study.

(D) is wrong because the author is not skeptical (doubting or questioning) of the results.

(E) is wrong because the author is not ambiguous (uncertain or vague) in his assessment of the study.

20. **B is correct.** The author describes the cultural transformation as "our society's massive shift toward electronic media for entertainment and information."

(A) is wrong because the increased availability of the Internet is just one of the factors in the changeover from reading to electronic media as the primary source of information and entertainment.

(C) is wrong because the passage is concerned with the decline of reading for both entertainment and information.

(D) is wrong because there is no mention of a decline in the number of students enrolled in literature classes.

(E) is wrong because declines in volunteerism and political participation are mentioned as effects of the decline in reading literature, not as the cultural transformation itself.

21. **B is correct.** The sentence in question is as follows: "Reading a book requires a degree of active attention and engagement." Used in this context, *involvement* best captures the meaning of *engagement*.

(A) and (C) are wrong because *contemplation* is "the act of thoughtful observation or study," and *focus* is "close or narrow attention." Both of these choices have to do with mental processes, when the point the author is originally trying to make is one of active participation.

(D) and (E) are wrong because the author is not suggesting that a person needs to make a *commitment* (meaning "a pledge or promise") to reading, nor is he suggesting that a person show *conviction* (meaning a "fixed or strong belief"). Both of these choices are too extreme for the word *engagement* in the context of this sentence.

22. **A is correct.** As stated in paragraph 6, "Reading a book requires a degree of active attention and engagement . . . By contrast, most electronic media such as television, recordings, and radio make fewer demands on their audiences, and indeed often require no more than passive participation."

(B) is wrong because while all reading involves the written word, not all electronic media involve spoken words.

(C) is wrong because both reading and electronic media could have both immediate and long-term consequences.

(D) is wrong because there is nothing in the passage to suggest a social versus political contrast between reading and electronic media.

(E) is wrong because both reading and electronic media can be entertaining and informational.

23. **D is correct.** The purpose of this passage is to report the results of "a comprehensive survey recently released by the National Endowment for the Arts."

(A) is wrong because the author does not criticize the study; he simply laments its findings.

(B) is wrong because there is no mention of the expense of the study.

(C) is wrong because the passage does not present an opposing viewpoint to be debated.

(E) is wrong because the author does not suggest a solution. As stated in the next-to-last paragraph, "There is surely no single solution to the present dilemma, just as there is no single cause. Each concerned group—writers, teachers, publishers, journalists, librarians, and legislators—will legitimately view the situation from a different perspective, and each will offer its own recommendations."

24. **C is correct.** As stated in the last paragraph, "Advanced literacy is a specific intellectual skill and social habit that depends on a great many educational, cultural, and economic factors. As more Americans lose this capability, our nation becomes less informed, active, and independent minded." Thus, the author could be said to agree that advanced literacy is essential to a free, innovative and productive society.

(A) is wrong because the passage makes no connection between a decline in reading and an increase in computer literacy.

(B) is wrong because there is nothing to support the idea that literary reading is not important in a technologically advanced society.

(D) is wrong because lines 35–37 specifically state, "The concerned citizen in search of good news about American literary culture will study the pages of this report in vain."

(E) is wrong because line 83 specifically states, "Reading is not a timeless, universal capability."

Section 3

1. **E is correct.** This vocabulary-in-context question asks you to find the word that best describes the look of someone who spends all her time in a dim library. *Pallor* (E), meaning "paleness" or "lack of color," is the correct answer. *Countenance* (A), meaning "appearance, especially the expression of the face," appears to fit; however, considering the context, it is not a better answer than *pallor*. *Repose* (B), which means "tranquility" or "peace," is incorrect, as is *comportment*

(C), which means "behavior" or "conduct." *Gait* (D), which means "a particular way of walking," is incorrect as well.

2. **B is correct.** If you were to come up with an answer to this question without looking at the choices, you would probably say the ankle had become "puffy" or "swollen." *Tumescent* (B), meaning "swollen" or "distended," is the best answer. (A) and (C) are wrong because *desiccated* (meaning "dry") and *bilious* (meaning "bad tempered" or "containing bile") have nothing to do with swollen and uncomfortable to walk on. Similarly, (D) and (E) are wrong because neither *trenchant* (meaning "sharp" or "pungent") nor *sullied* (meaning "soiled" or "stained") applies to an ankle that is difficult to walk on.

3. **A is correct.** This vocabulary-in-context question requires two words that complement each other and restate the qualities named in the second half of the sentence; namely, "inspired fear" and "commanded respect." On the basis of the first blank alone you can eliminate (B) and (D) because *petulant* means "unreasonably irritable or ill-tempered," and *tactical* means "carried out in support of naval or military operations." Turning your attention to the second blank, you can discount (C) and (E) because *facile*, which means "done or achieved with little effort or difficulty," and *exacting*, which means "making severe demands" or "rigorous," have nothing to do with fear or respect. The only possible answer is (A). Ali was described as *formidable* (causing fear or dread) and *redoubtable* (frightening or commanding respect).

4. **B is correct.** The phrase "help her bid for re-election" is a clue that the verb you are looking for in the second blank is one that will do something positive for the senator's standing with her constituents. This information allows you to eliminate (A) because *undermine* means "weaken," and weakening her standing cannot help the senator's re-election bid. Likewise, you can eliminate (D) and (E) because *curtail* means "to cut short or reduce," and *truncate* means "to shorten or cut off," and neither one would help the senator

get elected. Turning your attention to the first blank, you can eliminate (C) because *unobtrusive,* which means "not noticeable," does not really make sense as a modifier for "displays of wealth." That leaves only choice (B), which is best. Her *ostentatious* (meaning "pretentious" or "showy") displays of wealth have done little to *promote* (meaning "encourage" or "bolster") her standing among working-class families.

5. **C is correct.** From the phrases "fresh from hibernation" and "would eat everything in sight," you can logically infer that the bear is hungry. While choices such as *hirsute* (A), meaning "covered with hair," and *omnivorous* (E), meaning "eating both animal and vegetable foods," may be appropriate descriptions of a bear, neither is the best answer. *Servile* (B) meaning "abjectly submissive" or "slavish" is incorrect, and *insatiable* (D), meaning "impossible to satisfy" can be discounted because it is doubtful that this would be the best choice for a bear described as "surprisingly picky." *Ravenous* (C), meaning "extremely hungry," is the only choice that follows the logic of a bear that would seemingly "eat everything in sight."

6. **E is correct.** This two-blank sentence offers five suitable choices for the first blank, so, finding the right second-blank option will be the key to answering the question correctly. *Appeasing* (A), meaning "bringing peace, quiet, or calm to," and *placating* (C), meaning "allaying the anger of, especially by making concessions" do not work in the context of the sentence; one would not "calm" the public's trust by trying to cover up a scandal. Also, because the words are so close in meaning, neither one could be the best choice. *Gleaning* (B), meaning "gathering or collecting bit by bit," and *effectuating* (D), meaning "bringing about" or "producing," are words that could be used in reference to public trust. However, it seems more likely that the governor would glean or effectuate public trust by being honest rather than by "trying to cover up a scandal." Contextually, both are incorrect. (E) is the only answer that properly conveys the meaning of the sentence. The most *egregious* (meaning "excessive" or "outrageous") error the governor made was *breaching* (meaning "violating") the public's trust in him by trying to cover up the scandal.

7. **E is correct.** As stated in the first two sentence of Passage 1, "Volcanoes are mountains, but they are very different from other mountains; they are not formed by folding and crumpling or by uplift and erosion. Instead, volcanoes are built by the accumulation of their own eruptive products—lava, bombs (crusted over lava blobs), ashflows, and tephra (airborne ash and dust)."

(A) is wrong because there is no mention of height.

(B) is wrong because there is no mention of ruggedness.

(C) is wrong because there is no mention of age.

(D) is wrong because there is no mention of location.

8. **B is correct.** As stated in the third paragraph of Passage 1, "How explosive an eruption is depends on how runny or sticky the magma is. . . . . . If magma is thick and sticky, gases cannot escape easily. Pressure builds up until the gases escape violently and explode."

(A) is wrong because if magma is thin and runny, "gases can escape easily from it. When this type of magma erupts, it flows out of the volcano."

(C) is wrong because all magma is lighter than the solid rock around it and so it rises and collects in magma chambers. This does not affect the explosiveness of an eruption.

(D) is wrong because whether thick or thin, sticky or runny, magma pushes out through fissures in the Earth's surface. This does not indicate how explosive an eruption will be.

(E) is wrong because magma that has erupted is called lava, regardless of the explosiveness of the eruption.

9. **B is correct.** As stated in the last sentence of Passage 1, "Because there may be

hundreds or thousands of years between volcanic eruptions, people may not be aware of a volcano's dangers." The fact that a volcano has not erupted for many years does not mean that the volcano will not erupt some time in the future leaving death and destruction in its wake.

(A) is wrong because even nonexplosive eruptions can do great damage.

(C) is wrong because although a volcano may look like a mountain, it differs from other mountains as described in the first paragraph of Passage 1.

(D) is wrong because although lava flows rarely kill people, they do cause considerable damage to any buildings in their path.

(E) is wrong because, although volcanic ash looks like snow, it does not melt, and it can suffocate plants, animals, and humans.

10. **D is correct.** The words in italics are scientific terms for which the author provides definitions within the text. ("A *volcano* is most commonly a conical hill or mountain built around a vent that connects with reservoirs of molten rock below the surface of the Earth." "Magma that has erupted is called *lava*.")

(A) is wrong because the italicized words are used in their usual, not unusual, way.

(B) is wrong because the italicized words are not difficult to pronounce.

(C) is wrong because the italicized words are not foreign words.

(E) is wrong because the words are important to the understanding of the passage.

11. **A is correct.** The passage states that "Deep within the Earth it is so hot that some rocks slowly melt and become a thick flowing substance called *magma*." However, the passage does not mention the factors that contribute to hot temperatures deep inside the Earth.

(B) is wrong because it is answered in lines 22–35.

(C) is wrong because it is answered in lines 26–28.

(D) is wrong because it is answered in lines 15–17.

(E) is wrong because it s is answered in lines 29–30.

12. **C is correct.** A 123-year slumber means that Mount St. Helens had no eruptions going back 123 years from 1980. That puts the last eruption at 1857.

(A) is wrong because if Mount St. Helens had been "sleeping" for 123 years, it must have been active 123 years ago.

(B) is wrong because there is nothing to support the idea that Mount St. Helens erupts every 123 years.

(D) is wrong because there is no mention of when geologists began keeping records of volcanic eruptions.

(E) is wrong because if Mount St. Helens erupted 123 years ago, it could always erupt again.

13. **D is correct.** *Rising* is used in the following sentence: "Heat from a rising plume of volcanic ash melted glacial ice creating cement-like slurries of rock and ash called mudflows." Each of the answer choices is a possible meaning for *rising*. However, in context, the best meaning is *ascending*.

14. **B is correct.** Passage 2 states that the geologists were not surprised by Mount St. Helens' awakening because they had been studying Mount St. Helens for many years, and in 1975 they "published a report predicting Mount St. Helens was the volcano in the lower 48 states most likely to erupt by the end of the century." Thus, the assumptions they had made about Mount St. Helens based on extensive studies of deposits found around the volcano were proving to be correct.

(A) is wrong because the passage states only that geologists predicted that Mount St. Helens was the volcano in the lower 48 states most likely to erupt by the end of the century. The passage does not state that geologists were able to predict when it would erupt, only that it was most likely to erupt.

(C) is wrong because the passage provides no information to support the claim that the longer a volcano remains dormant, the more likely it is to become active.

(D) is wrong because there is no information in the passage to support this statement.

(E) is wrong because the information about heat rising from volcanic ash has nothing to do with why geologists were not surprised by the volcano's awakening. Rather, it is included in a description of factors leading up to the volcano's eruption. The passage states geologists were not surprised because extensive studies had indicated that Mount St. Helens was the volcano in the lower 48 states that was most likely to erupt by the end of the century.

15. **C is correct.** The author's use of vivid language is shown by such words as "triggered," "blast," "flattened," "scoured," "billowed," and "swept." Examples of dramatic images include these: "In less than three minutes, 230 square miles of forest lay flattened," ". . . concrete-like mudflows that scoured river valleys," "A plume of volcanic ash and pumice billowed out of the volcano reaching a height of 15 miles and transformed day into night."

(A) is wrong because the author does not use scientific analysis to describe the scene.

(B) is wrong because the author does not write in a detached way.

(D) is wrong because events are not presented in a strictly chronological order.

(E) is wrong because details are not presented in spatial order.

16. **E is correct.** A wasteland is barren land with no vegetation. The author mentions in line 75 that the landslides flattened the forest and in lines 78–79 that concrete-like mudflows scoured river valleys surrounding the mountain.

(A) is wrong because the landscape was covered in volcanic ash, not snow.

(B) is wrong because a wasteland is barren, not covered in waste matter.

(C) is wrong because the trees had been flattened and swept away.

(D) is wrong because the forest was no longer standing.

17. **D is correct.** Passage 1 explains the scientific phenomenon known as a volcano, telling how volcanoes are formed and what happens when they erupt. Passage 2 provides a description of one particular volcanic eruption, at Mount St. Helens in 1980.

(A) is wrong because Passage 2 does not refute the information given in Passage 1.

(B) is wrong because Passage 1 does not present a theory; it presents factual information about volcanoes.

(C) is wrong because Passage 2 does not take a position, and Passage 1 does not argue against it.

(E) is wrong because Passage 1 does not present a problem, and Passage 2 does not offer a solution.

18. **B is correct.** Passage 2 discusses the 1980 eruption of Mount St. Helens. Thus, it describes a specific volcanic eruption.

(A) is wrong because general information about volcanoes is presented in Passage 1, not in Passage 2.

(C) is wrong because neither passage offers advice.

(D) is wrong because historical background is provided in Passage 1, not in Passage 2.

(E) is wrong because neither passage makes an appeal to protect the environment.

19. **A is correct.** In line 36, Passage 1 states explicitly, "Explosive volcanic eruptions can be dangerous and deadly." Passage 2 supports this statement with its description of the damage done by the 1980 eruption of Mount St. Helens: "In less than 3 minutes, 230 square miles of forest lay flattened. The hot gas and magma melted the snow and ice that covered the volcano. The resulting floodwater mixed with the rock and debris

to create concrete-like mudflows that scoured river valleys surrounding the mountain. . . . By the following morning major eruptive activity had ceased and the landscape appeared to be a gray wasteland."

(B) is wrong because nonexplosive eruptions are discussed only in Passage 1.

(C) is wrong because slow-moving lava flows are mentioned only in Passage 1.

(D) is wrong because neither passage supports a specific timetable for volcanic eruptions.

(E) is wrong because earthquakes are discussed only in Passage 2.

CHAPTER 4

STRATEGIES FOR SENTENCE COMPLETION QUESTIONS

This chapter will give you . . .

- sample questions with step-by-step explanations
- strategies for answering this question type
- practice sets to sharpen your skills

The Sentence Completion questions on the SAT are designed to test your knowledge of word meanings along with your ability to understand the logical structure of a sentence. There are usually from five to eight Sentence Completion questions in any given Critical Reading section of the SAT.

FORMAT OF SENTENCE COMPLETION QUESTIONS

Each sentence completion question consists of a statement with one or two blanks. Each blank indicates a missing word. Following each sentence are five words or sets of words labeled A, B, C, D, and E. You are to select the word or set of words that, when inserted in the sentence, best fits the meaning of the sentence as a whole.

Often more than one pair of words among the answer choices will fit the structure of the sentence that appears in the question stem. However, in order to answer Sentence Completion questions correctly, you must determine which pair of words *best* completes the meaning of the sentence. To do this, you must consider both word meaning and logic.

Your SAT Coach Says . . .

"Do all the Sentence Completion questions first because they take less time than Reading Comprehension questions."

SAMPLE SENTENCE COMPLETION QUESTION EXPLAINED

Let's look at a sample question to see what's involved.

Anticipating a _____outcome, the candidate prepared an _____ speech.

- (A) divisive . . . adamant
- (B) reputable . . . apologetic
- (C) predictable . . . unresponsive
- (D) positive . . . acrimonious
- (E) favorable . . . acceptance

To answer this question, read the sentence focusing on the logical relationship between its parts. In this case, the nature of the outcome will determine what kind of speech the candidate will prepare. Now look at each of the answer choices to find the one that best reflects this relationship.

(A) is wrong because a *divisive* outcome (one that causes disagreement) is not likely to produce an *adamant* (unyielding or inflexible) speech.

(B) is wrong because a *reputable* outcome is a good one, and so it is unlikely to provoke an *apologetic* response.

(C) is wrong because a *predictable* (certain) outcome is not likely to result in an *unresponsive* speech.

(D) is wrong because a *positive* outcome is the desired outcome, and so it is not likely to result in an *acrimonious* (bitter) speech.

(E) is correct. A *favorable* outcome is most likely to result in the candidate's preparing an *acceptance* speech.

STRATEGIES FOR ANSWERING SENTENCE COMPLETION QUESTIONS

Here is a six-step strategic plan that you can use to answer Sentence Completion questions.

1. Read the sentence to get the overall meaning.
2. Look for clue words that show how sentence parts are related.
3. Use the clue words to anticipate the answer based on the relationship indicated.
4. Read the answer choices and select the one that is best.
5. Check your answer by reading the sentence with your answer choice in place.
6. If you still cannot determine the correct answer, eliminate answer choices that do not make sense. Then, guess from among the remaining answer choices.

> ### Your SAT Coach Says . . .
>
> "Circle clue words in your test book that show relationships."

USING CLUE WORDS

Use this chart to help you determine how sentence parts are frequently related in Sentence Completion questions.

Logical Relationship	Clues
Contrasting Ideas **Even though** the plane was late taking off, we arrived at our destination right on time.	although, but, despite, even though, however, instead of, nonetheless, not, on the contrary, rather, yet

Complementary Ideas *The hurricane destroyed homes all along the coastline; **furthermore,** it knocked down power lines, leaving millions without electricity.*	in addition, also, and, because, consequently, for, furthermore, likewise, moreover, similarly
Cause-and-Effect ***Because** they were so hot and thirsty after the ballgame, they could hardly wait to get a cold drink from the picnic cooler.*	accordingly, because, consequently, for, hence, in order to, since, so, therefore, thus
Definition or Explanation *The heat was unbearable; it never fell below 100 degrees the entire week.*	comma, semicolon, colon

Use the five-step strategy and what you have learned about sentence logic to answer the practice Sentence Completion questions that follow. Then compare your answer to the explanation given.

■ SAMPLE SENTENCE COMPLETION PRACTICE SET EXPLAINED

> <u>Directions:</u> Each sentence below has one or two blanks. Each blank indicates that something is missing. Following each sentence are five words or sets of words labeled A, B, C, D, and E. You are to select the word or set of words that, when inserted in the sentence, best fits the meaning of the sentence as a whole.

> ***Your SAT Coach Says . . .***
>
> "In choosing your answer, consider both word meaning and logic."

1. Despite our best efforts to protect the environment and keep it safe, until the problems of pollution are _____, the future of our environment seems, at best, _____.

    (A) created . . . gloomy
    (B) revoked . . . secure
    (C) solved . . . uncertain
    (D) replaced . . . revered
    (E) increased . . . unknown

1. Correct answer: C
    Despite is a clue that the sentence sets up a contrast. We want to keep the environment safe, but there are problems with pollution. The first blank requires a word that tells what we want to do about the problems of pollution. The best choice is to end them or solve them as in choice (C). Until

those problems can be *solved,* the future of the environment is not safe, but rather it is *uncertain.*

(A) and (E) can be eliminated because the first word makes no sense in the first blank.

(B) and (D) can be eliminated because the second word does not work in the second blank.

Your SAT Coach Says . . .

"Remember that words such as *although, but, despite,* and *however* often signal that a sentence completion question has a structure based on contrast, so look for words with opposite or different meanings rather than the same or similar meanings."

---

2. Knowledgeable dog owners recommend obtaining a purebred dog from a _____ breeder, one who is _____ and respected by customers and breeders alike.

(A) discerning . . . equivocal
(B) demanding . . . flexible
(C) churlish . . . charming
(D) reputable . . . admired
(E) humble . . . feared

2. Correct answer: D
The comma following the word *breeder* is a clue that the words that follow will define or explain what kind of breeder is recommended. Only choice (D) provides two words that can define or explain each other. A *reputable* breeder is one who is *admired* and respected.

(A) is wrong because a *discerning* (astute) breeder is not likely to be *equivocal* (vague or uncertain).

(B) is wrong because a *demanding* breeder is not likely to be *flexible.*

(C) is wrong because a *churlish* (rude or boorish) breeder is not likely to be *charming.*

(E) is wrong because a *humble* breeder is not likely to be *feared.*

Your SAT Coach Says . . .

"Remember that the use of a comma may signal that a sentence completion question has a structure based on definition."

---

3. The model of _____, he displayed impeccable manners and excellent taste.

(A) duplicity
(B) decorum
(C) depravity
(D) versatility
(E) efficiency

3. Correct answer: B
The comma in this sentence completion question is a clue that the missing word means the same as "impeccable manners and excellent taste." *Decorum,* which means "propriety and good taste in behavior, speech, or dress," is the best choice.

(A), (C), (D), and (E) are all wrong because they have nothing to do with good manners or taste. *Duplicity* (A) means "cunning or deception." *Depravity* (C) means "corruption or wickedness." *Versatility* (D) means "ability to do many things." *Efficiency* (E) means "effectiveness."

> ### *Your SAT Coach Says . . .*
>
> "Remember that Sentence Completion questions are generally arranged in order of difficulty, from easiest to hardest. Pace yourself accordingly."

4. The detectives believed that the fingerprint on the glass was _____ evidence; it definitely placed the defendant at the scene of the crime.

(A) negligible
(B) incorrigible
(C) incriminating
(D) inevitable
(E) inadmissible

4. Correct answer: C
The semicolon is a clue that the second part of the sentence describes or explains the first part of the sentence. Evidence that places someone at the scene of a crime is *incriminating;* it involves the person and makes that person look guilty.

(A) is wrong because *negligible* means "trifling or unimportant."
(B) is wrong because *incorrigible* means "incapable of being corrected or improved."
(D) is wrong because *inevitable* means "unavoidable."
(E) is wrong because *inadmissible* means "not allowed or accepted."

> ### *Your SAT Coach Says . . .*
>
> "Remember that words such as *because, for,* and *hence* often signal that a sentence completion question has a structure based on cause-and-effect, so look for words that express an expected causal relationship."

5. Carl had a reputation for being a _____ because he fearlessly skied down the steepest trails.

(A) leader
(B) dreamer
(C) coward
(D) clown
(E) daredevil

5. Correct answer: E
The word *because* is a clue that the sentence shows a cause-and-effect relationship. Skiing fearlessly down the steepest trails is likely to earn someone the reputation of being a *daredevil.* No other answer choice makes sense in this context.

6. Paradoxically, the effects of the hurricane were both _____ and _____; it demolished homes and businesses in its wake, but it spurred an economic revival by creating jobs for many previously unemployed workers.

    (A) destructive . . . constructive
    (B) tangible . . . intangible
    (C) empirical . . . scientific
    (D) practical . . . theoretical
    (E) fearsome . . . dreaded

6. Correct answer: A
Paradoxically in the first clause and *but* in the second clause are clues that the ideas in this sentence are in contrast to each other. Following the logic of the sentence the first effect was bad (homes and businesses were destroyed) and the second effect was good (jobs were created). Choice (A) best reflects these circumstances.

    (B) is wrong because the creation of jobs is not *intangible* (vague or untouchable).
    (C) is wrong because neither *empirical,* which means "practical," nor *scientific,* which means "systematic" or "derived from science," applies to the destruction of homes or the creation of jobs.
    (D) is wrong for the same reason as (C).
    (E) is wrong because *fearsome* and *dreaded* are synonyms, not antonyms.

Your SAT Coach Says . . .

"Remember that words such as *in addition, consequently, so,* and *also* often signal that a sentence completion question has a structure based on complementary ideas. With these questions, look for words among the answer choices that best complete the meaning of the sentence."

---

7. The museum's panel of experts was _____ collection of former curators and art historians; so each of them had _____ knowledge of the Renaissance.

    (A) an erudite . . . ample
    (B) a tenacious . . . extensive
    (C) a scholarly . . . scant
    (D) an educated . . . corpulent
    (E) a diversified . . . sparse

7. Correct answer: A

This question requires you to find an answer choice that complements (rather than contrasts) the other parts of the sentence. Complementary ideas provide additional support for the meaning of the sentence. The correct choice often has a similar meaning to another key word in the sentence. The panel was *erudite* (meaning "characterized by extensive knowledge" or "learned"). As a result, "each of them had *ample* knowledge of the Renaissance." Therefore, answer choice (A) is correct.

(B) is wrong because a panel of experts need not necessarily be *tenacious,* meaning "holding or tending to hold persistently to something, such as a point of view."

(C) and (E) are incorrect because their meanings do not make sense in the second blank. You can infer that if the panel is composed of experts, then they must surely have more than *scant* (C) or *sparse* (E) knowledge of the Renaissance.

(D) is wrong because *corpulent,* meaning "excessively fat," also does not fit the context of the sentence in the second blank.

Now take the time to apply what you have just learned about the structure and types of Sentence Completion questions to see how well you can use the strategies. When you are finished, use the answer key to score your work.

- You may find that certain types of structure are easier for you to deal with than others. Remember that Sentence Completion questions appear in order of their difficulty. Use the practice set to determine which types of questions give you the most difficulty.
- Review the strategies and clues discussed above and then try Practice B, focusing on the kinds of items that you found difficult. Remember that the more you practice with these items, the easier they will become for you to answer correctly.

▒▒▒ ON YOUR OWN: PRACTICE SET A

Directions: Each sentence below has one or two blanks. Each blank indicates that something is missing. Following each sentence are five words or sets of words labeled A, B, C, D, and E. You are to select the word or set of words that, when inserted in the sentence, best fits the meaning of the sentence as a whole.

E X A M P L E :

1. Despite our best efforts to protect the environment and keep it safe, until the problems of pollution are _____, the future of our environment seems, at best, _____.

    (A) created . . . gloomy
    (B) revoked . . . secure
    (C) solved . . . uncertain
    (D) replaced . . . revered
    (E) increased . . . unknown

    Correct Answer: C

1. During her _____ career, author Elfriede Jelinek has received numerous _____, including the 2004 Nobel Prize in Literature.

    (A) auspicious . . . accolades
    (B) inefficacious . . . awards
    (C) prosperous . . . censures
    (D) pernicious . . . citations
    (E) successful . . . invectives

2. Although the seminar's participants _____ for a morning introduction, they soon _____ until later on in the afternoon.

    (A) assembled . . . plundered
    (B) convened . . . adjourned
    (C) petitioned . . . repealed
    (D) gathered . . . assembled
    (E) converged . . . integrated

3. The company's hope was to _____ short-term sales expectations in order to reward investors and properly _____ the staff.

    (A) suspend . . . compensate
    (B) exceed . . . remunerate
    (C) surpass . . . indemnify
    (D) forecast . . . reward
    (E) determine . . . enervate

4. Having suffered numerous injuries over the course of her career, the gymnast demonstrated her _____ by overcoming adversity and winning the gold medal.

    (A) consternation
    (B) apprehension
    (C) viscosity
    (D) resilience
    (E) dexterity

5. During the soccer championship, the star mid-fielder fooled her defender as she _____ to the left and _____ dribbled the ball down the right side of the field.

    (A) lunged . . . ascetically
    (B) feinted . . . deftly
    (C) careened . . . maladroitly
    (D) staggered . . . haphazardly
    (E) lumbered . . . assiduously

6. When Clara saw the actor at the airport, she could not help noticing that everything about him seemed unreal; his skin appeared more orange than suntanned and his teeth were _____ white.

    (A) tautly
    (B) intrepidly
    (C) preternaturally
    (D) propitiously
    (E) unavailingly

7. Despite its innocuous appearance, the fish has a _____ sting.
    (A) deadly
    (B) benign
    (C) persistent
    (D) complacent
    (E) predictable

8. To help her unwind after a _____ week, there was nothing Celia enjoyed more than a drive through Vermont's _____ countryside.
    (A) hectic . . . bromidic
    (B) harried . . . fatuous
    (C) frenetic . . . obstreperous
    (D) sedate . . . bucolic
    (E) tumultuous . . . pastoral

ON YOUR OWN: PRACTICE SET A

ANSWERS AND EXPLANATIONS

1. Correct answer: A

   This question provides a good example of how you can narrow the possible options for the correct answer by focusing first on only one blank of a two-blank question. Logically, you can infer that if Ms Jelinek won the Nobel Prize in Literature, her career would not be considered *ineffi-cacious* (meaning "ineffective" or "not capable of producing a desired effect or result") or *pernicious* (meaning "tending to cause death or serious injury"), so you can eliminate both (B) and (D). By eliminating these choices, you are able to remove the second word of each pair (*awards* and *citations*, respectively) from consideration, a big advantage considering that both choices seem to fit. This leaves you with (A), (C), and (E). All three options provide good first-blank answers, but considering that *censures* are "expressions of strong disapproval" and *invectives* are "abusive expressions or denunciations," only choice (A) seems appropriate. During her *auspicious* (meaning "successful" or "favorable") career, Jelinek received numerous *accolades* (meaning "signs of respect or approval") including a Nobel Prize.

2. Correct answer: B

   The key to this sentence is the word "although." An "although" construction often signals that the answer choices you are looking for in a two-blank question will contrast with one another. Of the five sets of answer choices, only (B) offers an appropriate contrast. The participants *convened* (meaning "came together" or "assembled") for a morning introduction, but then they *adjourned* (meaning "suspended" or "closed the meeting") until later in the day. (A) is incorrect because it is unlikely that the seminar's participants would have *plundered* (meaning "raided" or "ravaged")

   until later on in the afternoon. (C) is incorrect because, although the participants may have *petitioned* (meaning "appealed") for a morning introduction, it makes no sense to say that they *repealed* (meaning "abolished") until later in the afternoon. (D) is incorrect because the answer choices complement, rather than contrast with, one another, and (E) is incorrect because *integrated* (meaning "to make into a whole by bringing all parts together") makes no sense in the context of the sentence.

3. Correct answer: B

   If the company seeks to reward investors, then sales would have to be good. Considering the first blank only, choices (B) and (C) both seem to work. However, when you look at the second blank, choice B is clearly better. The company hopes to *exceed* (meaning "outdo" or "surpass") sales expectations in order to reward investors and properly *remunerate* (meaning "pay" or "compensate") the staff. (A) is wrong because a company would not *suspend* (meaning "stop" or "hold back") sales expectations to reward investors, and (D) is wrong because merely forecasting (meaning "predicting") sales expectations does not produce rewards for investors or staff. (E) is wrong because *enervate* (meaning "weaken" or "unnerve") makes no sense in this context.

4. Correct answer: D

   Although not providing an exact restatement of the definition as many vocabulary-in-context questions do, this question does offer you a clue to getting the right answer. The phrase "overcoming adversity" as it relates to "having suffered numerous injuries" is the key to this question. Ask yourself: which answer choice most closely denotes "overcoming adversity"? *Resilience* (D), meaning "the ability to recover quickly from illness, change, or misfortune," is the correct answer choice. *Consternation* (A) is "the state of paralyzing dismay," and *apprehension* (B) is an "uneasy or fearful anticipation of the future;" both are incorrect in the context of the sentence. *Viscosity* (C), meaning "thickness" or "stickiness," is also incorrect. Occasionally on the SAT, you will encounter a question that seems to have more than one correct answer, and your task will be to settle on the best answer as it relates to the context of the question. With that in mind, eliminate *dexterity* (E), meaning "skill and grace in physical movement, especially in use of the hands" because it does not support the context of the sentence with regard to the gymnast "having suffered numerous injuries" and "overcoming adversity" as well as *resilience* does.

5. Correct answer: B

If you know which first blank-answer choice denotes the key word "fooled," you should be able to answer this question quickly and easily. If you do not, you still have a chance to answer correctly by selecting the proper second-blank word. *Feinted* (B), meaning "to perform a deceptive action calculated to divert attention from one's real purpose," is the best first-blank option, as its definition is the closest restatement of "fooled." Some of the other choices, such as *lunged* (A) and *careened* (C) seem to fit the first blank as well, however, each is paired with a word that is not indicative of the play of a "star mid-fielder." *Ascetically* means "in a way marked by self-discipline or self-denial, especially for spiritual improvement," and *maladroitly* means "in a way that is marked by a lack of skill or adeptness."

6. Correct answer: C

Knowing the definitions of the answer choices will help you answer this question correctly. Following the logic of the sentence, you can infer that if the actor's looks seemed unreal, and his skin was "or-

ange," then his teeth likely possessed a quality that makes them appear unnaturally white as well. *Tautly* (A) means "pulled tight," which makes no sense in describing someone's teeth. Likewise, (B), (D), and (E) are wrong because it makes little sense to describe teeth as *intrepidly* (meaning "fearlessly" or "courageously"), *propitiously* (meaning "favorably" or "advantageously"), or *unavailingly* (meaning "uselessly" or "ineffectually") white in the context of the sentence. *Preternaturally*, which means "abnormally" or "supernaturally," is the best choice to complement the actor's "orange" skin, making choice (C) the correct answer.

7. Correct answer: A

This sentence sets up a contrast in ideas by use of the word "despite." The "despite" construction provides you with a clue that the answer you are looking for will contrast with another word in the sentence: in this case *innocuous* (meaning "harmless"). Of the choices, only *deadly* (A), meaning "fatal," offers the proper contrast with *innocuous*. (B) is incorrect because *benign* and *innocuous* are often used synonymously. *Persistent* (D), which means "continuous," might make sense, but this choice fails to set up the contrast required by the word "despite." *Complacent* (D), which means "self-satisfied or smug," and *predictable* (E), which means "possible to foretell," make no sense in the context of the sentence.

8. Correct answer: E

You can eliminate (D) immediately because there would be no need to "unwind" after a *sedate* (meaning "serenely deliberate or composed") week. All of the other first-blank choices are appropriate, so, you will have to focus on the second-blank choices in order to select the correct answer. A *bromidic* (A) countryside would be one that is "stale, trite, or commonplace" and a *fatuous* (B) countryside would be one that is "vacuously, smugly, and unconsciously foolish." Neither is a good choice in the context of the sentence. *Obstreperous* (C), meaning "noisily and stubbornly defiant," is also incorrect as a description of the Vermont countryside. *Pastoral* (E), meaning "idyl-

lic" or "charmingly simple and serene" is a fitting description of the countryside, and *tumultuous* (meaning "noisy and disorderly") is an appropriate choice to describe Celia's week. Thus, (E) is the best answer.

ON YOUR OWN: PRACTICE SET B

Directions: Each sentence below has one or two blanks. Each blank indicates that something is missing. Following each sentence are five words or sets of words labeled A, B, C, D, and E. You are to select the word or set of words that, when inserted in the sentence, best fits the meaning of the sentence as a whole.

EXAMPLE:

1. Despite our best efforts to protect the environment and keep it safe, until the problems of pollution are _____, the future of our environment seems, at best, _____.

    (A) created . . . gloomy
    (B) revoked . . . secure
    (C) solved . . . uncertain
    (D) replaced . . . revered
    (E) increased . . . unknown

    Correct Answer: C

1. After the floodwaters receded, the townspeople began the long and _____ task of repairing and rebuilding in an attempt to get back to some _____ of life as they had previously known it.

    (A) arduous . . . semblance
    (B) difficult . . . consanguinity
    (C) affable . . . normalcy
    (D) rudimentary . . . affinity
    (E) despotic . . . modicum

2. The drive to the beach house had been _____; however, once they arrived the family enjoyed a(n)_____vacation.

    (A) heinous . . . virulent
    (B) verbose . . . churlish
    (C) rancorous . . . acrimonious
    (D) placid . . . carefree
    (E) disastrous . . . idyllic

3. Upon learning that their reservation had been canceled because their payment did not clear, the angry couple became _____, shouting at the desk clerk and threatening to sue the management.

    (A) amiable
    (B) belligerent
    (C) morose
    (D) extraneous
    (E) lavish

4. The sun had already set, and as Amanda walked down the sidewalk she could not help but notice how peaceful her neighborhood looked in the faint _____ light.

    (A) fervid
    (B) glowing
    (C) abstract
    (D) crepuscular
    (E) luminous

5. A strong yet _____ stone, cantera is ideal for architectural applications such as fountains, fireplaces, and columns.

    (A) obstinate
    (B) contumacious
    (C) absorbent
    (D) pestilent
    (E) malleable

6. Sam was always impeccably dressed at work; however, at home his _____ style seemed to limited to jeans and T-shirts.

    (A) leisurely
    (B) impetuous
    (C) wanton
    (D) sartorial
    (E) fallacious

▰▰▰ ON YOUR OWN: PRACTICE SET B

▰▰▰ ANSWERS AND EXPLANATIONS

1. Correct answer: A

    The first blank required a word that complements "long" to describe the task of repairing and rebuilding. Neither *affable* (C), meaning "pleasant," nor *rudimentary* (D), meaning "basic" or "elemental," fits the context of the sentence, so both can be discounted. *Despotic* (E), meaning "authoritarian," is also incorrect. Both *arduous* (A), meaning "laborious," and *difficult* (C), meaning "hard," fit the first blank; however, *consanguinity*, meaning "related by blood or a common ancestor" or "a close affinity or connection," is not the best match for the second blank. *Semblance* (A), meaning "an outward appearance" or "the barest trace," is a better match. Therefore, (A) is the correct answer.

2. Correct answer: E

    The key to this sentence is the word "however." When you encounter two-blank sentences on the SAT that contain words such as "however," "although," "despite," "but," "rather," and "yet," be aware that the answer choices you are looking for will likely contrast with one another. Of the choices, only (E) satisfies this requirement. After a *disastrous* (meaning "calamitous" or "extremely bad") drive, the family enjoyed an *idyllic* (meaning "pleasing and simple") vacation at the beach house. (A), (C), and (D) are incorrect because they all offer paired options that are synonymous or nearly synonymous. (B) is incorrect because *verbose* (meaning "wordy") makes no sense in the context of describing a drive.

3. Correct answer: B

    What kind of behavior would you expect from an "angry couple" who are "shouting," and "threatening"? Certainly, you can eliminate *amiable* (A), because an angry couple is unlikely to behave in a "friendly and agreeable" manner. As well, *lavish* (E) is inappropriate as it means "wasteful" or "rich." *Extraneous* (D), meaning "not essential" or "irrelevant," does not make sense in the context of the sentence. *Morose* (C) meaning "sullen" or "gloomy" is a possibility, but *belligerent* (B) meaning "ready to fight" is a better choice when you consider the clue words "angry," "shouting," and "threatening."

4. Correct answer: D

    The phrase "the sun had already set," provides a clue to this vocabulary-in-context question. Clearly, *glowing* (B) and *luminous* (E) are incorrect, as both words are inconsistent with the fact that "the sun had already set" and the light is "faint." It makes no sense to describe light as *abstract* (meaning "theoretical" or "difficult to understand") or *fervid* (meaning "passionate" or "zealous"). That leaves only (D), which is correct. *Crepuscular* means "dim" or "like twilight," which is a good description of the faint light visible once the sun has set.

5. Correct answer: E

    The "yet" construction of this sentence signals that the word you are looking for is "strong" *yet* something else as well. That is, cantera is strong, but it also possesses a quality that makes it "ideal for architectural applications." *Malleable* (E), meaning "capable of being shaped or formed," is the best answer. *Obstinate* (A), meaning "stubborn," and *contumacious* (B), meaning "disobedient" or "rebellious," are not words generally used to describe a stone. A stone that was *absorbent* (C) would likely not be a very good choice for use in construction of a fountain. *Pestilent* (D) is an adjective meaning "tending to cause death" or "likely to cause an epidemic disease."

6. Correct answer: D

    Sartorial (D), meaning "of or relating to clothing in general, or style or manner of dress," is the correct answer. (A) and (B) can be eliminated because neither *leisurely*, which means "deliberate" or "slow," nor *impetuous*, which means "impulsive" or "rash," fits the context of the sentence. The same is true of *wanton* (C), which means "lewd" or "immoral," and *fallacious* (E), which means "misleading" or "deceptive."

CHAPTER 5

STRATEGIES FOR CRITICAL READING COMPREHENSION QUESTIONS

This chapter will give you . . .

- sample questions with step-by-step explanations
- strategies for answering this question type
- practice sets to sharpen your skills

Passage-based Critical Reading questions test your ability to read, understand, analyze, and evaluate a variety of reading passages. The passages can be as short as 100 words or as long as 850 words and may be stand-alone passages or paired passages based on a related topic. The passages themselves come from many fields, including the humanities, social studies, natural sciences, and literature. Each passage or pair of passages is followed by questions based on its content.

FORMAT OF PASSAGE-BASED CRITICAL READING COMPREHENSION QUESTIONS

Irrespective of the type of passage(s) and the subject matter, you will find the following three main types of reading questions after each.

- *Vocabulary-in-Context Questions*—test your ability to determine the meaning of words based on their use in the passage.
- *Literal Comprehension Questions*—test your ability to understand information directly stated in the passage.
- *Extended Reasoning Questions*—test your ability to analyze information and evaluate an author's assumptions and techniques. These questions may ask you to recognize main ideas, make inferences, identify cause and effect, determine an author's tone, or follow an author's logic.

Each question is followed by five possible answer choices. Your job is to identify the best answer from among the choices presented.

STRATEGIES FOR PASSAGE-BASED CRITICAL READING QUESTIONS

Here's a helpful five-step plan that you can use for answering SAT Passage-Based Critical Reading questions.

1. Read any introductory text first to put the passage in context.
2. Skim the questions to focus on the information you will need. Ignore the answer choices for now.

3. Read the passage to get the big picture.

- Ask yourself: What's this passage all about? Why did the author write it?
- Mark up the passage or make notes in the margin as you read.

4. Read the questions with the answer choices.

- Choose the answer if you know it.
- If not, go back to the passage to find it.
- Use line references to help locate information.
- Cross out answer choices you can definitely eliminate.

5. Guess if you can eliminate even one or two of the answer choices.

- Try to answer all the questions based on a reading passage the first time around.
- If you have to go back to an unanswered question, you'll have to reread the passage, which takes valuable time.

Remember:

- The answer to a reading question can be found in or inferred from the passage(s).
- An answer choice that is true is not necessarily the correct answer. The correct choice must be both a true statement and the one that best answers the question.
- When a question refers to a numbered line go back to the passage and read the information around the line reference. It will clarify the question and help you choose the best answer.
- When comparing paired passages, be sure the answer you choose is true for both passages.

SAMPLE OF A LONG-PASSAGE READING QUESTION SET EXPLAINED

Here is a sample reading passage with four typical Critical Reading questions. Read the passage first. Then answer the questions based on what is stated or implied in the passage and the introductory material provided.

The following passage comes from an essay on nature by Ralph Waldo Emerson.

The inhabitants of cities suppose that the country landscape is pleasant only half the year. I please myself with the graces of the winter scenery, and believe that we are as much touched by it as by the genial influences of summer. To the attentive eye, each moment of the year has its own beauty, and in the same field, it beholds, every hour, a picture which was never seen before, and which shall never be seen again. The heavens change every moment, and reflect their glory or gloom on the plains beneath. The state of the crop in the surrounding farms alters the expression of the earth from week to week. The succession of native plants in the pastures and roadsides, which makes the silent clock by which time tells the summer hours, will make even the divisions of the day sen-

15 sible to a keen observer. The tribes of birds and insects, like the plants punctual to their time, follow each other, and the year has room for all. By water-courses, the variety is greater. In July, the blue pontederia or pickerel-weed blooms in large beds in the shallow parts of our pleasant river, and swarms with yellow butterflies in continual motion. Art cannot rival this pomp of purple and gold. Indeed the river is a perpetual gala, and boasts each month a new

20 ornament.

Your SAT Coach Says . . .

"Feel free to mark up the passage as you read. Highlight main ideas, important supporting details, and words that indicate special relationships."

---

1. The author's overall tone in this passage is best described as one of

   (A) frustration
   (B) disappointment
   (C) uncertainty
   (D) appreciation
   (E) curiosity

1. Correct answer: D
   The author is pleased with both "the graces of the winter scenery" and "the genial influences of summer." He says, "each moment of the year has its own beauty" and calls the river "a perpetual gala" that "boasts each month a new ornament." These phrases are evidence of the author's appreciation for the beauty of nature. Therefore, choice (D) is correct.
   There is no evidence in the passage to support choices (A), (B), (C), or (E).

Your SAT Coach Says . . .

"Look for specific words and phrases to support your answer choice."

---

2. The main idea of the passage is that the author

   (A) prefers summer to winter
   (B) laments the passing of time
   (C) finds beauty in every season
   (D) prefers the city to the country
   (E) thinks art is no rival for nature

2. Correct answer: C
   The overall message of this passage is the beauty to be found in every moment of the year. The fields change "every hour," the crops alter the expression of the earth "from week to week," tribes of birds and insects follow each other "and the year has room for all." All of these details point to choice (C) as the correct answer.

(A) is wrong because it is "the inhabitants of cities" who suppose that the country landscape is pleasant only half the year.

(B) is wrong because the author seems to celebrate the passing of time, looking forward to the changes each season brings.

(D) is wrong because the author contrasts his point of view with that of city dwellers.

(E) may be true, but it is only one detail mentioned in the passage, and not the main idea of the passage as a whole.

Your SAT Coach Says . . .

"Remember that virtually every sentence in a well-written passage relates to the main idea."

---

3. In line 4, "genial" most nearly means

(A) genuine
(B) esteemed
(C) generous
(D) amenable
(E) amiable

3. Correct answer: E

The word *genial* can mean "good natured," "friendly," "pleasant" or "healthful." The best synonym is *amiable* found in choice (E).

(A), (B), and (C) do not fit the context.

(D) may sound like *amiable,* but it means "responsive" or "obedient," which does not make sense in the context of the sentence.

Your SAT Coach Says . . .

"Substituting each answer choice in the original sentence is helpful in eliminating some obviously wrong answers."

---

4. Where can pontederia or pickerel-weed blooms be found growing?

(A) in river beds
(B) on farms
(C) in cities
(D) in fields
(E) in the country

4. Correct answer: A

In lines 16–17 of the passage, the author mentions pontederia or pickerel-weed blooms growing "in large beds in the shallow parts of our pleasant river." Therefore, (A) is the best answer choice. (E) might seem correct because Emerson is speaking about life in the country. However, the passage is specific about where in the country these blooms can be found. Therefore, (E) is incorrect. The other answer choices are not supported by details in the passage.

SAMPLE OF A SHORT-PASSAGE READING QUESTION SET EXPLAINED

Questions 1 and 2 are based on the following passage.

In this year of all years, Adams lost sight of education. Things began smoothly, and London glowed with the pleasant sense of fa-
Line miliarity and dinners. He sniffed with voluptuous delight the coal-smoke of Cheapside and reveled in the architecture of Oxford
5   Street. May Fair never shone so fair to Arthur Pendennis as it did to the returned American. The country never smiled its velvet smile of trained and easy hostess as it did when he was so lucky as to be asked on a country visit. He loved it all—everything;—had always loved it! He felt almost attached to the Royal Exchange. He
10   thought he owned the St. James Club. He patronized the Legation.

1. The narrator's attitude toward London is best described as one of

   (A) nostalgia
   (B) veneration
   (C) irreverence
   (D) familiarity
   (E) resignation

1. Correct answer: B

   (B) is the only choice that captures the passage's buoyant spirit
   (A) suggests a longing that is not evident in the passage
   (C) is too extreme.
   (D) does not reflect the lust for life that the narrator seems to possess
   (E) denotes a somber acceptance that is not found in the tone of the passage

2. The comparison in lines 6–8 (The country never . . . on a country visit) is intended to show how

   (A) much the narrator enjoyed country visits
   (B) much the narrator loved the country air
   (C) lucky the narrator felt to be invited to the country
   (D) rarely the narrator was invited to the country
   (E) welcome the narrator felt in the country

2. Correct answer: E

   (E) is correct because the clue "He loved it all—everything," indicates how the narrator felt in the country: he was at ease. There is little to differentiate (A) from (B) which should help to inform you that there is likely a better answer choice available. Moreover, both (C) and (D) are concerned with the narrator's invitations to the country, and there is little that separates one answer choice from the other.

Questions 3 and 4 are based on the following passage.

But this is not difficult, O Athenians, to escape death, but it is much
more difficult to avoid depravity, for it runs swifter than death. And
Line now I, being slow and aged, am overtaken by the slower of the two;
but my accusers, being strong and active, have been overtaken by
5   the swifter, wickedness. And now I depart, condemned by you to
death; but they condemned by truth, as guilty of iniquity and in-
justice: and I abide my sentence and so do they. These things, perhaps, ought so to be, and I think that they are for the best.

3. The narrator would probably agree with the statement that

(A) it is better to be unjust in the eyes of your detractors than it is to be
what they consider just
(B) it is nobler to die embracing the truth of the majority than it is to live
believing the lies of the minority
(C) people will always have their differences, but as long as they continue
to communicate they will find common ground
(D) discerning citizens realize that it is better to die old and alone than it
is to be young and live richly among your peers
(E) it is more important to defend the truth to your detractors than it is
to explain the truth to your supporters

3. Correct answer: A
(A) is correct because the author states that he considers his accusers depraved and acknowledges that he will comply with their death sentence.
There is no mention of who is in the majority (B), and the author would
likely not have been sentenced to death had he agreed with his accusers
(C). (D) is incorrect because there is no comparison of quality of life between the young and the old in the passage, and (E) is incorrect because
there is no indication the author feels it is more important to defend the
truth to his detractors than it is to explain it to his supporters. Rather, the
author seems content to let his detractors believe what they will.

4. The tone of the narrator's sentiments toward his accusers can best be described as one of

(A) malice
(B) defiance
(C) chicanery
(D) acquiescence
(E) derision

4. Correct answer: D
Of the five answer choices, only (D) reflects the mild tone and methodical
approach the narrator uses in addressing the actions of his accusers. The
other four choices all have negative connotations that do not reflect the
attitude of a man ready to comply with a death sentence. There is no support that his attitude is one of ill will (A), and by complying with their
death sentence, he is certainly not defying them (B). There is no indication that he is trying to deceive his accusers by trickery (C), nor does he
ridicule his accusers (E).

▨ RELATED-PASSAGE READING COMPREHENSION QUESTIONS

Some reading selections consist of a pair of passages that share a common topic or theme. Related passages may contain two long or two short passages. Questions based on Related passages will include standard Critical Reading questions such as those you have already studied. However, questions based on Related passages also include items that require you to compare or contrast the two passages, especially if the two passages are short.

Each question that follows a passage or pair of passages has five answer choices. Your task, as usual, is to select the one that best answers the question from among the choices given.

▨ SAMPLE OF A RELATED-PASSAGE READING QUESTION SET EXPLAINED

Here are two Related passages followed by four typical Critical Reading questions. Read the passages first. Then answer the questions based on what is stated or implied in the passages and the introductory material provided.

Questions 1–4 are based on the following passages.

The passages below are excerpts from *Chapters from My Autobiography* by Mark Twain. Passage 1 is written by Mark Twain himself. In Passage 2, Twain quotes the words of his young daughter, Susy.

Passage 1.

What I have been travelling toward all this time is this: the first critic that ever had occasion to describe my personal appearance
Line littered his description with foolish and inexcusable errors whose aggregate furnished the result that I was distinctly and distress-
5   ingly unhandsome. That description floated around the country in the papers, and was in constant use and wear for a quarter of a century. It seems strange to me that apparently no critic in the country could be found who could look at me and have the courage to take up his pen and destroy that lie. That lie began its course on
10 the Pacific coast, in 1864, and it likened me in personal appearance to Petroleum V. Nasby, who had been out there lecturing. For twenty-five years afterward, no critic could furnish a description of me without fetching in Nasby to help out my portrait. I knew Nasby well, and he was a good fellow, but in my life I have not felt
15 malignant enough about any more than three persons to charge those persons with resembling Nasby. It hurts me to the heart. I was always handsome. Anybody but a critic could have seen it. And it had long been a distress to my family—including Susy—that the critics should go on making this wearisome mistake, year after
20 year, when there was no foundation for it.

Passage 2.
Let us turn to Susy's biography now, and get the opinion of one who is unbiased:

From Susy's Biography
Papa's appearance has been described many times, but very incorrectly. He has beautiful gray hair, not any too thick or any too long,
Line   but just right; a Roman nose, which greatly improves the beauty of his features; kind blue eyes and a small mustache. He has a won-
5   derfully shaped head and profile. He has a very good figure—in short, he is an extraordinarily fine looking man. All his features are perfect, except that he hasn't extraordinary teeth. His complexion is very fair, and he doesn't wear a beard. He is a very good man and a very funny one. He has got a temper, but we all of us have in this
10   family. He is the loveliest man I ever saw or ever hope to see—and oh, so absent-minded. He does tell perfectly delightful stories. Clara and I used to sit on each arm of his chair and listen while he told us stories about the pictures on the wall.

1. The author's overall tone in Passage 1 is best described as

    (A) irate
    (B) appreciative
    (C) uncertain
    (D) humorous
    (E) jubilant

Your SAT Coach Says . . .

"Look carefully at the way the author uses words."

---

1. Correct answer: D
    The author states that the first critic who ever described his appearance "littered his description with foolish and inexcusable errors whose aggregate furnished the result that I was distinctly and distressingly unhandsome." That critic compared the author's appearance to that of Petroleum V. Nasby, a man the author describes as "a good fellow, but in my life I have not felt malignant enough about any more than three persons to charge those persons with resembling Nasby." To make matters worse, the author claims that other critics continue to make the same "wearisome mistake" year after year. On the other hand, the author proclaims that he was always handsome and "anybody but a critic could have seen it." All of this is said in a tongue-in-cheek way that gives the whole passage a humorous tone.

    (A) is wrong because the author is not angry, rather his words are meant to feign anger by poking fun at himself.
    (B) is wrong because nothing in the passage suggests that the author appreciates being described as "distressingly unhandsome."
    (C) is wrong because the author is not uncertain about what he has to say.
    (E) is wrong because the passage is humorous, but not joyous.

2. The depiction of Nasby in lines 13–16 ("I knew . . . resembling Nasby.") creates the impression of a man who

  (A) is seriously ill
  (B) is extremely unattractive
  (C) has made very few close friends
  (D) bears some resemblance to three people the author knows
  (E) has been a colleague of the author's for 25 years

Your SAT Coach Says . . .

"Go back and reread the lines referenced in the question."

---

2. Correct answer: B
   When the author says "in my life I have not felt malignant enough about any more than three persons to charge those persons with resembling Nasby," he means that there are very few people so unappealing to the author that he would suggest that they resemble Nasby.

  (A) is wrong because the word *malignant*, which can suggest illness, refers to the author's feelings toward other people; it has nothing to do with Nasby.
  (C) is wrong because the statement has nothing to do with the number of friends Nasby has.
  (D) is wrong because it is the author, not friends of the author, who has been compared to Nasby.
  (E) is wrong because nothing is said about the author and Nasby being colleagues.

3. Which of the following best describes the relationship between the two passages?

  (A) Passage 1 presents an argument that is refuted in Passage 2.
  (B) Passage 1 attacks a position that is defended by Passage 2.
  (C) Passage 1 offers an opinion that is supported by Passage 2.
  (D) Passage 2 presents an unbiased opinion that contrasts with the biased opinion expressed in Passage 1.
  (E) Passage 2 describes a misconception that is ignored by Passage 1.

Your SAT Coach Says . . .

"Check each answer choice against each passage."

---

3. Correct answer: C
   The author of Passage 1 claims that he has been mistakenly described as "distressingly unhandsome." The author of Passage 2 agrees that her father's appearance has been described incorrectly. She pictures her father as "an extraordinarily fine looking man" with beautiful gray hair, a Roman nose, kind blue eyes, and a small mustache. She says that he has a very good figure and that all his features are perfect (except his teeth). Thus, Passage 2 supports an opinion offered by Passage 1.

(A) is wrong because Passage 2 supports, rather than refutes, the opinion expressed in Passage 1.

(B) is wrong because Passage 1 does not attack the position taken by Passage 2.

(D) is wrong because as the author's daughter, Susy is not likely to be unbiased in her opinions about her father.

(E) is wrong because the misconception described in Passage 2 is also discussed in Passage 1.

4. Both passages assert that Twain

    (A) has not been properly described by critics.
    (B) greatly resembles Petroleum V. Nasby.
    (C) lectured on the Pacific coast in 1864.
    (D) makes up stories to amuse his daughters.
    (E) knew Nasby well.

Your SAT Coach Says . . .

"Eliminate any answer choice that is true for only one of the two passages."

---

4. Correct answer: A

In Passage 1, Twain complains that descriptions of his personal appearance are full of "foolish and inexcusable errors whose aggregate furnished the result that I was distinctly and distressingly unhandsome." In Passage 2 Susy says, "Papa's appearance has been described many times, but very incorrectly."

(B) is wrong because Nasby is mentioned only in Passage 1.

(C) is wrong because the lecture is mentioned only in Passage 1.

(D) is wrong because making up stories for his daughters is mentioned only in Passage 2.

(E) is wrong because Nasby is mentioned only in Passage 1.

▓ VOCABULARY-IN-CONTEXT QUESTIONS

Some of the questions on the Critical Reading section of the SAT ask you to define the meaning of a word as it is used in the context of the passage you have read. Such Vocabulary-in-Context questions will always give you a line indicator or some other reference so that you can easily find the word in the passage.

Some Vocabulary-in-Context questions deal with difficult words that you likely do not know. In other cases, a Vocabulary-in-Context question will be about an unusual meaning of an easier, familiar word. Regardless of which type of Vocabulary-in-Context question that you are dealing with, your goal is always the same: find the meaning of the word as it is used within the context of the passage.

STRATEGIES FOR VOCABULARY-IN-CONTEXT QUESTIONS

Below you will find four simple strategies that will help you to answer Vocabulary-in-Context questions correctly.

1. Use the line reference to locate the word.
2. Read the entire sentence.
3. Try to come up with a synonym on your own, and then look for your word among the answer choices.
4. If you can't come up with a synonym, try substituting each answer choice in the original sentence to see which one makes the most sense.

SAMPLE OF VOCABULARY-IN-CONTEXT QUESTIONS EXPLAINED

Use the reading and vocabulary strategies that you studied earlier to answer the sample questions that follow the passage.

> <u>Directions:</u> The passage below is followed by questions based on its content. Answer each question on the basis of what is stated or implied in the passage and the introductory material.

<u>Questions 1–3 are based on the following passage.</u>

The following excerpt is from a report on physical activity and health from the U.S. Department of Health and Human Services.

Participation in regular physical activity—at least 30 minutes of moderate activity on at least 5 days per week, or 20 minutes of vig-

Line orous physical activity at least three times per week—is critical to sustaining good health. Youth should strive for at least one hour

5 of exercise a day. Regular physical activity has beneficial effects on most (if not all) organ systems, and consequently it helps to prevent a broad range of health problems and diseases. People of all ages, both male and female, derive substantial health benefits from physical activity.

10 Regular physical activity is associated with lower mortality rates for both older and younger adults. Even those who are moderately active on a regular basis have lower mortality rates than those who are least active. Regular physical activity leads to cardiovascular fitness, which decreases the risk of cardiovascular disease

15 mortality in general and coronary artery disease mortality in particular. High blood pressure is a major underlying cause of cardiovascular complications and mortality. Regular physical activity can prevent or delay the development of high blood pressure, and reduces blood pressure in persons with hypertension.

20 Regular physical activity is also important for maintaining muscle strength, joint structure, joint functioning, and bone health. Weight-bearing physical activity is essential for normal skeletal development during childhood and adolescence and for achieving

and maintaining peak bone mass in young adults. Among post-
menopausal women, exercise, especially muscle strengthening (resistance) activity, may protect against the rapid decline in bone
mass. However, data on the effects of exercise on post-menopausal
bone loss are not clear-cut and the timing of the intervention (e.g.,
stage of menopausal transition) can influence the response. Regardless, physical activity including muscle-strengthening exercise
appears to protect against falling and fractures among the elderly,
probably by increasing muscle strength and balance. In addition,
physical activity may be beneficial for many people with arthritis.

Regular physical activity can help improve the lives of young
people beyond its effects on physical health. Although research has
not been conducted to conclusively demonstrate a direct link between physical activity and improved academic performance, such
a link might be expected. Studies have found participation in physical activity increases adolescents' self-esteem and reduces anxiety and stress. Through its effects on mental health, physical activity
may help increase students' capacity for learning. One study found
that spending more time in physical education did not have harmful effects on the standardized academic achievement test scores
of elementary school students; in fact, there was some evidence
that participation in a two-year health-related physical education
program had several significant favorable effects on academic
achievement.

Participation in physical activity and sports can promote social
well-being, as well as good physical and mental health, among
young people. Research has shown that students who participate in
interscholastic sports are less likely to be regular and heavy smok-
ers or use drugs, and are more likely to stay in school and have
good conduct and high academic achievement. Sports and physical activity programs can introduce young people to skills such as
teamwork, self-discipline, sportsmanship, leadership, and social-
ization. Lack of recreational activity, on the other hand, may contribute to making young people more vulnerable to gangs, drugs,
or violence.

Because physical inactivity is a risk factor for many diseases
and conditions, making physical activity an integral part of daily
life is crucial. There is a pressing need to encourage a more active
lifestyle among the American people. Clearly, the goal of a more
active population will be a challenge, requiring a commitment to
change on the part of individuals, families, work places, and communities. Both the public and private sectors will need to band together to promote more healthy habits for those of all ages. Schools
provide many opportunities to engage children in physical activity
as well as healthy eating. For adults, worksites provide opportunities to reinforce the adoption and maintenance of healthy lifestyle
behaviors. Perhaps the most important change, however, is at the
individual and family level. Each person must understand the value
of physical activity for his or her health and well-being and com-
mit to a lifestyle that is truly active.

1. In lines 10–11, "mortality rate" most nearly means

   (A) number of deaths
   (B) speed of recovery
   (C) intensity of exercise
   (D) seriousness of illness
   (E) degree of fitness

1. Correct answer: A
   Mortality rate is the proportion of deaths to the population of a region or nation. A lower mortality rate means fewer deaths. The word mortality appears several times in second paragraph. In each case, the word *death* can be substituted for mortality without changing the meaning of the sentence. The other answer choices have nothing to do with mortality rate.

2. In line 40, "stress" most nearly means

   (A) force
   (B) emphasis
   (C) importance
   (D) tension
   (E) significance

2. Correct answer: D
   "Stress" can mean any of the words offered as answer choices, depending upon the context in which it is used. In this case, the word *stress* occurs in the following sentence: "Studies have found participation in physical activity increases adolescents' self-esteem and reduces anxiety and stress." If you substitute each answer choice in the sentence, you will see that the only one that makes sense is "tension."

3. In line 60, "integral" most nearly means

   (A) entire
   (B) part of
   (C) essential
   (D) related to an integer
   (E) related to another part

3. Correct answer: C
   This is another question in which the word you are asked to define can mean any of the words given in the answer choices. The sentence in the passage, however, states "making physical activity an integral part of daily life is crucial." The word crucial is an indication that physical activity is "essential" to daily life. Therefore, answer choice (C) is correct.

   (A) is incorrect because physical activity is not a person's "entire" life.
   (B) is incorrect because the sentence already contains the word part, and it would be inappropriate to say that physical activity is part of part of life.
   (D) is incorrect because the sentence has nothing to do with mathematics, and integers are a kind of number.
   (E) is incorrect for the same reason that answer choice (B) is wrong.

Below you will find a variety of types of passages and questions that you encounter on the new SAT Critical Reading test.

- Review the strategies discussed above before you try the On Your Own: Practice Set A. You may find that certain types of questions are easier for you to deal with than others. For example, Vocabulary-in-Context questions are likely to be easier to answer than compare and contrast questions about two related passages.
- Focus on the kinds of items that you found difficult as you worked through the samples. Use the practice set to determine which types of questions continue to give you difficulty. Then, complete On Your Own: Practice Set B. Remember that the more you practice with these items, the less troublesome you are likely to find them.

ON YOUR OWN: PRACTICE SET A

Directions: The passages are followed by questions based on their content. Answer each question on the basis of what is stated or implied in the passages and any introductory material provided.

Questions 1–9 are based on the following passage.

In this excerpt from a short story written by Stephen Crane in 1896, a Civil War veteran discusses his battlefield experiences with the men gathered at the village grocery store.

OUT of the low window could be seen three hickory trees placed irregularly in a meadow that was re-
Line splendent in spring-time green. Farther away, the old dismal belfry of the village church loomed over the
5 pines. A horse meditating in the shade of one of the hickories lazily swished his tail. The warm sunshine made an oblong of vivid yellow on the floor of the grocery.

"Could you see the whites of their eyes?" said
10 the man who was seated on a soap-box.

"Nothing of the kind," replied old Henry warmly. "Just a lot of flitting figures, and I let go at where they 'peared to be the thickest. Bang!"

"Mr. Fleming," said the grocer—his deferential
15 voice expressed somehow the old man's exact social weight—"Mr. Fleming, you never was frightened much in them battles, was you?"

The veteran looked down and grinned. Observing his manner, the entire group tittered. "Well, I
20 guess I was," he answered finally. "Pretty well scared, sometimes. Why, in my first battle I thought the sky was falling down. I thought the world was coming to an end. You bet I was scared."

Every one laughed. Perhaps it seemed strange
25 and rather wonderful to them that a man should admit the thing, and in the tone of their laughter there was probably more admiration than if old

Fleming had declared that he had always been a lion. Moreover, they knew that he had ranked as an
30 orderly sergeant, and so their opinion of his heroism was fixed. None, to be sure, knew how an orderly sergeant ranked, but then it was understood to be somewhere just shy of a major-general's stars. So when old Henry admitted that he had been
35 frightened, there was a laugh.

"The trouble was," said the old man, "I thought they were all shooting at me. Yes, sir, I thought every man in the other army was aiming at me in particular, and only me. And it seemed so darned
40 unreasonable, you know. I wanted to explain to 'em what an almighty good fellow I was, because I thought then they might quit all trying to hit me. But I couldn't explain, and they kept on being unreasonable—blim!—blam!—bang! So I run!"

45 Two little triangles of wrinkles appeared at the corners of his eyes. Evidently he appreciated some comedy in this recital. Down near his feet, however, little Jim, his grandson, was visibly horror-stricken. His hands were clasped nervously, and his
50 eyes were wide with astonishment at this terrible scandal, his most magnificent grandfather telling such a thing.

"That was at Chancellorsville. Of course, afterward I got kind of used to it. A man does. Lots of
55 men, though, seem to feel all right from the start. I did, as soon as I 'got on to it,' as they say now; but at first I was pretty flustered. Now, there was young Jim Conklin, old Si Conklin's son—that used to keep the tannery—you none of you recollect him—

60 well, he went into it from the start just as if he was
born to it. But with me it was different. I had to get
used to it."

When little Jim walked with his grandfather he
was in the habit of skipping along on the stone
65 pavement in front of the three stores and the hotel
of the town and betting that he could avoid the
cracks. But upon this day he walked soberly, with
his hand gripping two of his grandfather's fingers.
Sometimes he kicked abstractedly at dandelions
70 that curved over the walk. Any one could see that
he was much troubled.

"There's Sickles's colt over in the medder,
Jimmie," said the old man. "Don't you wish you
owned one like him?"

75 "Um," said the boy, with a strange lack of interest. He continued his reflections. Then finally he
ventured: "Grandpa—now—was that true what
you was telling those men?"

"What?" asked the grandfather. "What was I
80 telling them?"

"Oh, about your running."

"Why, yes, that was true enough, Jimmie. It
was my first fight, and there was an awful lot of
noise, you know."

85 Jimmie seemed dazed that this idol, of its own
will, should so totter. His stout boyish idealism was
injured.

Presently the grandfather said: "Sickles's colt
is going for a drink. Don't you wish you owned
90 Sickles's colt, Jimmie?"

The boy merely answered: "He ain't as nice as
our'n." He lapsed then into another moody silence.

1. The major purpose of this story is to

(A) explain why a boy dislikes his grandfather
(B) show how a boy's image of a hero is shattered
(C) tell how a man learns to overcome his fear of
battle
(D) describe a battle scene during the Civil War
(E) portray the relationship between an officer and
his men

2. The question in line 9, "Could you see the whites of
their eyes?" most nearly means

(A) "Could you tell where the soldiers were look-
ing?"
(B) "What color were the enemy soldiers' eyes?"
(C) "Could you tell what kind of weapons the sol-
diers had?"
(D) "Were you close enough to see the enemy sol-
diers' eyes?"
(E) "Were the enemy soldiers aiming at you?"

3. In line 19, "tittered" most nearly means

(A) waited expectantly
(B) applauded appreciatively
(C) laughed nervously
(D) sneered scornfully
(E) grinned derisively

4. What was the reaction of the men at the grocery story
to Mr. Fleming's admission that he had been afraid
in battle?

(A) total disbelief
(B) continued admiration
(C) uncontrolled anger
(D) loss of respect
(E) complete frustration

5. Little Jim was "much troubled" (line 71) because

(A) the men at the grocery laughed at his grand-
father's story
(B) his grandfather told a story that was not true
(C) he discovered that his grandfather had run
from battle
(D) he learned that his grandfather was an orderly
sergeant
(E) he wished he owned Sickles's colt

6. The appearance of two "little triangles of wrinkles"
at the corners of his eyes (line 45) implies that
Mr. Fleming

(A) could not understand why he was being fired
upon
(B) was afraid of the enemy bullets
(C) was amused by his account of the battle
(D) was troubled by his actions
(E) was horror stricken at the terrible scandal

7. Mr. Fleming does not seem to be aware that

(A) Jim never knew that his grandfather had
fought in the Civil War
(B) the men in the grocery store are not interested
in his war stories
(C) people are laughing at him behind his back
(D) his grandson is greatly upset by his admission
of fear
(E) he is considered a hero by the townspeople

8. The characteristic that best describes Mr. Fleming is

(A) honesty
(B) pride
(C) hostility
(D) idealism
(E) hypocrisy

9. The passage is narrated from the point of view of

    (A) Jimmie
    (B) Mr. Fleming
    (C) the grocer
    (D) an observer who has partial knowledge of Jimmie
    (E) an observer who knows all about Jimmie including his thoughts

Questions 10–14 refer to the following passages.

Over the past 200 years, over 700 proposals have been introduced in Congress to reform or eliminate the Electoral College. There have been more proposals for Constitutional amendments on changing the Electoral College than on any other subject.

Passage 1.

The Electoral College protects rural communities and smaller states from the interests of urban cen-
Line ters and large states by requiring a distribution of popular support to elect a president. Without the
5   Electoral College a candidate can be elected by campaigning in and winning only the 10 largest cities in the country. The Electoral College forces candidates to pay attention to smaller states, which would otherwise be ignored. This process occa-
10   sionally results in giving the election to a candidate that did not win a majority of the popular vote. However, it is better than a process that gives the election to a candidate that is favored by a majority of voters but whose support is concentrated in a mi-
15   nority of regions or restricted to voters in large states.

Passage 2.

The Electoral College gives disproportionate voting power to the states, favoring the smaller states with more Electoral votes per person. (Wyoming
20   with 3 Electoral votes has one Elector for every 165,000 people, whereas Texas with 32 Electoral votes has one Elector for every 652,000 people.) Since all but two states allocate their Electoral votes on a winner-takes-all basis, there is little in-
25   centive for a candidate to campaign in a state that already favors that candidate or one in which the candidate has little chance of winning. As a result, presidential candidates actually campaign in only a few select states, the so-called "swing states," as
30   they battle for specific electoral votes. With no laws requiring them to vote for the candidate for whom they were selected, Electors in 21 states can simply vote as they please, without regard for the popular will of the state.

10. The author of Passage 2 uses the phrase "swing states" to suggest that these states

    (A) allow their Electors to vote as they please
    (B) are likely to vote for a third-party candidate
    (C) are not initially committed to one candidate or another
    (D) have a disproportionate number of Electoral votes per person.
    (E) do not allocate Electors on a winner-takes-all basis

11. The parenthetical remarks in lines 19–22 serve to

    (A) point out a problem with the author's reasoning
    (B) prove that the author is justified in supporting the Electoral College
    (C) indicate how the Electoral College has changed
    (D) show why the Electoral College has lasted for over 200 years
    (E) support the author's position with statistical evidence

12. Unlike Passage 2, Passage 1 suggests that

    (A) the Electoral College is unfair to voters in large cities
    (B) the Electoral College should be preserved
    (C) Electors should be required to vote for the candidates for whom they were selected
    (D) the Electoral College is inefficient and outmoded
    (E) allocating votes on a winner-takes-all basis is unfair to small states and rural communities

13. Which of the following best describes the relationship between the two passages?

    (A) Passage 1 presents a proposition that is supported by Passage 2.
    (B) Passage 1 explains a theory that is proved by Passage 2.
    (C) Passage 1 defends an institution that is attacked by Passage 2.
    (D) Passage 2 offers reasons for the outcome described in Passage 1.
    (E) Passage 2 presents an argument that elaborates on a point made in Passage 1.

14. Both passages are primarily concerned with

    (A) the voting power accorded to smaller states
    (B) preventing voting irregularities
    (C) ensuring that the winning candidate is supported by a majority of voters
    (D) the role of swing states in the voting process
    (E) allocating campaign resources

ON YOUR OWN: PRACTICE SET A

ANSWERS AND EXPLANATIONS

1. Correct answer: B

The focus of the story is Mr. Fleming's account of his lack of bravery in his first battle and young Jim's reaction to the story. The point of the story is stated in lines 85–87: "Jimmie seemed dazed that this idol, of its own will, should so totter. His stout boyish idealism was injured." Choice B best reflects this point.

(A) is wrong because there is no evidence that Jim comes to dislike his grandfather, but only that he is astonished that his grandfather would tell of such scandalous behavior.

(C) is wrong because although it is true that Mr. Fleming got used to the idea of fighting as the war wore on, this is not the major theme of this story.

(D) is wrong because the description of the battle is not the focus of the story.

(E) is wrong because the story does not provide a description of the relationship between an officer and his men.

2. Correct answer: D

The question is asked during the discussion of a battle. The point of the expression is to indicate just how close the enemy soldiers were.

(A) is wrong because the expression has nothing to do with where the soldiers were looking.

(B) is wrong because the expression is not really asking about eye color, but rather about how close the soldiers were.

(C) and (E) are wrong because the expression has nothing to do with weapons or where the soldiers were aiming.

3. Correct answer: C

The men in the grocery store treat Mr. Fleming with respect because of his "social weight" and his rank as an orderly sergeant. When the grocer asks if Fleming had been frightened in

battle, Fleming "looked down and grinned." In response, "the entire group tittered." The best synonym for *titter* is "giggle" or "laugh nervously."

(A) and (B) are wrong because neither one has anything to do with grinning or laughing.

(D) and (E) are wrong because the men are respectful of Mr. Fleming. At no point in the story do they treat Fleming *scornfully* (with disdain or contempt) or *derisively* (with ridicule).

4. Correct answer: B

As stated in lines 24–29, "Perhaps it seemed strange and rather wonderful to them that a man should admit the thing, and in the tone of their laughter there was probably more admiration than if old Fleming had declared that he had always been a lion."

(A) is wrong because there is no indication that the men did not believe Mr. Fleming.

(C) and (D) are wrong because there is no indication that anyone became angry or lost respect for Mr. Fleming.

(E) is wrong because there is nothing to indicate that the men became frustrated upon hearing the story.

5. Correct answer: C

In lines 43–44, Mr. Fleming admits that he was so frightened in his first battle that he actually turned and ran. Little Jim was "visibly horror-stricken. His hands were clasped nervously, and his eyes were wide with astonishment at this terrible scandal, his most magnificent grandfather telling such a thing." From this point on, Jim is moody and quiet, quite different from his usual playful self.

(A) is wrong because although the men at the grocery laughed at Mr. Fleming's story, that is not what troubles Jimmie.

(B) is wrong because the story Jimmie's grandfather told was true.

(D) is wrong because Jimmie already knew that his grandfather was an orderly sergeant.

(E) is wrong because when his grandfather asks Jimmie, "Don't you wish you owned Sickles's colt?" Jimmie replies, "He ain't as nice as our'n," so it does not seem that Jimmie wished he owned Sickles's colt.

6. Correct answer: C

Little triangles of wrinkles appear in the corners of a person's eyes when a person smiles. The implication is that Mr. Fleming was amused by his less than heroic reaction to his first experience on the battlefield.

(A) and (B) are wrong because neither confusion nor fear are typically expressed by smiling.

(D) and (E) are wrong because it is Jimmie, not Mr. Fleming, who was troubled and horror-stricken.

7. Correct answer: D

Mr. Fleming obviously finds humor in the story he tells of running away from his first battle. His grandson, on the other hand, is "visibly horror-stricken" at the "terrible scandal" of his grandfather's telling such a thing.

(A) is wrong because it is most likely that Jimmie did know of his grandfather's participation in the Civil War.

(B) is wrong because the men in the grocery store listen to his every word.

(C) is wrong because although the men laughed at his story, it was not done behind his back and "in the tone of their laughter there was probably more admiration than if old Fleming had declared that he had always been a lion."

(E) is wrong because it is likely that Fleming knew that he qualified as a hero because of his war activities.

8. Correct answer: A

Fleming is brutally honest about his actions during the battle of Chancellorsville. So honest that he completely shatters his grandson's illusions about his heroic grandfather.

(B) is wrong because a proud man would not be likely to tell such a story about himself.

(C) is wrong because there is nothing in the story to suggest that Fleming is hostile or angry. Rather, he is shown as friendly and well-liked.

(D) is wrong because Fleming is portrayed as a realist, not as someone who perceives things as he might wish them to be.

(E) is wrong because Fleming does not pretend to be better than he is.

9. Correct answer: E

The narrator of this story is not directly involved in the story but knows everything about Jimmie, including what he is thinking.

(A) is wrong because the story describes Jimmie's actions and thoughts in the third person ("*His* hands were clasped nervously, and *his* eyes were wide with astonishment . . .") not in the first person (*my* hands, *my* eyes).

(B) and (C) are wrong for the same reason. The actions of both Mr. Fleming and the grocer are described in the third person, not the first person.

(D) is wrong because the narrator knows not only what Jimmie is doing, but also what he is thinking.

10. Correct answer: C

The meaning of the phrase "swing states" can be found in the sentence before the one in which the phrase is used. "Since all but two states allocate their Electoral votes on a winner-takes-all basis, there is little incentive for a candidate to campaign in a state that already favors that candidate or one in which the candidate has no chance of winning." The next sentence states that candidates only campaign in "a few select states, the so-called 'swing states.'" Thus, it can be inferred that "swing states" are those states in which no one candidate has a clear majority of committed voters, and in which either candidate has a chance of winning.

CHAPTER 5 / STRATEGIES FOR CRITICAL READING COMPREHENSION QUESTIONS

(A) is wrong because the fact that Electors can vote as they please is introduced as another point in the argument. It has nothing to do with the idea of "swing states."

(B) is wrong because the passage does not mention third-party candidates.

(D) is wrong because it is smaller states such as Wyoming that are mentioned as having a disproportionate number of Electoral votes per person. Swing states are the ones whose votes could be won by either candidate.

(E) is wrong because only two states do not allocate their Electoral votes on a winner-takes-all basis.

11. Correct answer: E

The parenthetical information offers statistical evidence to support the author's claim that the Electoral College "gives disproportionate voting power to the states, favoring the smaller states with more Electoral votes per person."

(A) is wrong because the parenthetical information does not point out a problem with the author's reasoning.

(B) is wrong because the author does not support the Electoral College.

(C) is wrong because the information shows how Electoral votes relate to population; it has nothing to do with change over time.

(D) is wrong because the information does not offer a reason for the longevity of the Electoral College.

12. Correct answer: B

Passage 1 supports the Electoral College because it protects the interests of rural communities and small states that might otherwise be ignored in presidential elections. Passage 2 opposes the Electoral College for giving disproportionate voting power to the smaller states and forcing candidates to devote most of their campaign efforts to a select few states.

(A) is wrong because Passage 2, not Passage 1, claims that the Electoral College is unfair to voters in large cities.

(C) is wrong because Passage 1 never mentions the possibility that Electors could vote for a candidate other than the one for whom they had been selected.

(D) is wrong because Passage 1 supports the Electoral College. It does not claim that the Electoral College is inefficient or outmoded.

(E) is wrong because Passage 1 claims that the Electoral College protects the interests of small states and rural communities.

13. Correct answer: C

Passage 1 defends the Electoral College as the protector of the voting rights of rural communities and smaller states. Passage 2 attacks the Electoral College for giving too much power to smaller states by favoring them with more Electoral votes per person.

(A) is wrong because Passage 2 does not support Passage 1.

(B) is wrong because Passage 1 does not explain a theory.

(D) is wrong because the two passages do not provide an outcome and reasons for it.

(E) is wrong because Passage 2 does not elaborate on a point made in Passage 1.

14. Correct answer: A

Passage 1 claims that the Electoral College is necessary to protect the interest of voters in smaller states and Passage 2 claims that the Electoral College gives too much voting power to the smaller states. Thus, both passages are concerned with the voting power of smaller states.

(B) is wrong because neither passage mentions voting irregularities.

(C) is wrong because Passage 1 explicitly states that it is better to give the election to a candidate who did not win a majority of the popular vote but who has widespread support than to give it to a candidate who is favored by a majority of voters but whose support is concentrated in a few larger regions of the country.

(D) is wrong because the role of swing states is mentioned only in Passage 2.

(E) is wrong because there is no specific mention of how campaign resources should be allocated.

▉ ON YOUR OWN: PRACTICE SET B

Directions: The passages below are followed by questions based on their content. Answer each question on the basis of what is stated or implied in the passages and any introductory material provided.

Questions 1–9 are based on the passage below.

The excerpt below is from the website of the U.S. Environmental Protection Agency.

Coral reefs are among the world's richest ecosystems, second only to tropical rain forests in plant
Line and animal diversity. Coral reef ecosystems are rec-
ognized as valuable economic and environmental
5   resources. Although many people think coral reefs
are made of plants or rocks, they are actually made
of animals.

Corals are tiny animals that belong to the group
cnidaria (the "c" is silent). Other cnidarians in-
10   clude hydras, jellyfish, and sea anemones. Corals
are *sessile* animals, meaning they are not mobile
but stay fixed in one place. They feed by reaching
out with tentacles to catch prey such as small fish
and planktonic animals. Corals live in colonies
15   consisting of many individuals, each of which is
called a *polyp.* They secrete a hard calcium carbonate skeleton, which serves as a uniform base or
substrate for the colony. The skeleton also provides
protection, as the polyps can contract into the struc-
20   ture if predators approach. It is these hard skeletal
structures that build up coral reefs over time. The
calcium carbonate is secreted at the base of the
polyps, so the living coral colony occurs at the surface of the skeletal structure, completely covering
25   it. Calcium carbonate is continuously deposited by
the living colony, adding to the size of the structure.
Growth of these structures varies greatly, depending on the species of coral and environmental conditions—ranging from 0.3 to 10 centimeters per
30   year. Different species of coral build structures of
various sizes and shapes ("brain corals," "fan
corals," etc.), creating amazing diversity and complexity in the coral reef ecosystem. Various coral
species tend to be segregated into characteristic

35   zones on a reef, separated out by competition with
other species and by environmental conditions.

Virtually all reef-dwelling corals have a *symbiotic* (mutually beneficial) relationship with algae
called *zooxanthellae.* The plant-like algae live in-
40   side the coral polyps and perform photosynthesis,
producing food that is shared with the coral. In exchange the coral provides the algae with protection
and access to light, which is necessary for photosynthesis. The zooxanthellae also lend their color
45   to their coral symbionts. *Coral bleaching* occurs
when corals lose their zooxanthellae, exposing the
white calcium carbonate skeletons of the coral
colony. There are a number of stresses or environmental changes that may cause bleaching including
50   disease, excess shade, increased levels of ultraviolet radiation, sedimentation, pollution, salinity
changes, and increased temperatures.

Because the zooxanthellae depend on light for
photosynthesis, reef-building corals are found in
55   shallow, clear water where light can penetrate down
to the coral polyps. Reef-building coral communities also require tropical or sub-tropical temperatures, and exist globally in a band 30 degrees north
to 30 degrees south of the equator. Reefs are gen-
60   erally classified in three types. *Fringing reefs,* the
most common type, project seaward directly from
the shores of islands or continents. *Barrier reefs* are
platforms separated from the adjacent land by a bay
or lagoon. The longest barrier reefs occur off the
65   coasts of Australia and Belize. *Atolls* rest on the
tops of submerged volcanoes. They are usually circular or oval with a central lagoon. Parts of the atoll
may emerge as islands. Over 300 atolls are found
in the south Pacific.

70   Coral reefs provide habitats for a large variety
of organisms. These organisms rely on corals as a
source of food and shelter. Other creatures that call

coral reefs home include various sponges; mol-
luscs such as sea slugs, nudibranchs, oysters, and
75   clams; crustaceans like crabs and shrimp; many of
sea worms; echinoderms such as star fish and sea
urchins; other cnidarians such as jellyfish and sea
anemones; various types of fungi; sea turtles; and
many species of fish.
80   Coral reefs and their associated communities
of seagrasses, mangroves and mudflats are sensitive indicators of water quality and the ecological
integrity of the ecosystem. They tolerate relatively
narrow ranges of temperature, salinity, water clar-
85   ity, and other chemical and water quality characteristics. Reefs thus are excellent sentinels of the
quality of their environment. Proper monitoring
of reefs can identify changes in water quality or
impacts from land-based activities. Monitoring
90   changes in water quality can help local resource
managers understand the implications of actions
occurring in watersheds that are associated with
particular coral communities. These connections
will help in development of sound management
95   plans for coral reefs and other coastal and marine
resources.
        Humans have had a long association with reefs.
They are important fishery and nursery areas, and
more recently have proved to be very important
100 economically as tourist attractions. Reefs provide
protection from erosion to coastlines and sand for
beaches. However, reefs located near coastal populations are showing increasing signs of stress and
are not faring as well as reefs that are more distant
105 from centers of human population.

1. The primary purpose of this passage is to
    (A) raise concerns about the survival of the group
         cnidaria
    (B) examine the nature of coral reefs
    (C) describe the symbiotic relationship between
         corals and algae
    (D) prompt scientists to conduct more research on
         coral reefs
    (E) highlight the important benefits of coral reefs

2. Coral reefs are said to be like rain forests because
    both
    (A) include animals from the group *cnidaria*
    (B) are sensitive to changes in water quality
    (C) are made up of many different animals and
         plants
    (D) consist of various species segregated into
         zones
    (E) need to be carefully monitored

3. The exchange of services between the algae and the
    corals (lines 39–45) is an example of
    (A) diversity
    (B) photosynthesis
    (C) symbiosis
    (D) classification
    (E) environmental change

4. Coral bleaching can result from all of the following
    except
    (A) disease
    (B) increased temperatures
    (C) pollution
    (D) sea worms
    (E) change in salinity

5. It can be inferred from the passage that the author is
    in favor of
    (A) monitoring of coral reefs to detect changes
    (B) encouraging more tourists to visit reefs
    (C) supplying food for reef-dwelling corals
    (D) increasing water temperatures to encourage
         reef-building activities
    (E) preventing fishing and boating near coral reefs

6. According to paragraph 4, atolls are
    (A) the most common type of coral reef
    (B) separated from the shore by a bay or lagoon
    (C) coral reefs that project out into the sea directly
         from the shore
    (D) circular or oval-shaped reefs that surround a
         lagoon
    (E) most likely to be found off the coast of
         Australia

7. In this passage, *italics* are primarily used to
    (A) emphasize foreign words
    (B) highlight words that are difficult to spell
    (C) suggest that these words are not important to
         understanding the passage
    (D) point out terms that can have more than one
         meaning
    (E) call attention to scientific terms that are de-
         fined in the text

8. In line 103, "stress" most nearly means
    (A) significance
    (B) emphasis
    (C) urgency
    (D) weight
    (E) strain

9. All of the following questions can be explicitly answered by this passage EXCEPT:

    (A) What are *cnidaria*?
    (B) Where does the living coral occur?
    (C) What are the possible causes of coral bleaching?
    (D) What temperatures do reef-building coral communities require?
    (E) How many general classifications of coral reefs are there?

Questions 10–14 are based on the passages below.

Passage 1.

The results of a four-year scientific study conducted by an international team of 300 scientists
Line show that the Arctic is warming much more rapidly than previously known. Some areas in the Arctic
5 have warmed 10 times as fast as the world as a whole, which has warmed an average of 1 degree Fahrenheit (5/9°C) over the past century, and increasing greenhouse gases from human activities are projected to make the Arctic warmer still.
10   At least half of the summer sea ice in the Arctic is projected to melt by the end of this century, along with a significant portion of the Greenland Ice Sheet, as the region is expected to warm an additional 7 to 13°F (4–7°C) by 2100. These changes
15 will have major global impacts, such as contributing to global sea-level rise and intensifying global warming, according to the final report of the Arctic Climate Impact Assessment (ACIA).
     The assessment was commissioned by the Arctic Council (a ministerial intergovernmental forum
20 comprised of eight nations, including the United States, and six Indigenous Peoples organizations) and the International Arctic Science Committee (an international scientific organization appointed by
25 18 national academies of science). The assessment's projections are based on a moderate estimate of future emissions of carbon dioxide and other greenhouse gases, and incorporate results from five major global climate models used by the
30 Intergovernmental Panel on Climate Change.
     "The impacts of global warming are affecting people *now* in the Arctic," says Robert Corell, chair of the ACIA. "The Arctic is experiencing some of the most rapid and severe climate change on earth.
35 The impacts of climate change on the region and the globe are projected to increase substantially in the years to come."

Passage 2.

Should the Arctic Ocean become ice-free in summer, it is likely that polar bears would be driven
40 toward extinction. Bears depend on a frozen platform from which to hunt seals, the mainstay of their diet. Without ice, the bears are unable to reach their prey. If the reduced ice coverage results in more open water, cubs and young bears may also
45 not be able to swim the distances required to reach solid ice.
     In Canada, Hudson Bay's ice melts about three weeks earlier each spring than it did just 25 years ago. As a result, the time bears have on the ice, stor-
50 ing up energy for the summer and autumn when there is little available food, is becoming shorter. As the periods without food become longer, the overall body condition of these polar bears declines. This is particularly serious for bears that are
55 pregnant or have cubs, and for the cubs themselves. In Hudson Bay, scientists have found the main cause of death for cubs to be either lack of food or lack of fat on nursing mothers.
     For every week earlier the ice breaks up in
60 Hudson Bay, bears come ashore roughly 10 kg (22 lbs) lighter and in poorer condition. Rising temperatures in the southern Arctic, therefore, mean less sea ice, leading to less healthy bears. Poor body condition can lead to lower reproduction rates,
65 which in the long run could lead to local extinction.
     Because polar bears are a top predator in the Arctic, changes in their distribution or numbers could affect the entire arctic ecosystem. There is little doubt that ice-dependent animals such as
70 polar bears will be adversely affected by continued warming in the Arctic.

10. The information in Passage 2 supports which assumption in Passage 1?

    (A) Greenhouse gases will make the Arctic warmer still.
    (B) The Arctic Climate Impact Assessment was an international undertaking.
    (C) The impact of global warming is being felt in the Arctic now.
    (D) The assessment's projections were based on five major climate models.
    (E) Arctic warming will contribute to global sea-level rise.

11. Melting sea ice will result in all of the following EXCEPT:

    (A) a rise in global sea level
    (B) more greenhouse gases
    (C) intensified global warming
    (D) a decline in the health of adult polar bears
    (E) fewer polar bear cubs

12. Which of the following best describes the relationship between the two passages?

    (A) Passage 1 defends a study that is attacked in Passage 2.
    (B) Passage 1 offers a theory that is refuted in Passage 2.
    (C) Passage 2 provides a conclusion that follows from the evidence presented in Passage 1.
    (D) Passage 2 summarizes the argument presented in Passage 1.
    (E) Passage 2 presents evidence that supports a point made in Passage 1.

13. Both passages would agree that Arctic warming

    (A) is affected by greenhouse gases
    (B) contributes to global sea-level rise
    (C) is likely to drive polar bears to extinction
    (D) is increasing at a rapid rate
    (E) is harmful to polar bear cubs

14. In line 70, "adversely" most nearly means

    (A) indelibly
    (B) liberally
    (C) unpretentiously
    (D) publicly
    (E) unfavorably

▨ ON YOUR OWN: PRACTICE SET B
▨ ANSWERS AND EXPLANATIONS

1. Correct answer: B

Most of the passage is devoted to an examination of the nature of coral reefs—how they are formed, where they are formed, how they get their food and color.

(A) is wrong because although the passage raises concerns about the survival of coral reefs located near coastal populations, it does not raise concerns about the survival of the entire group *cnidaria*.

(C) is wrong because the symbiotic relationship between corals and algae is only one aspect of the entire coral reef ecosystem. It is not the subject of the entire passage.

(D) is wrong because the passage indicates a wealth of knowledge about coral reefs. The biggest danger to the reefs come from the land-based activities of humans.

(E) is wrong because the benefits of coral reefs are only one small part of the discussion about coral reefs.

2. Correct answer: C

Lines 2–3 state that coral reefs are "second only to tropical rain forests in plant and animal diversity." In other words, both ecosystems consist of many different animals and plants.

(A) is wrong because cnidarians include corals, hydras, jellyfish, and sea anemones, all of which live in the water, not in a rain forest.

(B) is wrong because only coral reefs are said to be sensitive to changes in water quality.

(D) is wrong because it is the coral species that are said to be segregated into characteristic zones on a reef.

(E) is wrong because nothing is said about the need to monitor rain forests.

3. Correct answer: C

Lines 37–38 define a symbiotic relationship as "mutually beneficial." The exchange of services between the algae (producing food for the coral) and the coral (providing protection and access to light for the algae) is a perfect example of symbiosis.

(A) is wrong because *diversity* means "variety," which has nothing to do with mutual help.

(B) is wrong because photosynthesis is the process by which green plants make food.

(D) is wrong because *classification* means "arrangement according to some systematic division into classes or groups."

(E) is wrong because environmental change has nothing to do with mutual benefit.

4. Correct answer: D

The stresses that result in coral bleaching are listed in lines 48–52: "There are a number of stresses or environmental changes that may cause bleaching including disease, excess shade, increased levels of ultraviolet radiation, sedimentation, pollution, salinity changes, and increased temperatures." Sea worms, which inhabit coral reefs but do not harm them, are missing from this list.

(A) is wrong because disease is listed as one of the stresses that may cause coral bleaching.

(B) is wrong because increased temperatures is one of the stresses that may cause bleaching.

(C) is wrong because pollution is listed as one of the stresses that may cause bleaching.

(E) is wrong because change in salinity is listed as one of the stresses that may cause bleaching.

5. Correct answer: A

In the next to last paragraph (lines 86–87), the author states that reefs are "excellent sentinels" of the quality of their environment. Proper monitoring of reefs can identify changes in water quality or impacts from land-based activities, which in turn can help local resource managers in the development of sound management plans for coral reefs and other marine resources.

(B) is wrong because there is nothing in the passage that supports the idea of encouraging more tourists to visit reefs.

(C) is wrong because nothing is said to indicate that reef-dwelling corals are lacking in the food they need to survive.

(D) is wrong because increased water temperatures result in coral bleaching, not in increased reef-building.

(E) is wrong because the author says nothing about preventing fishing and boating near coral reefs.

6. Correct answer: D

Lines 66–67 describe atolls as "usually circular or oval with a central lagoon."

(A) is wrong because fringing reefs are described as "the most common type" of reef.

(B) is wrong because barrier reefs are "separated from the adjacent land by a bay or lagoon."

(C) is wrong because the type of reef that projects out into the sea directly from the shore is the fringing reef.

(E) is wrong because Australia is mentioned only as the site of the longest barrier reefs.

7. Correct answer: E

The words in italics are scientific terms. Definitions for each of these terms are provided in the text immediately before or immediately after the term itself. For example, in lines 8–10 *cnidaria* is defined in the next sentence as the group of animals that includes corals, hydras, jellyfish, and sea anemones. In lines 11–12, *sessile* animals are defined in the same sentence as meaning animals that "are not mobile but stay fixed in one place."

(A) is wrong because words such as *symbiotic, coral bleaching,* and *fringing reefs* are not foreign words.

(B) is wrong because not all the words in italics are hard to spell.

(C) is wrong because using italics serves to make the words stand out, which suggests that they are important, not unimportant terms.

(D) is wrong because the words in italics are not multiple-meaning words.

8. Correct answer: E

The word *stress* occurs in the following sentence: "However, reefs located near coastal populations are showing increasing signs of stress and are not faring as well as reefs that are more distant from centers of human population." All of the choices are meanings for the word *stress;* however, the only one that makes sense in context is *strain.*

9. Correct answer: A

The article states that "Corals are tiny animals that belong to the group *cnidaria*" and that "other cnidarians include hydras, jellyfish, and sea anemones." However, the article never specifically defines *cnidaria* as a "phylum of more or less radially symmetrical invertebrate animals that lack a true body cavity and possess tentacles studded with nematocysts (a barbed threadlike tube that delivers a sting when propelled into attackers and prey).

(B) is wrong because it is answered in lines 58–59.

(C) is wrong because it is answered in lines 48–52.

(D) is wrong because it is answered in lines 56–58.

(E) is wrong because it is answered in lines 59–60.

10. Correct answer: C

The information that Hudson Bay's ice melts three weeks earlier in the spring than it did 25 years ago and the resulting decline in the body condition of Hudson Bay polar bears shows that the impact of global warming is already being felt in the Arctic.

(A), (B), (D), and (E) are all true statements, but none is supported by information in Passage 2.

11. Correct answer: B

The increase in greenhouse gases comes from human activities, not from melting sea ice.

(A) is wrong because rising global sea level is mentioned in Passage 1.

(C) is wrong because intensifying global warming is mentioned in Passage 1.

(D) is wrong because a decline in the health of polar bears is mentioned in Passage 2.

(E) is wrong because fewer polar bear cubs is mentioned in Passage 2.

12. Correct answer: E

Passage 1 makes the point that the effects of global warming are being felt in the Arctic now. Passage 2 presents evidence in support of this point: "In Canada, Hudson Bay's ice melts about three weeks earlier each spring than it did just 25 years ago." "For every week

earlier the ice breaks up in Hudson Bay, bears come ashore roughly 10 kg (22 lbs) lighter and in poorer condition."

(A) is wrong because Passage 2 does not attack the study presented in Passage 1.

(B) is wrong because Passage 2 does not refute the information in Passage 1.

(C) is wrong because Passage 2 does not offer a conclusion.

(D) is wrong because Passage 2 does not summarize Passage 1.

13. Correct answer: D

Passage 1 states that "the Arctic is warming much more rapidly than previously known." Passage 2 says that "Hudson Bay's ice melts about three week earlier each spring than it did just 25 years ago." Both of these statements support the idea that Arctic warming is increasing rapidly.

(A) is wrong because greenhouse gases are mentioned only in Passage 1.

(B) is wrong because a rise in sea level is mentioned only in Passage 1.

(C) is wrong because polar bear extinction is mentioned only in Passage 2.

(E) is wrong because polar bear cubs are mentioned only in Passage 2.

14. Correct answer: E

Adversely appears in the following sentence: "There is little doubt that ice-dependent animals such as polar bears will be adversely affected by continued warming in the Arctic." The entire passage has shown that Arctic warming has a negative effect on polar bears. *Adversely* means "unfavorably."

(A) is wrong because *indelibly* means "permanently."

(B) is wrong because *liberally* means "freely" or "generously."

(C) is wrong because *unpretentiously* means "not grandly."

(D) is wrong because *publicly* means "openly."

CHAPTER 6

SAT CRITICAL READING PRACTICE EXAM I

ANSWER SHEET

Directions

- Remove this Answer Sheet from the book and use it to record your answers to this test.
- This test will require 1 hour and 10 minutes to complete. Take this test in one sitting.
- The times for each section are indicated at the start of the section. Sections 1 and 2 are each 25 minutes long, and Section 3 is 20 minutes long.
- Work on only one section at a time. If you finish a section before time has run out, check your work on that section only.

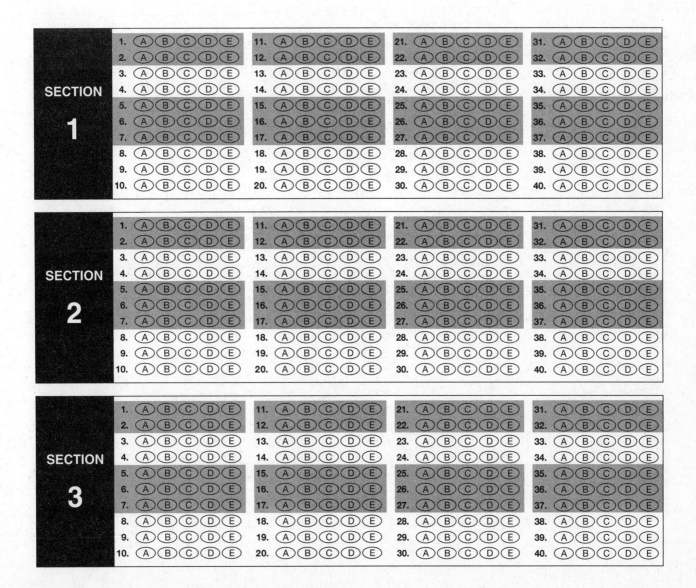

■ SECTION 1 QUESTIONS

Time—25 Minutes

24 Questions

Directions: This section consists of sentence completion questions and questions based on reading passages. For each question, select the answer you think is best and record your choice by filling in the corresponding oval on the answer sheet.

Directions: Each sentence below has one or two blanks. Each blank indicates that something is missing. Following each sentence are five words or sets of words labeled A, B, C, D, and E. You are to select the word or set of words that, when inserted in the sentence, best fits the meaning of the sentence as a whole.

E X A M P L E :

1. Despite our best efforts to protect the environment and keep it safe, until the problems of pollution are _____, the future of our environment seems, at best, _____.

    (A) created . . . gloomy
    (B) revoked . . . secure
    (C) solved . . . uncertain
    (D) replaced . . . revered
    (E) increased . . . unknown

    Correct Answer: C

1. Before the book was _____, references to several living people were _____.

    (A) banned . . . deleted
    (B) published . . . expurgated
    (C) printed . . . informed
    (D) reviewed . . . added
    (E) denounced . . . clarified

2. History has shown that two of the most _____ patriots of the Revolutionary War were Samuel Adams and John Hancock.

    (A) destitute
    (B) dolorous
    (C) captious
    (D) eminent
    (E) spontaneous

3. Despite her _____ temper, the actress typically displayed a _____ demeanor.

    (A) modest . . . humble
    (B) caustic . . . maniacal
    (C) explosive . . . timid
    (D) irascible . . . insolent
    (E) manageable . . . courteous

4. As her guests warmly _____ themselves in front of the fireplace, the hostess returned to the kitchen.

    (A) ensconced
    (B) expounded
    (C) remitted
    (D) immolated
    (E) capitulated

5. The _____ buffet featured an array of sandwiches, salads, and desserts, which the guests _____ within minutes.

    (A) enigmatic . . . extrapolated
    (B) fanciful . . . ascertained
    (C) fetid . . . consumed
    (D) enticing . . . devoured
    (E) sumptuous . . . imbibed

6. For Maurice to arrive on time, he had to _____ himself from the web of traffic in which he was currently stuck.

    (A) recuse
    (B) extricate
    (C) buttress
    (D) disavow
    (E) elucidate

GO ON TO THE NEXT PAGE

7. Knowing that the bonuses being offered were not
    easily _____, the union decided not to _____
    the new contract.

    (A) attainable . . . ratify
    (B) reachable . . . nullify
    (C) restricted . . . validate
    (D) limited . . . certify
    (E) obtainable . . . repudiate

8. The ending of the movie was so _____ that many
    questions the audience had were left unanswered.

    (A) derivative
    (B) lucid
    (C) explicit
    (D) indubitable
    (E) equivocal

Directions: The passages below are followed by questions based on their content. Questions that follow a pair of related passages may also ask about the relationship between the paired passages. Answer each question on the basis
of what is stated or implied in the passages and any introductory material provided.

Questions 9–12 are based on the following passages.

Passage 1.

After dominating the land for 130 million years,
dinosaurs suddenly disappeared from the face of
Line Earth at the end of the Cretaceous Period, about 65
million years ago, when a giant asteroid slammed
5   into what is now Mexico's Yucatan Peninsula. The
impact blasted a 180 kilometer-wide (100 miles)
crater deep into the Earth. The heat of impact sent
a searing vapor cloud speeding northward, which,
within minutes, set the North American continent
10 aflame. Following the fireball, lingering airborne
debris triggered darkness and a decline in the
global temperature that made Earth uninhabitable
not only for dinosaurs but also for many other
plants and animals.

Passage 2.

15 Dinosaurs faded away into extinction as a result of
volcanism. During the late Cretaceous Period, there
was a marked increase in volcanic activity. Huge
volcanic eruptions spewed forth floods of lava. In
India, the Deccan eruption alone could have cov-
20 ered the entire surface of the Earth with a lava layer
10 feet thick if it had spread evenly over the continents and oceans. Over a period of several million
years, this volcanic activity created enough soot
and dust to block out sunlight. The resulting cli-
25 mate change was unfavorable to dinosaurs, and
slowly they began to die off.

9. Like Passage 1, Passage 2 does which of the
    following?

    (A) explains a study
    (B) offers a solution
    (C) quotes an authority
    (D) takes a stand
    (E) presents both sides of an issue

10. Unlike the author of Passage 1, the author of Passage
    2 believes that

    (A) the Age of Dinosaurs ended 130 million years
        ago
    (B) dinosaurs died out gradually
    (C) an extraterrestrial event was responsible for
        the death of the dinosaurs
    (D) dinosaurs lived for 65 million years
    (E) dinosaurs are not really extinct

11. Both authors would most likely agree with which of
    the following statements?

    (A) Dinosaurs could not adapt to declining global
        temperatures.
    (B) Dinosaurs were wiped off the face of the earth
        by a giant asteroid.
    (C) Most dinosaurs were destroyed by violent vol-
        canic eruptions.
    (D) Global warming contributed to the disappear-
        ance of dinosaurs.
    (E) As dinosaurs grew larger, they could not find
        enough food to sustain themselves.

GO ON TO THE NEXT PAGE

12. Which best expresses the relationship between Passage 2 and Passage 1?

    (A) Passage 2 presents findings that negate Passage 1.

    (B) Passage 2 provides a scientific example of the theory advanced in Passage 1.

    (C) Passage 2 offers an alternative to the theory presented in Passage 1.

    (D) Passage 2 questions the data presented in Passage 1.

    (E) Passage 2 is more scientific than Passage 1.

Questions 13–24 are based on the following passage.

This excerpt comes from *To Build a Fire,* a short story written by Jack London in the early 1900s.

Day had broken cold and gray, exceedingly cold and gray, when the man turned aside from the main
Line Yukon trail and climbed the high earth-bank, where a dim and little-traveled trail led eastward through
5 the fat spruce timberland. It was a steep bank, and he paused for breath at the top, excusing the act to himself by looking at his watch. It was nine o'clock. There was no sun nor hint of sun, though there was not a cloud in the sky. It was a clear day, and yet
10 there seemed an intangible pall over the face of things, a subtle gloom that made the day dark, and that was due to the absence of sun. This fact did not worry the man.

The man flung a look back along the way he
15 had come. The Yukon lay a mile wide and hidden under three feet of ice. On top of this ice were as many feet of snow. It was all pure white, rolling in gentle undulations where the ice-jams of the freeze-up had formed. North and south, as far as his
20 eye could see, it was unbroken white, save for a dark hair-line that curved and twisted from around the spruce-covered island to the south, and that curved and twisted away into the north, where it disappeared behind another spruce-covered island.
25 But all this—the mysterious, far-reaching hair-line trail, the absence of sun from the sky, the tremendous cold, and the strangeness and weird-ness of it all—made no impression on the man. It was not because he was long used to it. He was a
30 newcomer in the land, a *chechaquo,* and this was his first winter. The trouble with him was that he was without imagination. He was quick and alert in the things of life, but only in the things, and not in the significances. Fifty degrees below zero meant
35 eighty-odd degrees of frost. Such fact impressed him as being cold and uncomfortable, and that was all. It did not lead him to meditate upon his frailty as a creature of temperature, and upon man's frailty

in general, able only to live within certain narrow
40 limits of heat and cold; and from there on it did not lead him to the conjectural field of immortality and man's place in the universe.

As he turned to go on, he spat speculatively. There was a sharp, explosive crackle that startled
45 him. He spat again. And again, in the air, before it could fall to the snow, the spittle crackled. He knew that at fifty below spittle crackled on the snow, but this spittle had crackled in the air. Un-doubtedly it was colder than fifty below—how
50 much colder he did not know. But the temperature did not matter. He was bound for the old claim on the left fork of Henderson Creek, where the boys were already. They had come over across the divide from the Indian Creek country, while he had come
55 the roundabout way to take a look at the possibili-ties of getting out logs in the spring from the islands in the Yukon.

At the man's heels trotted a dog, a big native husky, the proper wolf-dog, gray-coated and with-
60 out any visible or temperamental difference from its brother, the wild wolf. The animal was depressed by the tremendous cold. It knew that it was no time for travelling. Its instinct told it a truer tale than was told to the man by the man's judgment. In re-
65 ality, it was not merely colder than fifty below zero; it was colder than sixty below, than seventy below. It was seventy-five below zero. Since the freezing-point is thirty-two above zero, it meant that one hundred and seven degrees of frost ob-
70 tained. The dog did not know anything about ther-mometers. Possibly in its brain there was no sharp consciousness of a condition of very cold such as was in the man's brain. But the brute had its in-stinct. It experienced a vague but menacing appre-
75 hension that subdued it and made it slink along at the man's heels, and that made it question eagerly every unwonted movement of the man as if ex-pecting him to go into camp or to seek shelter some-where and build a fire. The dog had learned fire,
80 and it wanted fire, or else to burrow under the snow and cuddle its warmth away from the air.

13. The imagery in lines 1–14 establishes a mood of

    (A) promise

    (B) serenity

    (C) hostility

    (D) foreboding

    (E) regret

GO ON TO THE NEXT PAGE

14. As used in line 1, "broken" most nearly means

   (A) dawned
   (B) separated
   (C) shattered
   (D) interrupted
   (E) cracked

15. The statement that "It was a steep bank, and he paused for breath at the top, excusing the act to himself by looking at his watch," (lines 5–7) suggests that

   (A) the man was worried about running late
   (B) the man was not accustomed to such activity
   (C) the man was disoriented by the extreme cold
   (D) the man was farther ahead of schedule than he thought
   (E) the man expected to see the sun

16. In line 30, the term *chechaquo* refers to the man's

   (A) knowledge of logging
   (B) spirit of adventure
   (C) inexperience with Yukon winters
   (D) ability to follow a winding trail
   (E) ability to recognize signs of danger

17. In line 44, the author includes the detail of "a sharp, explosive crackle that startled him" primarily to emphasize

   (A) the man's fragile state of mind
   (B) how eerily quiet it had become
   (C) that the temperature was dropping
   (D) the danger the man was in
   (E) it was colder than the man thought

18. The author of the passage qualifies the man's judgment of the cold by

   (A) having him continue on a "little-travelled trail"
   (B) mentioning that the cold does not worry the man
   (C) subjectively indicating that the weather was tremendously cold
   (D) explaining that it was the man's first winter on the Yukon trail
   (E) including the statement that the man was "quick and alert in the things of life"

19. By saying that the man was quick and alert "in the things of life" but not in the "significances" (lines 32–34) the author means that the man was

   (A) observant but not thoughtful
   (B) fast but not accurate
   (C) watchful but careless
   (D) perceptive but reckless
   (E) ready but not able

20. In line 43, "speculatively" is closest in meaning to

   (A) appropriately
   (B) unexpectedly
   (C) experimentally
   (D) especially
   (E) quickly

21. The discussion of spitting into the air (lines 43–48) serves primarily to suggest

   (A) the strangeness of the landscape
   (B) the severity of the cold
   (C) the courage of the man
   (D) the frustration of the dog
   (E) the gloom of the day

22. In context, the word "obtained" (lines 69–70) most nearly means

   (A) amassed
   (B) procured
   (C) acquired
   (D) existed
   (E) realized

23. Which word best describes how the author regards the man in the story?

   (A) clever
   (B) cautious
   (C) foolish
   (D) ambitious
   (E) ruthless

24. With which of the following statements is the author most likely to agree?

   (A) The man is right to press on.
   (B) The dog is unfazed by the cold.
   (C) The man is jealous of the dog.
   (D) The dog is wiser than the man.
   (E) The sun will make the day more bearable.

END OF SECTION

IF YOU FINISH BEFORE TIME IS UP, CHECK YOUR WORK ON THIS SECTION ONLY.

SECTION 2 QUESTIONS

Time—25 Minutes

24 Questions

Directions: This section consists of sentence completion questions and questions based on reading passages. For each question, select the answer you think is best and record your choice by filling in the corresponding oval on the answer sheet.

Directions: Each sentence below has one or two blanks. Each blank indicates that something is missing. Following each sentence are five words or sets of words labeled A, B, C, D, and E. You are to select the word or set of words that, when inserted in the sentence, best fits the meaning of the sentence as a whole.

EXAMPLE:

1. Despite our best efforts to protect the environment and keep it safe, until the problems of pollution are _____, the future of our environment seems, at best, _____.

    (A) created . . . gloomy
    (B) revoked . . . secure
    (C) solved . . . uncertain
    (D) replaced . . . revered
    (E) increased . . . unknown

    Correct Answer: C

1. The first speaker gave such a _____ speech on the subject that every speaker who followed her seemed _____.

    (A) detailed . . . problematic
    (B) comprehensive . . . redundant
    (C) narrow . . . repetitive
    (D) thorough . . . reasonable
    (E) generic . . . superfluous

2. Both _____ and _____, the river's path was quiet and winding.

    (A) tranquil . . . sinuous
    (B) turbulent . . . circuitous
    (C) cacophonous . . . meandrous
    (D) serene . . . rigid
    (E) raucous . . . convoluted

3. The court's refusal to reverse the decision, despite overwhelming evidence, led many to believe it had _____ justice.

    (A) impelled
    (B) accelerated
    (C) impeded
    (D) hastened
    (E) expedited

4. Based on almost no research, the company's plan to go ahead with the expansion seemed rather _____.

    (A) judicious
    (B) heedful
    (C) circumspect
    (D) arbitrary
    (E) prudent

5. Although the effects of the tornado were _____, it brought the town together through a sense of _____.

    (A) ruinous . . . camaraderie
    (B) destructive . . . aversion
    (C) deleterious . . . apostasy
    (D) innocuous . . . goodwill
    (E) benign . . . fellowship

GO ON TO THE NEXT PAGE

Directions: The passages below are followed by questions based on their content. Answer each question on the basis of what is stated or implied in the passages and any introductory material provided.

Questions 6 and 7 are based on the following passage.

Who says engineers don't know how to have fun? In 1958, William Higinbotham designed the first
Line video game while working at the Brookhaven National Laboratory: a U.S. nuclear research lab in
5 Upton, New York. Named "Tennis for Two," the game was developed as entertainment for the laboratory's annual visitors' days in an effort to add a bit of excitement to what was then, a particularly staid event. According to Higinbotham, head of the
10 Instrumentation Division, "It might liven the place up to have a game that people could play, and which would convey the message that our scientific endeavors have relevance for society."

6. The quote from Higinbotham helps explain that

(A) he was involved in bringing science out of the lab and into the home

(B) he knew that many people were indifferent to how science affects their daily lives

(C) he realized most people felt removed from the importance of scientific research

(D) his research lab was at the forefront of developing science for entertainment purposes

(E) he was aware that people were looking for ways in which science could enhance their lives

7. This passage primarily serves to

(A) explain the origin of a popular cultural phenomenon

(B) compare an early video game to those made today

(C) support the general idea that scientific research is tedious

(D) explain the type of research conducted at the laboratory

(E) inform the reader about the life of William Higinbotham

Questions 8 and 9 are based on the following passage.

In this very attitude did I sit when I called to him,
Line rapidly stating what it was I wanted him to do—namely, to examine a small paper with me. Imag-
5 ine my surprise, nay, my consternation, when without moving from his privacy, Bartleby in a singularly mild, firm voice, replied, "I would prefer not to."

I sat awhile in perfect silence, rallying my stunned faculties. Immediately it occurred to me
10 that my ears had deceived me, or Bartleby had entirely misunderstood my meaning. I repeated my request in the clearest tone I could assume. But in quite as clear a one came the previous reply, "I would prefer not to."

8. The narrator's tone implies that he

(A) is rarely denied a request for assistance

(B) is incapable of working on his own

(C) did not voice his request clearly

(D) often required the help of others

(E) is constantly annoyed by those he works with

9. In context, "rallying my stunned faculties" most nearly means

(A) gathering his surprised staff

(B) processing Bartleby's refusal

(C) thinking aloud

(D) realizing he had misconstrued Bartleby's reply

(E) noticing he had asked for help impolitely

Questions 10–18 are based on the following passage.

The following passage is from *Homespun Heroines and Other Women of Distinction,* a collection of biographies of history-making black women compiled and edited by teacher and writer Hallie Q. Brown. It tells the story of Phillis Wheatley, the former slave who became a noted American poet.

In the year 1761, a little slave girl about seven years
Line old, stood in the market place in Boston, Massachusetts, with a number of others to be sold as chattel.
5 The little girl had been brought from far off Africa. She stood a pitiful looking object with no clothing save a piece of dirty, ragged carpet tied around her. Mrs. John Wheatley had several slaves, but they were growing too old to be active and she
10 wished to purchase a young girl, whom she could train up in such a manner as to make a good domestic. For this purpose she went to the slave market and there she saw the little girl who appeared to

GO ON TO THE NEXT PAGE

be in ill health, which no doubt was due to the suffering she endured in the slave-ship on the long voy-
15 age. Mrs. Wheatley was a kind, religious woman and though she considered the sickly look of the child an objection, there was something so gentle and modest in the expression of her dark countenance and her large mournful eyes that her heart was
20 drawn toward her and she bought her in preference to several others who looked more robust. She took her home in her chaise, gave her a bath and dressed her in clean clothes. They could not at first understand her and she resorted to signs and gestures for
25 she spoke only her native African dialect and a few words of broken English. Mrs. Wheatley gave her the name of Phillis Wheatley, little dreaming that it, and the little slave girl she had rescued, would become renowned in American history.
30   Phillis soon learned to speak English, but she could tell nothing of herself nor when she was torn from her parents by the slave-traders, nor where she had been since that time. The poor, little orphan had gone through so much suffering and terror that her
35 mind had become bewildered concerning the past.
       The only thing that clung to her about Africa was seeing her mother pour out water before the rising sun which would indicate that the mother descended from some remote tribe of sun-worshippers. And
40 that sight of her mother doing reverence before the great luminous orb coming as it did out of the nowhere, but giving light and cheer to the world, naturally impressed the child's imagination so deeply that she remembered it when all else was forgotten
45 about her native land. In the course of a year and a half a wonderful change took place in the little, forlorn stranger. She not only learned to speak English correctly, but was able to read fluently in any part of the Bible. She possessed uncommon intelligence
50 and a great desire for knowledge. She was often found trying to make letters with charcoal on the walls and fences. Mrs. Wheatley's daughter became her teacher. She found this an easy task for the pupil learned with astonishing quickness. At the same
55 time she showed such an amiable, affectionate disposition that all members of the family became much attached to her. Her gratitude to her motherly benefactress was unbounded and her greatest delight was to do anything to please her. At the age
60 of fourteen she began to write poetry. Owing to such uncommon manifestations of intelligence, she was never put to hard household work. She became the companion of Mrs. Wheatley and her daughter. Her poetry attracted attention and friends
65 of Mrs. Wheatley lent her books which she read with great eagerness. She soon acquired a good knowledge of geography, history and English poetry. After a while she learned Latin which she so far

mastered as to be able to read it understandingly.
70 There was no law in Massachusetts against slaves learning to read and write and Mrs. Wheatley did everything to encourage her love of learning. She always called her affectionately "My Phillis" and seemed to be as proud of her attainments as if she
75 had been her own daughter. Phillis was very religious and at the age of sixteen joined the Orthodox Church that worshipped in the Old-South Meetinghouse in Boston. Her character and deportment were such that she was considered an ornament to
80 the church. Clergymen and other literary persons who visited Mrs. Wheatley's home took a great deal of notice of her. Her poems were brought forward to be read by the company and were often praised.

10. Mrs. Wheatley chose Phillis over other healthier looking young girls at the slave market primarily because of Phillis's

(A) ragged clothes
(B) ability to speak English
(C) uncommon intelligence
(D) modest expression and mournful eyes
(E) African heritage

11. The "great luminous orb" in line 41 refers to

(A) the Earth
(B) the sun
(C) Phillis's mother
(D) Africa
(E) Mrs. Wheatley

12. Phillis became the companion of Mrs. Wheatley and her daughter mainly because Phillis

(A) was an orphan
(B) could not speak English
(C) showed uncommon intelligence
(D) was frail and sickly
(E) was very religious

13. As used in line 55, "amiable" most nearly means

(A) amenable
(B) ambivalent
(C) reproachable
(D) genial
(E) impudent

GO ON TO THE NEXT PAGE →

14. The statement that Phillis was "never put to hard household work" (line 62) suggests that

(A) the Wheatleys' feelings toward slavery were ambivalent
(B) the Wheatleys no longer believed in the institution of slavery
(C) the Wheatleys considered Phillis their daughter
(D) Phillis was treated differently from the other slaves
(E) Phillis had not yet returned to good health

15. The statement in lines 70–72 ("There was. . . . . learning.") implies that

(A) Phillis learned to read and write without telling Mrs. Wheatley
(B) Mrs. Wheatley taught Phillis to read and write, even though it was against the law
(C) Mrs. Wheatley sent Phillis to school in another state
(D) some states had laws against teaching slaves to read and write
(E) Massachusetts was a state that had no laws

16. Mrs. Wheatley used the term "My Phillis" (line 73) to show that Phillis is

(A) her daughter
(B) her personal slave
(C) someone who is not to be given hard household chores
(D) different from other domestics named Phillis
(E) someone she is very fond of

17. The author regards Phillis Wheatley as a "Woman of Distinction" because of Wheatley's

(A) poetry
(B) knowledge of geography and history
(C) mastery of Latin
(D) church work
(E) great love of books

18. The tone of this passage is both

(A) objective and angry
(B) disappointed and critical
(C) factual and inspirational
(D) hopeful and moralistic
(E) humorous and ironic

Questions 19–24 are based on the following passage.

Astronomers with NASA's Chandra X-ray Observatory have found a pulsating star only 10,000 light
Line   years from Earth that is rapidly cooling down. The object discovered by the astronomers is a type of
5   whirling neutron star known as a pulsar. The remnant of a once bright and burning star, a pulsar spins and flashes radiation like a lighthouse on a distant point. Understanding how pulsars function could help explain how nuclear forces and magnet-
10   ism work in our universe.

First identified by Asian astronomers in the year 1181, pulsar 3C58 should have a temperature of about 1.5 million degrees Celsius. However, puzzled scientists have found the star's temperature
15   to be far below that.

"We now have strong evidence that, in slightly more than 800 years, the surface of the 3C58 pulsar has cooled to a temperature of slightly less than a million degrees Celsius," said Patrick Slane of the
20   Harvard–Smithsonian Center for Astrophysics in Cambridge, Mass. "A million degrees may sound pretty hot, but for a young neutron star, that's like the frozen tundra in Green Bay, Wisc."

Neutron and pulsar stars are what astronomers
25   believe are left after a regular star collapses in a supernova explosion. When the star implodes, electrons and protons in its core violently smash into one another, destroying themselves to form neutrons and tinier neutrinos. A powerful shockwave
30   then blasts away the star's outer material, leaving only a concentrated core of neutrons behind.

Once the new star is formed, high-speed collisions between neutrons and other particles inside the core create even more neutrinos. The neutrinos in-
35   teract weakly with the neutrons, causing them to easily escape the star and take heat energy with them. If the number of departing neutrinos climbs, so will the cooling rate of the star. The fact that 3C58's temperature plummeted so quickly leads astronomers to be-
40   lieve its core is abuzz with neutrino activity.

Researchers wonder if the pulsar's rapid cooling is triggered by something new in the mix of particles inside the core. One idea is that a higher number of protons survived the supernova explosion, or
45   perhaps the core is infested with small specks of matter known as pion condensates.

Aside from the star's swift change in temperature, scientists also detected loops of magnetic energy surrounding the pulsar. Jets of high-energy
50   particles can also be seen shooting out of the pulsar. Evidence from these and similar discoveries suggests that pulsars with defined magnetic fields are powerful generators of high-energy particles. Why pulsar 3C58 has cooled off so quickly remains
55   a mystery. Determining the cause could reveal valuable details about the fundamental ways matter and energy interact in the universe.

GO ON TO THE NEXT PAGE ➤

19. The scientists are "puzzled" (line 14) because

    (A) the pulsar is cooling down
    (B) the pulsar is more than 800 years old
    (C) the pulsar is a young neutron star
    (D) the temperature of the pulsar is lower than expected
    (E) the temperature of the pulsar is 1.5 million degrees

20. The primary purpose of this passage is to

    (A) explain a widely held scientific theory
    (B) describe the activity of neutrons and neutrinos
    (C) report on an unusual scientific discovery
    (D) present a practical application for astronomy
    (E) describe the role of nuclear forces and magnetism in the universe

21. The quotation in lines 21–23 ("A million. . . . . Wisc.") serves to reinforce the point that

    (A) the cooling of the pulsar has been significant
    (B) a million degrees is very hot for a neutron star
    (C) the star's outer material has been blasted away by a powerful shockwave
    (D) Green Bay is the best place from which to observe the neutron star
    (E) the temperature of a neutron star increases with age

22. According to the passage, neutrinos result from

    (A) the combination of electrons and neutrons
    (B) the cooling of a neutron star
    (C) violent collisions between electrons and protons
    (D) weak interaction with neutrons
    (E) high-impact collisions between protons and neutrons

23. Which of the following is not offered as a possible explanation for the cooling of pulsar 3C58?

    (A) an increased number of departing neutrinos
    (B) greater neutrino activity in the core
    (C) more protons surviving the supernova explosion
    (D) an infestation of pion condensates in the core
    (E) the collapse of a star in a supernova explosion

24. Analysis of the loops of magnetic energy surrounding pulsar 3C58 and the particles seen shooting out of it suggests that

    (A) more neutrinos are departing the pulsar
    (B) pulsars are powerful generators of high-energy particles.
    (C) higher numbers of protons survived the supernova explosion
    (D) the core of the pulsar is infested with pion condensates
    (E) a pulsar is the remnant of a once bright and burning star

END OF SECTION

IF YOU FINISH BEFORE TIME IS UP, CHECK YOUR WORK ON THIS SECTION ONLY.

SECTION 3 QUESTIONS

Time—20 Minutes

19 Questions

Directions: This section consists of sentence completion questions and questions based on reading passages. For each question, select the answer you think is best and record your choice by filling in the corresponding oval on the answer sheet.

Directions: Each sentence below has one or two blanks. Each blank indicates that something is missing. Following each sentence are five words or sets of words labeled A, B, C, D, and E. You are to select the word or set of words that, when inserted in the sentence, best fits the meaning of the sentence as a whole.

EXAMPLE:

1. Despite our best efforts to protect the environment and keep it safe, until the problems of pollution are _____, the future of our environment seems, at best, _____.

   (A) created . . . gloomy
   (B) revoked . . . secure
   (C) solved . . . uncertain
   (D) replaced . . . revered
   (E) increased . . . unknown

   Correct Answer: C

---

1. Lacking any interesting qualities, the _____ movie featured cheap special effects, an unlikely plot, and ridiculously bad acting.

   (A) classic
   (B) hilarious
   (C) insipid
   (D) optimistic
   (E) uproarious

2. Because of her _____ handling of the case, the lawyer was asked if she would be interested in becoming a junior partner in the _____ law firm.

   (A) idiosyncratic . . . reverent
   (B) callous . . . punitive
   (C) adroit . . . humble
   (D) deft . . . venerable
   (E) inept . . . estimable

3. Leaving the computer store with an armload of merchandise, Amir could not help but feel that the _____ salesperson had misled him into buying more than he really needed.

   (A) beguiling
   (B) anachronistic
   (C) industrious
   (D) observant
   (E) disparate

4. Although financial analysts had initially praised the company's president for his business _____, they soon realized his ethical conduct was _____ lacking.

   (A) development . . . refreshingly
   (B) acumen . . . woefully
   (C) decisions . . . innocuously
   (D) finesse . . . timorously
   (E) strategy . . . provincially

5. One of the most _____ songwriters of her generation, Joni Mitchell has written and recorded over three hundred songs since 1968.

   (A) successful
   (B) independent
   (C) prolific
   (D) pretentious
   (E) inscrutable

6. The Underground Railroad was a network of _____ routes, often informal and _____, by which slaves were able to escape from the southern United States.

   (A) clandestine . . . impromptu
   (B) public . . . extemporaneous
   (C) covert . . . organized
   (D) surreptitious . . . convenient
   (E) train . . . improvised

GO ON TO THE NEXT PAGE

Directions: The two passages below are followed by questions based on their content and on the relationship between the passages. Answer each question on the basis of what is stated or implied in the passages and any introductory material provided.

Questions 7–19 are based on the following passages.

Passage 1 is from an appeal to Congress made by former slave Frederick Douglass in 1845. Passage 2 is from a speech made by women's rights activist Susan B. Anthony after her arrest for casting an illegal vote in the presidential election of 1872.

Passage 1.

A very limited statement of the argument for impartial suffrage, and for including the negro in the
Line body politic, would require more space than can be reasonably asked here. It is supported by reasons as
5 broad as the nature of man, and as numerous as the wants of society. Man is the only government-making animal in the world. His right to a participation in the production and operation of government is an inference from his nature, as direct
10 and self-evident as is his right to acquire property or education. It is no less a crime against the manhood of a man, to declare that he shall not share in the making and directing of the government under which he lives, than to say that he shall not acquire
15 property and education. The fundamental and unanswerable argument in favor of the enfranchisement of the negro is found in the undisputed fact of his manhood. He is a man, and by every fact and argument by which any man can sustain his right to vote,
20 the negro can sustain his right equally. It is plain that, if the right belongs to any, it belongs to all. The doctrine that some men have no rights that others are bound to respect, is a doctrine which we must banish as we have banished slavery, from which it em-
25 anated. If black men have no rights in the eyes of white men, of course the whites can have none in the eyes of the blacks. The result is a war of races, and the annihilation of all proper human relations.

Passage 2.

The preamble of the Federal Constitution says:
30 "We, the people of the United States, in order to form a more perfect union, establish justice, insure domestic tranquility, provide for the common defense, promote the general welfare, and secure the blessings of liberty to ourselves and our posterity,
35 do ordain and establish this Constitution for the United States of America."

It was we, the people, not we, the white male citizens; but we, the whole people, who formed the Union. And we formed it, not to give the blessings
40 of liberty, but to secure them; not to the half of ourselves and the half of our posterity but to the whole people—women as well as men. And it is a downright mockery to talk to women of the enjoyment of the blessings of liberty while they are denied the
45 use of the only means of securing them provided by this democratic-republican government—the ballot.

For any state to make sex a qualification that must ever result in the disfranchisement of one en-
50 tire half of the people, is to pass a bill of attainder, or, an ex post facto law, and is therefore a violation of the supreme law of the land. By it the blessings of liberty are forever withheld from women and their female posterity.

55 To them this government has no just powers derived from the consent of the governed. To them this government is not a democracy. It is not a republic. It is an odious aristocracy; a hateful oligarchy of sex; the most hateful aristocracy ever established on
60 the face of the globe; an oligarchy of wealth, where the rich govern the poor. An oligarchy of learning, where the educated govern the ignorant, or even an oligarchy of race, where the Saxon rules the African, might be endured; but this oligarchy of sex,
65 which makes father, brothers, husband, sons, the oligarchs over the mother and sisters, the wife and daughters, of every household—which ordains all men sovereigns, all women subjects, carries dissension, discord, and rebellion into every home of the
70 nation.

Webster, Worcester, and Bouvier all define a citizen to be a person in the United States, entitled to vote and hold office.

The only question left to be settled now is: Are
75 women persons? And I hardly believe any of our opponents will have the hardihood to say they are not. Being persons, then, women are citizens; and no state has a right to make any law, or to enforce any old law, that shall abridge their privileges or
80 immunities. Hence, every discrimination against women in the constitutions and laws of the several states is today null and void, precisely as is every one against Negroes.

GO ON TO THE NEXT PAGE ➔

7. Both passages are primarily concerned with

   (A) banishing slavery
   (B) the right to run for and hold office
   (C) the right to vote
   (D) the difference between democracy and aristocracy
   (E) civil disobedience

8. The author of Passage 1 is similar to the author of Passage 2 in that both are

   (A) former slaves
   (B) members of a disenfranchised group
   (C) under arrest at the time of their speech
   (D) strongly opposed to war
   (E) unlikely to gather any support for their positions

9. The authors of Passage 1 and Passage 2 differ in that

   (A) the author of Passage 1 reflects the views typical of a Southerner, while the author of Passage 2 reflects the views typical of a Northerner of the time
   (B) the author of Passage 1 directs his remarks to a predominantly black audience and the author of Passage 2 direct her remarks to a mostly white audience
   (C) the author of Passage 2 opposes the solution proposed by the author of Passage 1
   (D) the author of Passage 1 bases the right to vote on being a man, while the author of Passage 2 bases the right to vote on being a person
   (E) the author of Passage 1 cites citizenship as a requirement for voting while the author of Passage 2 cites property ownership as the requirement for voting

10. Both authors would agree that

    (A) it is better to be impartial in deciding who should vote and who should not
    (B) an oligarchy is the most hateful of all forms of government
    (C) the right to vote should be tied to education and property ownership
    (D) women have a subservient place in a democracy
    (E) There can be no peace when civil rights are denied to large segments of the population

11. In Passage 1, the author compares the right to participate in government to the right to

    (A) hold a job
    (B) own property
    (C) have a family
    (D) wage war
    (E) move from place to place

12. By calling for "impartial suffrage" (lines 1–2) the author of Passage 1 means

    (A) elections should be fair and just
    (B) Congress should act to end suffering
    (C) men and women should have the same voting rights
    (D) blacks and whites should have the same voting rights
    (E) requirements for U.S. citizenship should be the same for all

13. In line 19 of Passage 1, "sustain" most nearly means

    (A) carry
    (B) encourage
    (C) support
    (D) suffer
    (E) nourish

14. The statement in Passage 1 that "If black men have no rights in the eyes of white men, of course the whites can have none in the eyes of blacks" primarily suggests that

    (A) women of both races will have equal rights
    (B) the author believes the racial divide can never be bridged
    (C) white men will have no rights in a separate black society
    (D) black men will afford white men the same rights they receive from white men
    (E) the author believed the Civil War was imminent

15. The main purpose of Passage 1 is to

    (A) plead for voting rights for black men
    (B) appeal for voting rights for all citizens
    (C) remove a source of racial tension
    (D) praise Congress for voting to end slavery
    (E) advocate respect for all men

16. In lines 30–36, the author of Passage 2 quotes the Preamble to the Constitution in order to

    (A) provide a historical overview
    (B) imply that the Constitution is unfair to women
    (C) elicit sympathy for her position
    (D) give strength and authority to her argument
    (E) demonstrate her superior intellect

GO ON TO THE NEXT PAGE

17. To the author of Passage 2, the "most hateful aristocracy ever established" (line 59) is

    (A) rule by monarchs over subjects
    (B) rule by the educated over the ignorant
    (C) rule by one sex over the other
    (D) rule by one race over another
    (E) rule by one ethnic group over another

18. Passage 2 is primarily intended to

    (A) illustrate an important difference between men and women
    (B) explain why women should have the right to vote
    (C) clarify the meaning of the Preamble to the Constitution
    (D) define the word citizen
    (E) provide an example of a law that does not discriminate

19. In line 79 of Passage 2, "abridge" means most nearly

    (A) shorten
    (B) condense
    (C) summarize
    (D) abbreviate
    (E) curtail

END OF SECTION

IF YOU FINISH BEFORE TIME IS UP, CHECK YOUR WORK ON THIS SECTION ONLY.

ANSWER KEY

Section 1

1. B	7. A	13. D	19. A
2. D	8. E	14. A	20. C
3. C	9. D	15. B	21. B
4. A	10. B	16. C	22. D
5. D	11. A	17. E	23. C
6. B	12. C	18. D	24. D

Section 2

1. B	7. A	13. D	19. D
2. A	8. A	14. D	20. C
3. C	9. B	15. D	21. A
4. D	10. D	16. E	22. C
5. A	11. B	17. A	23. E
6. C	12. C	18. C	24. B

Section 3

1. C	6. A	11. B	16. D
2. D	7. C	12. D	17. C
3. A	8. B	13. C	18. B
4. B	9. D	14. D	19. E
5. C	10. E	15. A	

ANSWERS AND EXPLANATIONS

Section 1

1. **B is correct.** The key word in this sentence is *before*. *Before* sets up a logical structure for the sentence and informs the reader that before *this* can occur, *that* must occur. (A) and (E) can be discounted almost immediately because names do not have to be deleted before a book is banned, and they have to be clarified before a book can be denounced. Also, (D) is incorrect because by the time a book is reviewed, it is too late to add any material to the manuscript. A reference (C) is an inanimate object, and therefore cannot be informed of anything. (B) is the correct choice and the only one that contains proper logic; *before the book was published, the names of several living people were expurgated.* To *expurgate* something from a book is to remove erroneous or objectionable material from it.

2. **D is correct.** Getting the correct answer to this question will be made easier by knowing the definitions of the five answer choices. Which choice best reflects a description of two famous (rather than infamous) historical figures? A *destitute* (A) person lacks the means to support himself, and a *dolorous* (B) person is one who exhibits grief or sorrow. Someone who is *captious* (C) is most often critical or acrimonious, and *spontaneous* (E) is not appropriate in the context of the question. *Eminent* (D) denotes a person of prominence or high ranking and is the correct answer.

3. **C is correct.** *Despite* is the key word in this sentence, and it is often used in sentence completion questions to signal a contrast between the correct answers in two-blank questions. An easy way to demonstrate this point is with this sentence: *Despite a cloudy morning, the afternoon was sunny.* The structure of the sentence is designed to stress one characteristic of the subject in the first clause ("cloudy") and then to contrast this characteristic with another characteristic in the second clause ("sunny"). In this sentence, choices (A), (B), and (E) can be easily dis-

counted because there is too little contrast between the choices for the first blank and the choices for the second blank to justify the use of *despite*. *Modest* and *humble* are synonymous, and there is not enough of a difference between *caustic* and *maniacal*, or *manageable* and *courteous* in the context of the sentence to juxtapose the two meanings. Even if you do not know that *irascible* means "easily angered" and *insolent* means "rude" (D), you should be able to determine that (C) is the correct answer by noting the contrast between an *explosive* temper and a *timid* demeanor.

4. **A is correct.** Answering this question correctly depends almost entirely on knowing the definitions of the five answer choices you must choose from. *Ensconced* (A) is the correct answer, meaning "to settle oneself comfortably or securely." *Expounded* (B) is to have "given a detailed statement," and *remitted* (C) is most often used to describe having "transmitted money in payment" or "to restore to a former condition or position." To *immolate* (D) is "to kill oneself by fire," and *capitulate* is "to surrender or give up resistance."

5. **D is correct.** This type of sentence completion is known as a vocabulary-in-context question. To answer this type of question, you need to look at how the answer choices can be used in the context of the sentence. In addition, the more you know the definitions of the answer choices, the greater chance you have of answering correctly. Often the best way to answer a two-blank question is by focusing on either the first or second blank and eliminating any obviously wrong answers. Focusing on the second blank, you know that because buffets are not *extrapolated* (which means "inferred by projecting unknown information") or *ascertained* (which means "discovered through examination"), (A) and (B) can be discounted. Similarly, a buffet with "sandwiches, salads, and desserts," cannot be *imbibed* (drank), so choice (E) is not correct. Although you may not know that *fetid* (C) means having an

offensive odor, you should know that *enticing* (D) is used synonymously with "appealing." Therefore, (D) is the correct answer.

6. **B is correct.** *Extricate* (B), meaning "to release from an entanglement or difficulty" or "to disengage" is the correct answer. To *recuse* (A) is "to disqualify or seek to disqualify from participation in a decision," as in, *the judge recused himself from the case due to the close relationship he had with the defendant.* To *buttress* (C) is "to sustain, prop, or bolster," and to *disavow* (D) is "to disclaim knowledge or responsibility for" an event or situation. To *elucidate* (E) is defined as "to make clear or plain," or "to clarify especially by explanation."

7. **A is correct.** Some of the most challenging sentence completion questions will deal with sentences that have two negatives. This sentence contains a negative in both clauses of the sentence, and the second clause, which begins with *the union decided not to* is explained by the introductory word *knowing.* For sentences such as this one, it may be helpful to figure out which types of words should fill in the blanks before you look at the answer choices. For example, focus on the first blank of the sentence and which of the words available follow the logic of the sentence. In context, (C) and (D) do not make sense, so they can be eliminated. Now move on to the second blank, and you should notice that two of the remaining three choices, *nullify* (B) and *repudiate* (E) have meanings that are similar enough as to be indistinguishable. This leaves you with (A), the correct answer, and the only option that contextually follows the logic of the sentence.

8. **E is correct.** The word "unanswered" offers a context clue in that "something about the ending of the movie left the audience with unanswered questions." With questions like this one, it is often best to try to fill in the blank with an answer of your own before studying the answer choices. Words such as "ambiguous" and "confusing" come to mind, as these are words that could describe a movie's ending and leave the audience with unanswered questions. *Equivocal* (meaning

"open to two or more interpretations and often intended to mislead") is the only choice that conveys the meaning of the sentence. So, (E) is correct.

9. **D is correct.** Both passages take a stand on the issue of dinosaur extinction. Passage 1 supports the theory that the impact of a giant asteroid caused a rapid extinction of the dinosaurs and Passage 2 supports the theory that increased volcanic activity caused a gradual extinction of the dinosaurs.

(A) is wrong because neither passage explains a study.

(B) is wrong because no solutions are offered.

(C) is wrong because neither passage offers a quote from an authority.

(E) is wrong because each passage presents only one side of the argument it supports.

10. **B is correct.** A major difference between the positions taken by the two authors is the rate at which the dinosaurs died off. According to the author of Passage 1, "dinosaurs suddenly disappeared from the face of the Earth. . . . when a giant asteroid slammed into what is now Mexico's Yucatan Peninsula." According to the author of Passage 2, dinosaurs "faded away into extinction" and "slowly" died off.

(A) is wrong because both passages indicate that the Age of Dinosaurs ended at the end of the Cretaceous Period, which was about 65 million years ago.

(C) is wrong because the author of Passage 2 believes that increased volcanic activity was responsible for the death of the dinosaurs. Passage 1 attributes the extinction of the dinosaurs to an extraterrestrial event.

(D) is wrong because both authors would agree that dinosaurs became extinct about 65 million years ago, not that they lived for 65 million years.

(E) is wrong because both authors state that dinosaurs are extinct.

11. **A is correct.** As stated in Passage 1, "Following the fireball, lingering airborne debris triggered darkness and a decline in the global temperature that made Earth uninhabitable not only for dinosaurs but also for many other plants and animals." As stated in Passage 2, "volcanic activity created enough soot and dust to block out sunlight. The resulting climate change was unfavorable to dinosaurs, and slowly they began to die off." Thus both authors agree that declining temperatures were ultimately responsible for dinosaur extinction because the dinosaurs could not successfully adapt to cooler temperatures.

(B) is wrong because only Passage 1 mentions a giant asteroid.

(C) is wrong because only Passage 2 mentions volcanic activity.

(D) is wrong because both passages discuss global cooling, not global warming, as a cause of dinosaur extinction.

(E) is wrong because there is no support for this statement in either passage.

12. **C is correct.** Passage 1 supports the theory that a giant asteroid caused the extinction of the dinosaurs. Passage 2 supports an alternative theory of dinosaur extinction, one based on increased volcanic activity.

(A) is wrong because the findings of Passage 2 do not necessarily negate the findings of Passage 1.

(B) is wrong because Passage 2 does not provide an example of the theory discussed in Passage 1.

(D) is wrong because Passage 2 does not mention the data presented in Passage 1.

(E) is wrong because neither passage is more or less scientific than the other.

13. **D is correct.** Mood is the pervading spirit or feeling of a passage as transmitted by the author's choice of words. In this passage the day is described as "exceedingly cold and gray" with "no sun nor hint of sun, though there was not a cloud in the sky." There was "an intangible pall over the face of things, a subtle gloom that made the day dark." And yet, despite these warning signs, the man was not worried. Taken together this information imparts a sense of impending misfortune or foreboding.

(A) is wrong because there are no words in the paragraph that indicate good things to come.

(B) is wrong because the description does not create a feeling of serenity or tranquility.

(C) is wrong because the description of the day does not evoke hostility or anger.

(E) is wrong because the description is not tinged with regret or sorrow.

14. **A is correct.** All of the choices are definitions of the word *broken*, but only choice (A) makes sense in context. The day was cold and gray, when it came into being or dawned.

15. **B is correct.** Clearly, the facts that the man is traveling a little-used path, is unsure about the actual temperature, and does not notice that the dog seems almost hesitant to follow indicate that the man is not accustomed to such activity. In addition, the passage states that the man "was a newcomer," and "this was his first winter."

(A) is wrong because the passage states only that it is nine o'clock in the morning and makes no mention that the man is running late.

(C) is wrong because even though it is extremely cold out, there is no evidence, at this point, that the man is disoriented.

(D) is wrong because no mention is made of the man being ahead of schedule, only that "the boys were already" there.

(E) is wrong, because although the passage makes note of the sun's absence, there is nothing to indicate the man expected to see it.

16. **C is correct.** *Chechaquo* appears in the following sentence: "He was a newcomer in the land, a *chechaquo*, and this was his first winter." From the context it is clear that the

word refers to the fact that the man is a new-comer to the Yukon and, therefore, has little experience with the extreme cold of a Yukon winter. Actually, *chechaquo* is a Chinook word meaning "tenderfoot" or "newcomer to the Yukon."

(A) is wrong because there is nothing to suggest that *chechaquo* has anything to do with logging.

(B) is wrong because there is nothing to suggest that *chechaquo* means spirit of adventure.

(D) is wrong because there is nothing in the context of the sentence to suggest that *chechaquo* has anything to do with the ability to follow a trail.

(E) is wrong because the context of the sentence makes (C) the best choice.

17. **E is correct.** The man was startled because he was not expecting to hear his spit-tle crackle before it fell to the snow. The passage goes on to say that the man knew "that at fifty below spittle crackled on the snow, but this spittle had crackled in the air. Undoubtedly it was colder than fifty below."

(A) is wrong because the passage contains no information describing the man's fragile state of mind.

(B) is wrong because there is no mention that the setting has become "eerily quiet."

(C) is wrong, because although it is ex-tremely cold, there is no evidence that the temperature was dropping.

(D) is wrong because at this point in the pas-sage, it is difficult to know if the man is in danger or not. Indeed, he does not seem to believe himself to be in danger because the passage states that "the tem-perature did not matter."

18. **D is correct.** The author qualifies the man's judgment of the cold by explaining that the man was "a newcomer in the land, a *cheqaquo*," and "not because he was long used to it." These statements indicate that had the man been more familiar with the cli-

mate, he likely would have exercised greater caution in his journey.

(A) is wrong because the point that the man is on a "little-travelled trail" by itself does not indicate the man's poor judg-ment of the cold. Indeed, even when the man "flung a look back along the way he had come," all he saw was snow and ice indicating that even on the busier path he was the only one about that day.

(B) is wrong because at the point in the pas-sage that the author mentions the man as "being cold and uncomfortable, and that was all," the reader has yet to be given the details of the spittle crackling and the dog's depression. Both are de-tails that might have caused the man to alter his plans had he been aware of their significance, and not just their existence.

(C) is wrong because most people would not agree with the statement that a tempera-ture of seventy-five below zero was "sub-jectively" cold.

(E) is wrong because the statement that the man was "quick and alert in the things of life" would indicate that the man pos-sessed better judgment in regard to the cold than he appears to have.

19. **A is correct.** In lines 37–42, the author goes on to explain that knowing how cold it was "did not lead him to meditate upon his frailty as a creature of temperature, and upon man's frailty in general, able only to live within certain narrow limits of heat and cold; and from there on it did not lead him to the conjectural field of immortality and man's place in the universe." Thus, although he observed that the temperature was lower than fifty below zero, he did not think about the consequences of the cold.

(B) is wrong because significance has to do with importance or meaning, not accu-racy.

(C) is wrong because significance has noth-ing to do with carelessness.

(D) is wrong because significance has noth-ing to do with recklessness.

(E) is wrong because significance has nothing to do with ability to act.

20. C is correct. *Speculatively* is used in the following sentence: "As he turned to go on, he spat speculatively." Two lines later the passage says, "He knew that at fifty below spittle crackled on the snow, but this spittle had crackled in the air. Undoubtedly it was colder than fifty below. . . ." The implication is that he spat in the air as an experiment to see just how cold it was. Thus, *experimentally,* is closest in meaning to *speculatively* in this sentence. No other choice makes sense in the context of this sentence.

21. B is correct. The man knew that "at fifty below spittle crackled on the snow." Obviously he wanted to test the temperature of the air. When he found that his spittle "had crackled in the air," he realized that the temperature was even lower than fifty below, which indicates very severe cold.

(A) is wrong because spitting in the air has nothing to do with the strangeness of the landscape.

(C) is wrong because spitting in the air is not a courageous act. In fact, knowing how cold the day was made the notion of pressing on a foolish idea.

(D) is wrong because the man's spitting in the air had nothing to do with the dog's being frustrated. The dog was agitated because he saw no sign that the man would seek shelter or build a fire.

(E) is wrong because spitting in the air had nothing to do with making the day gloomy.

22. D is correct. The word *obtained* appears in the following sentence: "Since the freezing-point is thirty-two above zero, it meant that one hundred and seven degrees of frost obtained." Although each of the answer choices is a meaning of *obtained,* in this context, choice (D) fits best.

23. C is correct. The day is described as "exceedingly cold and gray." The man determines that "it was colder than fifty below," and yet he continues to travel on. Even the dog "was depressed by the tremendous cold.

It knew that it was no time for travelling." Under these circumstances, the best description of the man's actions is foolish.

(A) is wrong because *clever* means "intelligent" and the author describes the man as "without imagination."

(B) is wrong because a cautious man would not venture out in such severe weather.

(D) is wrong because although the man displays some ambition, the overall impression created by the author is one of foolish boldness.

(E) is wrong because the man is not portrayed as ruthless or cruel.

24. D is correct. As stated in lines 61–64, "The animal was depressed by the tremendous cold. It knew that it was no time for travelling. Its instinct told it a truer tale than was told to the man by the man's judgment." These statements clearly support choice (D).

(A) is wrong because the passage offers no support for the idea that the man is right to press on. In fact, it offers support for the idea of turning back or finding shelter.

(B) is wrong because the passage indicates that the dog was "depressed by the tremendous cold" and it experienced "a vague but menacing apprehension that subdued it and made it slink along at the man's heels."

(C) is wrong because there is nothing in the passage to suggest that the man is jealous of the dog.

(E) is wrong because the passage states that "there was no sun or hint of sun." There is nothing to suggest that the sun is likely to appear that day.

Section 2

1. B is correct. This type of logic-based question contrasts the first speaker to every speaker that followed her. Try thinking of a word for each blank before you look at the answer choices. This will give you an idea of the type of contrast you are looking for and help you eliminate some of the choices almost immediately. In this sentence both (A) and (D) can be discounted because they are not pairs of words that set up a contrast between the speeches given. A *detailed* speech is not likely to make other speeches *problematic* (uncertain), and a *thorough* speech is not likely to make others *reasonable* (sound or sensible). Similarly, (E) is wrong because a *generic* (general or universal) speech is not likely to make other speeches *superfluous* (unnecessary). (C) is incorrect as well because a *narrow* speech would not likely be followed by others that were *repetitive*. However, a *comprehensive* speech (one that is complete or all-inclusive) is likely to make all other speeches *redundant* (unnecessary or superfluous).

2. **A is correct.** This vocabulary-in-context question asks you to find two words that describe the river's path. One word has to mean "quiet," and the other has to mean "winding," because both of these words are included in the sentence as descriptions of the river's path. *Tranquil* means "free of commotion or disturbance," and *sinuous* means "characterized by many curves or turns." (A) is the correct answer.

3. **C is correct.** The phrase "despite overwhelming evidence" provides a clue that suggests the court has made an error in its refusal to reverse the decision. Knowing that an error has presumably been made, the question is to figure out how this affected justice. By making an error, would the court have quickened justice? In all likelihood, no, so you can eliminate *accelerated* (B), *hastened* (D), and *expedited* (E) as all of these are synonymous with "quickened." *Impelled* (A) is used most often to mean "urged to action through moral pressure," and this answer is incorrect as well. *Impeded* (C) means "obstructed the progress of," and this is the only possible correct answer.

4. **D is correct.** The key to this sentence is the phrase "Based on almost no research." Using this phrase, ask yourself: would a company's decision to expand based on almost no research be *judicious* (meaning "sound" or "wise")? How about *prudent*

(meaning "cautious" or "careful")? Because neither seems appropriate, you can eliminate (A) and (E). *Heedful* (B), meaning "paying close attention" or "mindful" and *circumspect* (C), meaning "aware of circumstances and potential consequences" are incorrect as well. *Arbitrary* (D), meaning "determined by chance, whim, or impulse," is the correct answer.

5. **A is correct.** The first thing you should notice about this question is that it has two parts or clauses. The first clause begins with "Although" and the second clause begins with "it brought the town together." The word *although* provides a clue that the two parts of the sentence will contrast with each other. Because the first clause concerns the effects of a tornado, which are likely to be negative, the second clause should concern something positive. Choices (D) and (E) can be eliminated because the effects of a tornado are not likely to be *innocuous* (harmless) or *benign* (kindly). Although choices (B) and (C) provide negative words for the first blank, they fail to provide a contrasting positive word for the second blank. The correct choice is (A). The effects were *ruinous* (disastrous) but they brought the town together through a sense of *camaraderie* (friendship).

6. **C is correct.** The clue that the game "would convey the message that our scientific endeavors have relevance for society" acknowledges Higinbotham's awareness of how the populace views scientific research.

(B) is wrong because while Higinbotham recognizes how the population views the impact of scientific research on daily life, he never categorizes the viewpoint as *indifferent*. There is no support in the passage for either (A) or (D).

(E) misconstrues the quote by equating *relevance* with *enhancement*.

7. **A is correct.** The passage is a brief history describing the invention of the first video game.

(B) is wrong because the passage makes no comparisons to current video games.

(C) is wrong because although the passage implies the work may be technical in nature, it never describes the work as tedious.

(D) is wrong because the passage makes no attempt to explain the type of research conducted at the laboratory.

(E) is wrong because the passage contains very little history on the life of Higinbotham.

8. **A is correct.** The passage contains numerous phrases to support this answer including, "imagine my surprise, nay, my consternation" and "rallying my stunned faculties."

(B) and (D) are outside the scope of this passage.

(C) may appear to be correct because of the narrator's thought that "my ears had deceived me," but the incredulous tone comes more from being denied assistance than from being misunderstood.

(E) is too extreme.

9. **B is correct.** The fact that the narrator is stunned and must sit a moment collecting his thoughts is enough information to indicate that the narrator cannot believe that Bartleby has refused him.

(A) and (C) are wrong because there is no indication that the narrator gathers his surprised staff (A) or that he is merely thinking aloud (C).

(D) and (E) are wrong because neither one makes sense within the context of the quotation.

10. **D is correct.** As stated in lines 17–21, ". . . there was something so gentle and modest in the expression of her dark countenance and her large mournful eyes that her heart was drawn toward her and she bought her in preference to several others who looked more robust."

(A) is wrong because the ragged clothes were not what drew Mrs. Wheatley to Phillis.

(B) is wrong because Phillis learned to speak English after coming to live with the Wheatleys.

(C) is wrong because Phillis's intelligence became obvious only after she came to live with the Wheatleys.

(E) is wrong because Phillis was not the only girl at the marketplace who was of African heritage.

11. **B is correct.** The previous sentence mentions that Phillis remembers seeing her mother pour out water before the rising sun. The next sentence mentions "the great luminous orb" that gives light and cheer to the world. Taken together, it is obvious that the great luminous orb refers to the sun.

(A) is wrong because nothing in the text supports the Earth as being the great luminous orb.

(C) is wrong because the passage states that the mother pours water before the rising sun, not that she is the sun.

(D) is wrong because nothing in the text supports Africa as being the great luminous orb.

(E) is wrong because Mrs. Wheatley came into Phillis's life after the time of this memory.

12. **C is correct.** As stated in the last paragraph, Phillis "possessed uncommon intelligence and a great desire for knowledge." She quickly learned to read and write, and by the age of fourteen she was writing poetry. "Owing to such uncommon manifestations of intelligence, she was never put to hard household work. She became the companion of Mrs. Wheatley and her daughter."

(A) is wrong because the fact that Phillis was an orphan is not what made her the companion of Mrs. Wheatley and her daughter.

(B) is wrong because Phillis became the companion of Mrs. Wheatley and her daughter after she had learned to speak English.

(D) is wrong because Mrs. Wheatley was moved to purchase Phillis because she looked so frail and sickly, but it was Phillis's intelligence that made her a good companion for the Wheatleys.

(E) is wrong because the fact that Phillis was religious is not what made her a good companion.

13. **D is correct.** *Amiable* is used in the following sentence: "At the same time she showed such an amiable, affectionate disposition that all members of the family became much attached to her." From the context, *amiable* is most likely to mean something positive. *Genial*, which means "pleasant" or "good natured," is the best synonym for *amiable*.

(A) is wrong because *amenable* means "responsive" or "obedient."

(B) is wrong because *ambivalent* means "conflicted."

(C) is wrong because *reproachable* means "shameful" or "disgraceful."

(E) is wrong because *impudent* means "disrespectful" or "insolent."

14. **D is correct.** The fact that Phillis was "never put to hard household work" implies that the other slaves were put to hard household work. The passage contains numerous descriptions of Phillis that seemed to have endeared her to the Wheatleys including her "amiable, affectionate disposition," "uncommon intelligence," and "ability to read fluently in any part of the Bible." However, the fact that she became "the companion of Mrs. Wheatley and her daughter" should make it clear that she was treated differently from the other slaves.

(A) and (B) are wrong because there is no evidence that the Wheatleys' feelings toward slavery were ambivalent or that they no longer believed in the institution of slavery.

(C) is wrong because the passage never states that the Wheatleys considered Phillis their daughter. In fact, the passage says only that she became their "companion."

(E) is wrong because the passage gives no indication that Phillis continued to experience the poor health she was in when the Wheatleys first purchased her.

15. **D is correct.** By saying that there was no law in Massachusetts against slaves learning to read and write, the author implies that there were such laws in other states.

(A) is wrong because Mrs. Wheatley "did everything to encourage her love of learning."

(B) is wrong because Mrs. Wheatley lived in Massachusetts, and Massachusetts had no law against teaching slaves to read and write.

(C) is wrong because there is nothing in the passage to support the idea that Phillis was sent to school in Massachusetts or any other state. The passage implies that Phillis was taught at home by Mrs. Wheatley's daughter.

(E) is wrong because the only law mentioned is the one against slaves learning to read and write. There is no reason to believe that Massachusetts had no laws at all.

16. **E is correct.** As stated in lines 72–75, "She always called her affectionately 'My Phillis' and seemed to be as proud of her attainments as if she had been her own daughter."

(A) is wrong because Phillis is not Mrs. Wheatley's daughter.

(B) is wrong because Mrs. Wheatley regarded Phillis as a companion, not a personal slave.

(C) is wrong because it has nothing to do with why Mrs. Wheatley used the term "My Phillis."

(D) is wrong because there is nothing to support the idea of there being other domestics named Phillis in the household.

17. **A is correct.** The introductory remarks indicate that Phillis Wheatley was included in Hallie Q. Brown's book *Homespun Heroines and Other Women of Distinction* because Wheatley was "a noted American poet."

(B) is wrong because although Phillis learned a great deal about geography and history in her reading, this knowledge is not the basis for her being included in Hallie Q. Brown's book.

(C) is wrong because Phillis's knowledge of Latin is not the basis for her being included as a "Woman of Distinction."

(D) is wrong because church work is not the basis of Phillis's inclusion in Brown's book.

(E) is wrong because Phillis's love of books is not the reason for her being a "Woman of Distinction."

18. **C is correct.** This account of Phillis Wheatley's life is both factual and inspirational as it tells the story of a young slave who overcomes great adversity to become a renowned American poet.

(A) is wrong because the tone is not angry.

(B) is wrong because the tone is neither disappointed nor critical.

(D) is wrong because the tone is not moralistic.

(E) is wrong because the tone is neither humorous nor ironic.

19. **D is correct.** As stated in lines 12–15, "pulsar 3C58 should have a temperature of about 1.5 million degrees Celsius. However, puzzled scientists have found the star's temperature to be far below that." The scientists are puzzled because the expected temperature of the pulsar should be much higher than the million degrees it now registers.

(A) is wrong because the pulsar is expected to cool down, just not so rapidly.

(B) and (C) are wrong because the scientists are not puzzled by the age of the pulsar.

(E) is wrong because the scientists expected the temperature to be 1.5 million degrees. They are puzzled because it is much cooler than that.

20. **C is correct.** The passage reports the discovery of a pulsar that is cooling down more rapidly than would normally be expected.

(A) is wrong because, although the passage mentions that scientists would have expected the temperature to cool down more slowly, it does not explain a scientific theory.

(B) is wrong because the description of the activity of neutrons and neutrinos is only one aspect of the passage, not its primary purpose.

(D) is wrong because the passage does not provide a practical application for the science of astronomy.

(E) is wrong because the passage merely mentions the role of nuclear forces and magnetism in the universe. It does not describe that role.

21. **A is correct.** The scientist says, "A million degrees may sound pretty hot, but for a young neutron star, that's like the frozen tundra in Green Bay, Wisc." He is making the point that a million degrees is actually cold for a young neutron star.

(B) is wrong because the scientist's words mean just the opposite.

(C) is wrong because the quote has nothing to do with the shockwave that blasts away the star's outer material.

(D) is wrong because Green Bay is used only as an example of an extremely cold place.

(E) is wrong because the passage indicates that neutron stars cool as they age.

22. **C is correct.** As stated in lines 26–29, "When the star implodes, electrons and protons in its core violently smash into one another, destroying themselves to form neutrons and tinier neutrinos."

(A) is wrong because neutrinos result from the destruction of neutrons and protons, not the combination of electrons and neutrons.

(B) is wrong because neutrinos are formed when the star is very hot. As neutrinos depart, they take heat energy with them, thus lowering the temperature of the star.

(D) is wrong because it takes violent collisions, not weak interactions, to destroy the electrons and protons and form neutrons and neutrinos.

(E) is wrong because the passage states that the collisions are between protons and electrons, not protons and neutrons.

23. **E is correct.** Scientists believe that neutron and pulsar stars are what are left after a regular star collapses in a supernova explosion. The explosion has nothing to do with the cooling of pulsar 3C58 or any other pulsar.

(A) is wrong because it is mentioned in line 36–40.

(B) is wrong because it is mentioned in lines 52–53.

(C) is wrong because it is mentioned in line 43–44.

(D) is wrong because it is mentioned in lines 45–46.

24. **B is correct.** The answer is found in lines 47–53: "Aside from the star's swift change in temperature, scientists also detected loops of magnetic energy surrounding the pulsar. Jets of high-energy particles can also be seen shooting out of the pulsar. Evidence from these and similar discoveries suggests that pulsars with defined magnetic fields are powerful generators of high-energy particles."

(A), (C), (D), and (E) are all true. However, none of these choices is mentioned in connection with the analysis of the loops of magnetic energy surrounding the pulsar or the particles seen shooting out of the pulsar.

Section 3

1. **C is correct.** The phrase "lacking any interesting qualities" is the key to solving this vocabulary-in-context question. When you encounter this type of question on the SAT, look for the answer choice that is defined or explained in the sentence. *Insipid* (C), meaning "lacking qualities, that excite, stimulate, or interest," is the correct answer. Occasionally, on the SAT, you will come across a question such as this one, which seems to have more than one correct answer. When you do, remember to choose the *best* answer. Although it may not be incorrect to refer to this movie as *hilarious, classic, optimistic,* or *uproarious* (meaning "loud and full" or "boisterous"), keep in mind that only *insipid* is actually defined by the sentence. Thus, (C) is the best answer.

2. **D is correct.** The key to this sentence is the phrase "the lawyer was asked if she would be interested in becoming a junior partner." Logically, you can conclude that if her law firm is extending such an offer, then the manner in which she handled the case was likely not (B) *callous* or (E) *inept* (meaning "inappropriate"). *Idiosyncratic* (A), meaning "peculiar to the individual," is not a strong choice because there is limited contextual evidence provided about the lawyer to justify its selection. *Adroit* (C), meaning "skillful and adept under pressing conditions," and *deft* (D), meaning "quick and skillful," both work well in the first blank, so you will likely base your decision on which of these choices contains the most appropriate second-blank option. Again, lacking the contextual evidence to support *humble, venerable* (meaning "commanding respect by virtue of age, dignity, character, or position") is the better option. Because of her *deft* handling of the case, she was asked to become a partner in the *venerable* law firm.

3. **A is correct.** The word "misled" is the key to this sentence, along with the negative connotations the word implies. Look at the answer choices and ask yourself: "which choices can I eliminate based on a lack of negative connotations?" You should be able to discount *industrious* (C) and *observant* (D) because both these answers suggest positive, rather than negative, attributes. *Anachronistic* (B) means "chronologically misplaced," and *disparate* (E) means "fundamentally distinct or different in kind." There is no contextual evidence to support using either of these choices, and both can be eliminated. *Beguiling* (A), meaning "misleading by means of pleasant or alluring methods," is the correct answer.

4. **B is correct.** The use of the word "although" is a clue that the sentence sets up a contrast. The company president possessed a good quality and a bad quality. In this sentence, virtually all of the first blank options work, so you will need to concentrate on the context of the second clause. It is not likely that financial analysts would find a company president's ethical conduct *refreshingly* or *innocuously* (meaning "harmlessly") lacking. So, both (A) and (C) can be eliminated. *Timorously* (D), meaning "in a timid way," and *provincially* (E), meaning "in a narrow or self-centered way" are also incorrect. The best choice is that the analyst praised the president for his business *acumen* (meaning "keen judgment" or "insight"), but found his ethical conduct *woefully* (meaning "sadly" or "pitifully") lacking, making (B) the correct answer.

5. **C is correct.** This vocabulary-in-context question requires you to find the word that best restates the description of the songwriter as someone who "has written and recorded over three hundred songs since 1968." Although there may not be anything technically incorrect about referring to Mitchell as *independent* (B), there is no contextual evidence to justify this answer as the best choice. The same can be said for *successful* (A), not glaringly incorrect, but unlikely to be the best choice. There is nothing in the sentence that should lead you to choose *pretentious* (D), meaning "ostentatious" or "demanding or claiming distinction or merit." *Inscrutable* (E) meaning "difficult to fathom or understand" also lacks contextual evidence. *Prolific* (C), meaning "producing abundant works or results," is the correct answer.

6. **A is correct.** The Underground Railroad was neither underground nor a railroad, but rather the name for a secret network of people and routes set up to help slaves escape to freedom. So choices (B) and (E) can be eliminated. *Clandestine, covert,* and *surreptitious* are all synonyms for *secret* and all can work in the first blank, so turn your attention to the second blank choices. The word "informal" offers a context clue that suggests you

should look for a word that comes close to it in meaning. Neither *organized* (C) nor *convenient* (D) seem to match as well as *impromptu*, which means "spontaneous" or "prompted by the occasion rather than being planned in advance." Choice (A), *clandestine . . . impromptu* is the correct answer.

7. **C is correct.** Both passages are concerned with suffrage, the right to vote.

(A) is wrong because only Passage 1 mentions banishing slavery.

(B) is wrong because the right to run for and hold office is secondary to the primary concern of both passages, the right to vote.

(D) is wrong because only Passage 2 mentions differences between democracy and aristocracy.

(E) is wrong because neither passage advocates civil disobedience.

8. **B is correct.** The introduction provides the information that Passage 1 was written by a former slave and Passage 2 by a woman. Thus both are members of a group that does not have the right to vote.

(A) is wrong because only the author of Passage 1 was a former slave.

(C) is wrong because only the author of Passage 2 has been arrested.

(D) is wrong because neither author mentions opposition to war.

(E) is wrong because both authors are members of large groups (blacks and women, respectively) and, therefore, are likely to attract many supporters to their cause.

9. **D is correct.** The author of Passage 1 bases his appeal for "the enfranchisement of the negro" on "the undisputed fact of his manhood." The author of Passage 2 bases her argument on the fact that a citizen is defined as "a person in the United States, entitled to vote and hold office. . . . Being persons, then, women are citizens," and thus have the right to vote.

(A) is wrong because neither author reflects the typical view of a Southerner or a Northerner.

(B) is wrong because Passage 1 is described as "an appeal to Congress," which is not a predominantly black audience. There is no mention of the audience to whom Passage 2 is addressed.

(C) is wrong because the author of Passage 2 would favor rights for blacks as well as women as evidenced by the last sentence of the passage: "Hence, every discrimination against women in the constitutions and laws of the several states is today null and void, precisely as is every one against Negroes."

(E) is wrong because the author of Passage 1 does not mention citizenship and the author of Passage 2 does not mention property ownership as requirements for voting.

10. **E is correct.** As stated in Passage 1, "If black men have no rights in the eyes of white men, of course the whites can have none in the eyes of the blacks. The result is a war of races, and the annihilation of all proper human relations." The author of Passage 2 voices a similar view when she says, ". . . this oligarchy of sex, which makes father, brothers, husband, sons, the oligarchs over the mother and sisters, the wife and daughters, of every household—which ordains all men sovereigns, all women subjects, carries dissension, discord, and rebellion into every home of the nation."

(A) is wrong because it is not a statement either author would be likely to support.

(B) is wrong because only the author of Passage 2 mentions the idea of an oligarchy. Some forms of oligarchy she might be willing to endure, but the oligarchy of sex she finds most hateful.

(C) is wrong because neither author makes the case for education or property ownership as a requirement for voting rights.

(D) is wrong because the author of Passage 2 would certainly not agree with this idea.

11. **B is correct.** As stated in lines 7–11, "His right to a participation in the production and operation of government is an inference from his nature, as direct and self-evident as is his right to acquire property or education."

(A) is wrong because the author never mentions the right to hold a job.

(C) is wrong because the author never mentions the right to have a family

(D) is wrong because the author never mentions the right to wage war.

(E) is wrong because the author never mentions the right to move from place to place.

12. **D is correct.** The author is calling for equal voting rights for blacks and whites. Because at the time only white men could vote, the author's appeal is for an extension of this right to black men as well. As stated in lines 18–21, ". . . by every fact and argument by which any man can sustain his right to vote, the negro can sustain his right equally. It is plain that, if the right belongs to any, it belongs to all."

(A) is wrong because *suffrage* means "voting," not "elections."

(B) is wrong because *suffrage* is not the same as suffering.

(C) is wrong because the author refers only to men in this passage.

(E) is wrong because the passage does not discuss citizenship requirements.

13. **C is correct.** The word *sustain* is used in the following sentence: "He is a man, and by every fact and argument by which any man can sustain his right to vote, the negro can sustain his right equally." In this context *support* is the best fit.

(A), (B), (D), and (E) are also meanings for the word *sustain;* however, in this sentence, *support* is the best choice.

14. **D is correct.** The author's speech is based on recognizing equality between black men and white men. He emphasizes this with the statement that "if the right belongs

to any, it belongs to all." Thus, the author is imploring Congress to understand that if white men intend to deny black men their rights, then in the eyes of black men, white men will have no rights, as well.

(A) is incorrect because no mention is made of black and white women having equal rights. In fact, the passage makes no mention of women at all.

(B) is incorrect because the author never mentions a "racial divide" or states that he believes that it will never be bridged. He does, however, imply that equality cannot be achieved by giving the right to vote to white men at the exclusion of black men.

(C) is incorrect because the author makes no mention of a separate black society.

(E) is incorrect because the author offers no evidence that the Civil War is imminent. He does state that the result of denying black men the same rights given to white men will be "a war of races, and the annihilation of all proper human relations." However, there is no specific mention of the Civil War.

15. **A is correct.** The author is appealing for voting rights for black men. As stated in lines 15–20, "The fundamental and unanswerable argument in favor of the enfranchisement of the negro is found in the undisputed fact of his manhood. He is a man, and by every fact and argument by which any man can sustain his right to vote, the negro can sustain his right equally."

(B) is wrong because the author mentions only "the negro," not all citizens.

(C) is wrong because although the author says that racial tension will result if black men do not have the same rights as white men, the main purpose of the passage is to appeal for black suffrage and for including blacks in the body politic.

(D) is wrong because although the author mentions that slavery has been banished, this is not the primary purpose of the passage.

(E) is wrong because although the author would be likely to favor respect for all men, in this passage he is arguing specifically for the right to vote.

16. **D is correct.** The author quotes the Preamble to the Constitution to give weight to her argument that women should have the right to vote. She argues that the Union was formed by *all* the people—men and women—to secure the blessings of liberty for all, and the only way to secure those blessings is by means of the ballot.

(A) is wrong because the Preamble is not intended to provide a historical overview.

(B) is wrong because the author does not imply that the Constitution is unfair, but rather that its provisions are unfairly applied.

(C) is wrong because the Preamble is not likely to elicit sympathy for a position.

(E) is wrong because the author is not attempting to demonstrate her intellect, but rather to give weight to her argument.

17. **C is correct.** As stated in lines 56–61, "To them this government is not a democracy. It is not a republic. It is an odious aristocracy; a hateful oligarchy of sex; the most hateful aristocracy ever established on the face of the globe; an oligarchy of wealth, where the rich govern the poor."

(A) is wrong because the author never mentions a monarchy.

(B) is wrong because the author says she might endure an oligarchy of the educated over the ignorant.

(D) is wrong because the author might also endure an oligarchy of race.

(E) is wrong because the author never mentions ethnicity.

18. **B is correct.** The whole point of the passage is to show that women should have the right to vote both because they are a part of "We, the people" and because as persons they meet the definition of a citizen.

(A) is wrong because the point of the passage is to lobby for voting rights for women.

(C) is wrong because the Preamble is not given in order to be explained but simply to support the author's argument about voting rights for women.

(D) is wrong because the definition of citizen is only one part of the passage, not its primary intent.

(E) is wrong because the passage does not provide a law that does not discriminate.

19. **E is correct.** The word *abridge* is used in the following sentence: "Being persons, then, women are citizens; and no state has a right to make any law, or to enforce any old law, that shall abridge their privileges or immunities." In this context, the best synonym for *abridge* is *curtail*.

(A), (B), (C), and (D) are all meanings for *abridge;* however, in this sentence, (E) is best.

CHAPTER 7

SAT CRITICAL READING PRACTICE EXAM II

ANSWER SHEET

Directions

- Remove this Answer Sheet from the book and use it to record your answers to this test.
- This test will require 1 hour and 10 minutes to complete. Take this test in one sitting.
- The times for each section are indicated at the start of the section. Sections 1 and 2 are each 25 minutes long, and Section 3 is 20 minutes long.
- Work on only one section at a time. If you finish a section before time has run out, check your work on that section only.

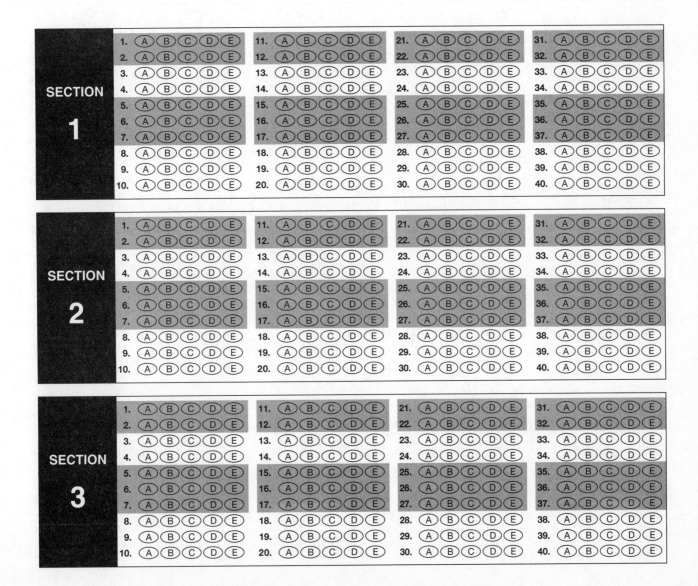

SECTION 1 QUESTIONS

Time—25 Minutes

24 Questions

Directions: This section consists of sentence completion questions and questions based on reading passages. For each question, select the answer you think is best and record your choice by filling in the corresponding oval on the answer sheet.

Directions: Each sentence below has one or two blanks. Each blank indicates that something is missing. Following each sentence are five words or sets of words labeled A, B, C, D, and E. You are to select the word or set of words that, when inserted in the sentence, best fits the meaning of the sentence as a whole.

EXAMPLE:

1. Despite our best efforts to protect the environment and keep it safe, until the problems of pollution are _____, the future of our environment seems, at best, _____.

   (A) created . . . gloomy
   (B) revoked . . . secure
   (C) solved . . . uncertain
   (D) replaced . . . revered
   (E) increased . . . unknown

   Correct Answer: C

---

1. Considering she'd only read a synopsis, Marian's critique of the book seemed _____.

   (A) sensible
   (B) benevolent
   (C) recalcitrant
   (D) justified
   (E) premature

2. Perhaps the best known constellation in the sky, Orion is occasionally visible throughout the northern hemisphere and _____ with the naked eye.

   (A) imperceptible
   (B) audible
   (C) discernible
   (D) diminished
   (E) subjugated

3. Often described as _____ and _____, the candidate was unwilling to compromise and prone to dividing the sides over an issue.

   (A) reticent . . . divisive
   (B) intransigent . . . factious
   (C) reserved . . . pugnacious
   (D) taciturn . . . quarrelsome
   (E) opinionated . . . conciliatory

4. After _____ denying all allegations of impropriety, the senator sheepishly _____ that his accusers were, in fact, right all along.

   (A) listlessly . . . agreed
   (B) vociferously . . . repudiated
   (C) vehemently . . . conceded
   (D) apathetically . . . acquiesced
   (E) ardently . . . disputed

5. Clearly trying to _____ the lawyer in front of the court, the judge _____ him for arriving at the trial unprepared.

   (A) compliment . . . ridiculed
   (B) belittle . . . lauded
   (C) commend . . . denigrated
   (D) disparage . . . derided
   (E) discredit . . . extolled

6. For _____ results with the product, the manufacturer advised customers to carefully read the manual or download the _____ tutorial from its Web site.

   (A) optimum . . . comprehensive
   (B) superior . . . abbreviated
   (C) unparalleled . . . selective
   (D) median . . . compendious
   (E) conventional . . . extensive

GO ON TO THE NEXT PAGE

7. By the time Abe sat down for dinner, the biscuits had vanished, the gravy had _____, and the roast had dried out.

(A) protruded
(B) debilitated
(C) disintegrated
(D) coagulated
(E) eviscerated

8. Once the scouts realized they had left their water behind, Julia and Marie, ever the _____, set out to look for the nearest stream.

(A) ingénues
(B) prodigies
(C) thespians
(D) prognosticators
(E) pragmatists

Directions: The passages below are followed by questions based on their content. Questions that follow a pair of related passages may also ask about the relationship between the paired passages. Answer each question on the basis of what is stated or implied in the passages and any introductory material provided.

Questions 9 and 10 are based on the following passage.

The celestial spectacle known as the northern lights occurs as the result of millions of light particles
Line being emitted from an energy collision between atmospheric gas molecules and huge quantities of
5 solar particles. The solar particles travel from the sun at over a million kilometers per hour and take 2 to 3 days to reach Earth's atmosphere. As they approach, they are trapped by Earth's magnetic field and directed to a donut-shaped oval located above
10 the North Pole. Although attempts to pinpoint when and where the phenomenon will appear are largely futile, 90% of the most stellar displays take place in the northern regions of Alaska, Russia, Greenland, and Canada during late fall and early
15 spring.

Questions 11 and 12 are based on the following passage.

To date, the most famous and successful American woman artist is Georgia O'Keeffe. Born in 1887 in
Line Wisconsin, O'Keeffe's mesmerizing, almost surreal paintings of Western landscapes, larger-than-life
5 flowers, and animal skulls are known worldwide. O'Keeffe attended the Chicago Institute of Art and later the Art Student League in New York City. Her first solo exhibition was in 1918, and by the mid-1920s her paintings were commanding prices of
10 $25,000. O'Keeffe eventually settled in New Mexico, surrounded by the desert and mountains that became the focal point of her best known works. "All the earth colors of the painter's pallet are out there in the many miles of badlands," she once
15 commented.

9. The primary purpose of this article is to

(A) elicit support for further research
(B) encourage people to view the northern lights
(C) validate a predominant theory of astronomy
(D) explain a natural phenomenon
(E) describe the spectral beauty of the northern lights

10. The author suggests that

(A) the northern lights are easier to view on the second day than the third
(B) aurora borealis is similar in scale and size to the northern lights
(C) much of how the northern lights occur is still unknown
(D) the northern lights are rarely seen
(E) predicting when and where the phenomenon will occur is an inexact science

11. The quote from Georgia O'Keeffe (lines 13–14) suggests that

(A) the desert is more colorful than she had once thought
(B) she made her paints with materials found in the desert
(C) her fondness for the desert endured despite its rough terrain
(D) her paintings reflected the bleak earth tones found in the desert
(E) a wide spectrum of color is represented in the desert

GO ON TO THE NEXT PAGE ➡

12. The first sentence of the passage (To date....
O'Keeffe) implies that

(A) most well-known women artists are not
American

(B) no other American woman artist has attained
the same fame and fortune

(C) there are other, more successful women artists
from other countries

(D) there are very few successful American
women artists

(E) many American women artists who are more
successful followed O'Keeffe

Questions 13–24 are based on the following passages.

The passages that follow present two perspectives on life
in the United States during the nineteenth century.

Passage 1.

I was asked not long ago to tell something about the
sports and pastimes that I engaged in during my
Line youth. Until that question was asked it had never
occurred to me that there was no period of my life
5   that was devoted to play. From the time that I can
remember anything, almost every day of my life
has been occupied in some kind of labour; though
I think I would now be a more useful man if I had
had time for sports. During the period that I spent
10   in slavery I was not large enough to be of much
service, still I was occupied most of the time in
cleaning the yards, carrying water to the men in the
fields, or going to the mill, to which I used to take
the corn, once a week, to be ground. The mill was
15   about three miles from the plantation. This work I
always dreaded. The heavy bag of corn would be
thrown across the back of the horse, and the corn
divided about evenly on each side; but in some
way, almost without exception, on these trips, the
20   corn would so shift as to become unbalanced and
would fall off the horse, and often I would fall with
it. As I was not strong enough to reload the corn
upon the horse, I would have to wait, sometimes for
many hours, till a chance passer-by came along
25   who would help me out of my trouble. The hours
while waiting for some one were usually spent in
crying. The time consumed in this way made me
late in reaching the mill, and by the time I got my
corn ground and reached home it would be far into
30   the night. The road was a lonely one, and often led
through dense forests. I was always frightened. The
woods were said to be full of soldiers who had deserted from the army, and I had been told that the
first thing a deserter did to a Negro boy when he
35   found him alone was to cut off his ears. Besides,
when I was late in getting home I knew I would always get a severe scolding or a flogging.

Passage 2.

The summers we spent in the country, now at one
place, now at another. We children, of course,
40   loved the country beyond anything. We disliked the
city. We were always wildly eager to get to the
country when spring came, and very sad when in
the late fall the family moved back to town. In the
country we of course had all kinds of pets—cats,
45   dogs, rabbits, a coon, and a sorrel Shetland pony
named General Grant. When my younger sister
first heard of the real General Grant, by the way,
she was much struck by the coincidence that some
one should have given him the same name as the
50   pony. (Thirty years later my own children had *their*
pony Grant.) In the country we children ran bare-
foot much of the time, and the seasons went by in a
round of uninterrupted and enthralling pleasures—
supervising the haying and harvesting, picking ap-
55   ples, hunting frogs successfully and woodchucks
unsuccessfully, gathering hickory-nuts and chest-
nuts for sale to patient parents, building wigwams in
the woods, and sometimes playing Indians in too re-
alistic manner by staining ourselves (and inciden-
60   tally our clothes) in liberal fashion with poke-cherry
juice. Thanksgiving was an appreciated festival, but
it in no way came up to Christmas. Christmas was
an occasion of literally delirious joy. In the evening
we hung up our stockings—or rather the biggest
65   stockings we could borrow from the grown-ups—
and before dawn we trooped in to open them while
sitting on father's and mother's bed; and the bigger
presents were arranged, those for each child on its
own table, in the drawing-room, the doors to which
70   were thrown open after breakfast. I never knew any
one else have what seemed to me such attractive
Christmases, and in the next generation I tried to reproduce them exactly for my own children.

13. In Passage 1, line 2, "engaged" means most nearly

(A) pledged
(B) occupied
(C) meshed
(D) participated
(E) reserved

GO ON TO THE NEXT PAGE →

14. The author's "trouble" in line 25 is

   (A) not being able to have the corn ground at the mill
   (B) having to travel alone in the dark
   (C) not knowing the way through the woods
   (D) facing a flogging for being late
   (E) not being able to reload the corn that had fallen off the horse

15. The author of Passage 1 was always frightened on his way home from the mill for all of the following reasons EXCEPT:

   (A) There were few people on the road at night.
   (B) The woods were full of soldiers.
   (C) He feared having his ears cut off.
   (D) He knew he would be flogged for being late.
   (E) He thought he might be kidnapped.

16. The author of Passage 1 would apparently agree that childhood recollections are

   (A) best served by focusing only on the positive
   (B) an important aspect in gaining adult perspective
   (C) a constant source of optimism
   (D) some of the happiest of his life
   (E) often not worth revisiting

17. The statement in Passage 1 that "the first thing a deserter did to a Negro boy when he found him alone was to cut off his ears" primarily serves to

   (A) illustrate one of the author's greatest childhood fears
   (B) provide a cautionary tale for a new generation of young people
   (C) sum up the author's overall view of growing up a slave
   (D) describe a specific situation the author encountered
   (E) provide a counterpoint to the good times he experienced

18. Passage 2 serves mainly to

   (A) recount the author's experience working on a farm in summer
   (B) provide a description of the author's summer home
   (C) describe the joys of being in the country
   (D) convey the author's love of family celebrations
   (E) explain the significance of the pony's name

19. In lines 46–51, the author includes the story of the pony's name primarily to

   (A) show his love for animals
   (B) poke good-hearted fun at his sister
   (C) point up the difficulty of raising a pony
   (D) show his love for his own children
   (E) emphasize the friendship between the Roosevelt and Grant families

20. All of the following can be explicitly answered by Passage 2 EXCEPT:

   (A) Where did the author and his siblings prefer to spend their childhood summers?
   (B) What types of pets did the author and his siblings have in the country?
   (C) How did the author and his siblings spend their time in the country?
   (D) Where did the author and his siblings stay while in the country?
   (E) How did the author feel about Thanksgiving?

21. The statement in Passage 2 that "I never knew any one else have what seemed to me such attractive Christmases, and in the next generation I tried to reproduce them exactly for my own children" (lines 70–74) primarily suggests that

   (A) the author wanted his children to follow his example
   (B) the author missed the Christmases from his childhood
   (C) the author went to great lengths trying to recreate his childhood Christmases
   (D) the author carried on certain traditions because he thought his children would enjoy them, too
   (E) the author wanted his children to know the value of carrying on traditions

22. The contrast between the descriptions provided by the two passages is essentially one between

   (A) fantasy and reality
   (B) acceptance and rejection
   (C) bleakness and richness
   (D) humility and pride
   (E) fame and fortune

GO ON TO THE NEXT PAGE ➡

23. In both passages the authors describe
    (A) slavery
    (B) childhood memories
    (C) holiday celebrations
    (D) a pet pony
    (E) haying and harvesting

24. Both passages are told from the point of view of
    (A) an adult looking back on his own life
    (B) a child describing his life
    (C) an adult describing another person's life
    (D) a child describing events that happened to someone else
    (E) an adult filled with nostalgia for the past

END OF SECTION

IF YOU FINISH BEFORE TIME IS UP, CHECK YOUR WORK ON THIS SECTION ONLY.

SECTION 2 QUESTIONS

Time—25 Minutes

24 Questions

> Directions: This section consists of sentence completion questions and questions based on reading passages. For each question, select the answer you think is best and record your choice by filling in the corresponding oval on the answer sheet.

> Directions: Each sentence below has one or two blanks. Each blank indicates that something is missing. Following each sentence are five words or sets of words labeled A, B, C, D, and E. You are to select the word or set of words that, when inserted in the sentence, best fits the meaning of the sentence as a whole.
>
> EXAMPLE:
>
> 1. Despite our best efforts to protect the environment and keep it safe, until the problems of pollution are _____, the future of our environment seems, at best, _____.
>
>   (A) created . . . gloomy
>   (B) revoked . . . secure
>   (C) solved . . . uncertain
>   (D) replaced . . . revered
>   (E) increased . . . unknown
>
>   Correct Answer: C

1. After staying up all night and working _____ to finish the project, Gerard finally _____ to sleep.

   (A) haltingly . . . deferred
   (B) interminably . . . succumbed
   (C) incessantly . . . dissented
   (D) perpetually . . . refuted
   (E) intermittently . . . surrendered

2. The decision to go whitewater rafting was ultimately _____; once on board, there would be no turning back.

   (A) misguided
   (B) didactic
   (C) ponderous
   (D) inculpable
   (E) irrevocable

3. For much of his career, Andy Warhol was considered a _____ artist for _____ other people's images in his own work, often without acknowledgment.

   (A) treacly . . . ignoring
   (B) conciliatory . . . allocating
   (C) questionable . . . bestowing
   (D) controversial . . . appropriating
   (E) contentious . . . mocking

4. The mayor's suggestion to raise property taxes in order to _____ a new stadium was met with _____ response from homeowners.

   (A) construct . . . an exuberant
   (B) eradicate . . . a desiccate
   (C) subsidize . . . an ambivalent
   (D) suppress . . . a disdainful
   (E) build . . . an encouraging

5. A regular at rummage sales, who was often seen carting away boxfuls of books, Ms. Tompkins could be said to have a _____ for accumulation.

   (A) propensity
   (B) repulsion
   (C) consortium
   (D) knack
   (E) perspective

GO ON TO THE NEXT PAGE

Directions: The passages below are followed by questions based on their content. Questions that follow a pair of related passages may also ask about the relationship between the paired passages. Answer each question on the basis of what is stated or implied in the passages and any introductory material provided.

Questions 6–9 are based on the following passages.

Passage 1.

Hybrid-electric vehicles (HEVs) are among the most fuel efficient vehicles available today. Combining the best features of the internal combustion engine with an electric motor, hybrids can signifi-
5 cantly improve fuel economy without sacrificing performance or driving range. In addition, hybrids are environmentally friendly, emitting less global warming and smog-forming emissions than most conventional vehicles.
10   HEVs are primarily propelled by an internal combustion engine, just like conventional vehicles. However, they also convert energy normally wasted during coasting and braking into electricity, which is stored in a battery until needed by the electric
15 motor. The electric motor is used to assist the engine when accelerating or hill climbing and in low-speed driving conditions where internal combustion engines are least efficient. Some HEVs also automatically shut off the engine when the vehicle comes to
20 a stop and restart it when the accelerator is pressed, thus preventing wasted energy from idling.

Passage 2.

Today there are substantial differences among energy sources that are used to create electricity. Conventional methods of electricity generation in
25 the United States use fossil or nuclear fuels—forms of power generation that can be harmful to human health and the environment. Newer technologies capture renewable energy sources such as wind, solar, geothermal, low impact (or small)
30 hydropower, biomass, and biogas, to create electricity. These renewable sources are continuously replenished by nature and significantly reduce the environmental impacts of electricity generation. Currently, less than 2% of the nation's energy sup-
35 ply is generated from non-hydro renewable resources. The majority of our nation's electricity is generated from fossil fuels.

6. The author of Passage 1 would most likely regard the development of wind and solar energy as
    (A) impractical as alternative sources of energy
    (B) less important than finding new sources of fossil fuel for energy production
    (C) inconsistent with sound energy policy
    (D) important steps toward more environmentally friendly ways to produce power
    (E) essential to increasing the fuel economy of hybrid cars

7. All of the following are true of renewable resources EXCEPT:
    (A) They reduce the environmental impacts of energy production.
    (B) They are constantly replenished naturally.
    (C) They are often harmful to human health.
    (D) They currently generate less than 2% of the nation's energy supply.
    (E) They can take the place of fossil or nuclear fuels.

8. As with the author of Passage 1, the author of Passage 2 does which of the following?
    (A) explains a study
    (B) quotes an authority
    (C) suggests a solution
    (D) takes sides in an argument
    (E) presents the pros and cons of an issue

9. Both passages seem to be discouraging
    (A) continued reliance on conventional energy sources
    (B) development of new energy sources
    (C) investing in new technologies
    (D) increased energy production
    (E) production of internal combustion engines

GO ON TO THE NEXT PAGE

Questions 10–16 are based on the following passage.

An allergic reaction involves two features of the human immune response. One is the production of immunoglobulin E (IgE), a type of protein called an antibody that circulates through the blood. The other is the mast cell, a specific cell that occurs in all body tissues but is especially common in areas of the body that are typical sites of allergic reactions, including the nose and throat, lungs, skin, and gastrointestinal tract.

The ability of a given individual to form IgE against something as benign as food is an inherited predisposition. Generally, such people come from families in which allergies are common—not necessarily food allergies but perhaps hay fever, asthma, or hives. Someone with two allergic parents is more likely to develop food allergies than someone with one allergic parent.

Before an allergic reaction can occur, a person who is predisposed to form IgE to foods first has to be exposed to the food. As this food is digested, it triggers certain cells to produce specific IgE in large amounts. The IgE is then released and attaches to the surface of mast cells. The next time the person eats that food, it interacts with specific IgE on the surface of the mast cells and triggers the cells to release chemicals such as histamine. Depending upon the tissue in which they are released, these chemicals will cause a person to have various symptoms of food allergy. If the mast cells release chemicals in the ears, nose, and throat, a person may feel an itching in the mouth and may have trouble breathing or swallowing. If the affected mast cells are in the gastrointestinal tract, the person may have abdominal pain or diarrhea. The chemicals released by skin mast cells, in contrast, can prompt hives.

Food allergens (the food fragments responsible for an allergic reaction) are proteins within the food that usually are not broken down by the heat of cooking or by stomach acids or enzymes that digest food. As a result, they survive to cross the gastrointestinal lining, enter the bloodstream, and go to target organs, causing allergic reactions throughout the body.

The complex process of digestion affects the timing and the location of a reaction. If people are allergic to a particular food, for example, they may first experience itching in the mouth as they start to eat the food. After the food is digested in the stomach, abdominal symptoms such as vomiting, diarrhea, or pain may start. When the food allergens enter and travel through the bloodstream, they can cause a drop in blood pressure. As the allergens reach the skin, they can induce hives or eczema, or when they reach the lungs, they may cause asthma.

All of this takes place within a few minutes to an hour.

In adults, the most common foods to cause allergic reactions include: shellfish such as shrimp, crayfish, lobster, and crab; peanuts, a legume that is one of the chief foods to cause severe anaphylaxis, a sudden drop in blood pressure that can be fatal if not treated quickly; tree nuts such as walnuts; fish; and eggs.

In children, the pattern is somewhat different. The most common food allergens that cause problems in children are eggs, milk, and peanuts. Adults usually do not lose their allergies, but children can sometimes outgrow them. Children are more likely to outgrow allergies to milk or soy than allergies to peanuts, fish, or shrimp.

The foods that adults or children react to are those foods they eat often. In Japan, for example, rice allergy is more frequent. In Scandinavia, codfish allergy is more common.

10. The passage focuses primarily on which aspect of allergies?

(A) which foods cause allergies
(B) how allergic reactions work
(C) the differences between allergic reactions in children and adults
(D) how immunoglobulin E is produced
(E) the definition of an allergen

11. Which of the following could best be substituted for "predisposition" in line 12 without changing the meaning of the sentence?

(A) antibody
(B) allergen
(C) prediction
(D) reaction
(E) susceptibility

12. All of the following are considered allergic reactions EXCEPT:

(A) itching in the mouth
(B) difficulty in swallowing
(C) abdominal pain
(D) presence of mast cells
(E) skin rashes

GO ON TO THE NEXT PAGE

13. According to the passage which of the following is most responsible for the ability of an individual to produce immunoglobin E against food?

    (A) heredity
    (B) body type
    (C) chemicals in food
    (D) food proteins
    (E) mast cells

14. The author suggests that histamine is

    (A) a substance that alleviates allergic reactions
    (B) a protein in food that is not affected by heat or stomach acids
    (C) a chemical released by mast cells as part of an allergic reaction
    (D) the food fragment that is responsible for an allergic reaction
    (E) the substance that triggers cells to produce IgE in large amounts

15. According to the passage, the biggest difference between children's allergies and adults' allergies is that children

    (A) are more likely to be allergic to shellfish and adults to dairy products
    (B) are likely to produce more immunoglobulin E than adults do
    (C) may outgrow allergies, but adults are not likely to lose their allergies
    (D) are more likely to react to foods they eat often than adults are
    (E) have more mast cells than adults do

16. Which sentence best supports the idea that people seldom react to a food the first time they encounter it?

    (A) An allergic reaction involves two features of the human immune response (lines 1–2).
    (B) The ability of a given individual to form IgE against something as benign as food is an inherited predisposition (lines 10–12).
    (C) Someone with two allergic parents is more likely to develop food allergies than someone with one allergic parent (lines 15–17).
    (D) Before an allergic reaction can occur, a person who is predisposed to form IgE to foods first has to be exposed to the food (lines 18–20).
    (E) The complex process of digestion affects the timing and the location of a reaction (lines 44–45).

Questions 17–24 are based on the following passage.

"The President shall from time to time give to Congress information of the State of the Union and recommend to their Consideration such measures as he shall judge necessary and expedient" (Article II, Sec. 3, U.S. Constitution).

On a cold January morning, the President rode in a carriage drawn by six horses from his residence on Cherry Street in New York to Federal Hall for a joint meeting of the two bodies of Congress, the House of Representatives and the Senate. When George Washington personally delivered the first annual message to Congress on January 8, 1790, he was aware of his constitutional duty to deliver his message and of the precedent he was setting for future presidents.

The President's focus, however, was on the very concept of union itself. Washington and his administration were concerned with the challenges of establishing a nation and maintaining a union. The experiment of American democracy was in its infancy. Aware of the need to prove the success of the "union of states," Washington included a significant detail in his speech. Instead of datelining his message with the name of the nation's capital, New York, Washington emphasized unity by writing "United States" on the speech's dateline.

Since Washington's first speech to Congress, U.S. Presidents have "from time to time" given Congress an assessment of the condition of the union. Presidents have used the opportunity to present their goals and agenda through broad ideas or specific details. The annual message or "State of the Union" message's length, frequency, and method of delivery have varied from President to President and era to era.

For example, Thomas Jefferson thought Washington's oral presentation was too kingly for the new republic. Likewise, Congress's practice of giving a courteous reply in person at the President's residence was too formal. Jefferson detailed his priorities in his first annual message in 1801 and sent copies of the written message to each house of Congress. The President's annual message, as it was then called, was not spoken by the President for the next 112 years. The message was often printed in full or as excerpts in newspapers for the American public to read.

The first President to revive Washington's spoken precedent was Woodrow Wilson in 1913. Although controversial at the time, Wilson delivered

GO ON TO THE NEXT PAGE

his first annual message in person to both houses of Congress and outlined his legislative priorities.

55 With the advent of radio and television, the President's annual message has become not only a conversation between the President and Congress but also an opportunity for the President to communicate with the American people at the same time. Calvin Coolidge's 1923 speech was the first annual message broadcast on radio. Franklin Roosevelt began

60 using the phrase "State of the Union" in 1935, which became the common name of the President's annual message. Roosevelt's successor, Harry Truman, also set a precedent in 1947 when his State of the Union speech became the first to be broadcast on television.

65 Most annual messages outline the President's legislative agenda and national priorities in general or specific terms. James Monroe in 1823 discussed the centerpiece of his foreign policy, now known as the Monroe Doctrine, which called on European

70 countries to end western colonization. Lincoln famously expressed his desire for slave emancipation in 1862, and Franklin Roosevelt spoke about the now-famous four freedoms during his State of the Union message in 1941.

75 Whatever the form, content, delivery method or broadcast medium, the President's annual address is a backdrop for national unity. The State of the Union gives the President an opportunity to reflect on the past while presenting his hopes for the future

80 to Congress, the American people and the world.

17. The author most likely included the quotation from the U.S. Constitution in lines 1–5 in order to

(A) suggest that the author is very knowledgeable about the Constitution
(B) illustrate the wording used in the Constitution
(C) explain the reason for the State of the Union address
(D) demonstrate how different Presidents have interpreted the same provision
(E) point out the difference between a constitutional duty and a custom

18. The phrase "from time to time" in line 1 has been interpreted to mean

(A) once in a while
(B) in a timely manner
(C) annually
(D) at a convenient time
(E) when time allows

19. U.S. Presidents deliver State of the Union messages primarily because they

(A) are following a tradition started by George Washington
(B) are required to do so by the U.S. Constitution
(C) need to fulfill campaign promises
(D) want to thank their supporters
(E) are trying to unify opposing factions

20. Thomas Jefferson's State of the Union address differed from Washington's address in that Jefferson

(A) spoke first to the Senate and then to the House of Representatives
(B) presented more frequent messages than did Washington
(C) broadcast his message on radio
(D) sent written copies of his message to each house of Congress
(E) required a formal reply at the President's residence

21. Washington drew attention to the idea of unity for the new nation by

(A) giving the speech in New York
(B) delivering his speech in person
(C) speaking at Federal Hall
(D) addressing a joint meeting of the two houses of Congress
(E) using *United States* instead of *New York* in the speech's dateline

22. In the first half of the twentieth century, the State of the Union address was forever changed by

(A) the advent of radio and television
(B) the Monroe Doctrine
(C) Woodrow Wilson
(D) Franklin Roosevelt's four freedoms speech
(E) newspaper coverage of the speech

GO ON TO THE NEXT PAGE

23. In line 76, "medium" most nearly means

   (A) middle state
   (B) means of communication
   (C) surrounding substance
   (D) oracle
   (E) proclamation

24. Which generalization about the State of the Union address is most strongly supported by the passage?

   (A) In general, State of the Union addresses are very similar from administration to administration.
   (B) Every President since Washington has delivered a State of the Union speech before a joint session of Congress.
   (C) State of the Union addresses are designed to increase the popularity of the President in the eyes of the world.
   (D) Although they vary greatly in style and content, all State of the Union addresses reflect the agenda of the man in office.
   (E) Each administration can decide whether or not to present a State of the Union address.

END OF SECTION

IF YOU FINISH BEFORE TIME IS UP, CHECK YOUR WORK ON THIS SECTION ONLY.

SECTION 3 QUESTIONS

Time—20 Minutes

19 Questions

Directions: This section consists of sentence completion questions and questions based on reading passages. For each question, select the answer you think is best and record your choice by filling in the corresponding oval on the answer sheet.

Directions: Each sentence below has one or two blanks. Each blank indicates that something is missing. Following each sentence are five words or sets of words labeled A, B, C, D, and E. You are to select the word or set of words that, when inserted in the sentence, best fits the meaning of the sentence as a whole.

EXAMPLE:

1. Despite our best efforts to protect the environment and keep it safe, until the problems of pollution are _____, the future of our environment seems, at best, _____.

   (A) created . . . gloomy
   (B) revoked . . . secure
   (C) solved . . . uncertain
   (D) replaced . . . revered
   (E) increased . . . unknown

   Correct Answer: C

---

1. When the owner provided a _____ certificate of authenticity, the art historian declared the painting a forgery.

   (A) legitimate
   (B) spurious
   (C) perfunctory
   (D) substantiated
   (E) incantational

2. Much of Langston's Hughes' poetry tries to _____ the rhythms of blues music, the music he _____ to be the true expression of his spirit.

   (A) emulate . . . believed
   (B) abjure . . . deemed
   (C) capture . . . doubted
   (D) forgo . . . considered
   (E) eschew . . . maintained

3. Although the rain was torrential, Sheila stayed dry in her new raincoat that was _____ to water.

   (A) susceptible
   (B) elliptical
   (C) impervious
   (D) salient
   (E) ostensible

4. The curator was _____ in her care of the museum, often working late into the night to keep the galleries in _____ condition.

   (A) fastidious . . . imprudent
   (B) meticulous . . . impeccable
   (C) negligent . . . pristine
   (D) unscrupulous . . . flawless
   (E) vituperative . . . immaculate

5. Wary of defeat, the rebel factions _____ into a single army to fight the approaching invaders.

   (A) coalesced
   (B) diffused
   (C) assuaged
   (D) importuned
   (E) supplicated

6. Initially standing by his _____ alibi, the main suspect in the embezzlement scandal later _____ it and agreed to cooperate with the prosecution.

   (A) improbable . . . abated
   (B) solid . . . voided
   (C) unshakable . . . retracted
   (D) tenuous . . . recanted
   (E) dubious . . . relented

GO ON TO THE NEXT PAGE

Directions: The passages below are followed by questions based on their content. Answer each question on the basis of what is stated or implied in the passages and any introductory material provided.

Questions 7–19 are based on the following passage.

In this excerpt from *Life on the Mississippi,* Mark Twain tells of his boyhood ambition to become a steamboatman

My father was a justice of the peace, and I supposed he possessed the power of life and death over all
Line men and could hang anybody that offended him. This was distinction enough for me as a general
5   thing; but the desire to be a steamboatman kept intruding, nevertheless. I first wanted to be a cabin-boy, so that I could come out with a white apron on and shake a tablecloth over the side, where all my old comrades could see me; later I thought I would
10 rather be the deckhand who stood on the end of the stage-plank with the coil of rope in his hand, because he was particularly conspicuous. But these were only day-dreams,—they were too heavenly to be contemplated as real possibilities. By and by one
15 of our boys went away. He was not heard of for a long time. At last he turned up as apprentice engineer or "striker" on a steamboat. This thing shook the bottom out of all my Sunday-school teachings. That boy had been notoriously worldly, and I just
20 the reverse; yet he was exalted to this eminence, and I left in obscurity and misery. There was nothing generous about this fellow in his greatness. He would always manage to have a rusty bolt to scrub while his boat tarried at our town, and he would sit
25 on the inside guard and scrub it, where we could all see him and envy him and loathe him. And whenever his boat was laid up he would come home and swell around the town in his blackest and greasiest clothes, so that nobody could help remembering
30 that he was a steamboatman; and he used all sorts of steamboat technicalities in his talk, as if he were so used to them that he forgot common people could not understand them. He would speak of the "labboard" side of a horse in an easy, natural way
35 that would make one wish he was dead. And he was always talking about "St. Looy" like an old citizen; he would refer casually to occasions when he "was coming down Fourth Street," or when he was "passing by the Planter's House," or when there was a
40 fire and he took a turn on the brakes of "the old Big Missouri;" and then he would go on and lie about how many towns the size of ours were burned down there that day. Two or three of the boys had long been persons of consideration among us because
45 they had been to St. Louis once and had a vague general knowledge of its wonders, but the

day of their glory was over now. They lapsed into a humble silence, and learned to disappear when the ruthless "cub"-engineer approached. This fellow
50 had money, too, and hair oil. Also an ignorant silver watch and a showy brass watch chain. He wore a leather belt and used no suspenders. If ever a youth was cordially admired and hated by his comrades, this one was. No girl could withstand his charms.
55 He "cut out" every boy in the village. When his boat blew up at last, it diffused a tranquil contentment among us such as we had not known for months. But when he came home the next week, alive, renowned, and appeared in church all battered up
60 and bandaged, a shining hero, stared at and wondered over by everybody, it seemed to us that the partiality of Providence for an undeserving reptile had reached a point where it was open to criticism.

7. In the first sentence, the author's impression of his father can best be described as

    (A) childishly naïve
    (B) unflinchingly melancholic
    (C) brusquely resigned
    (D) resolutely somber
    (E) uncompromisingly wistful

8. The author perceives his father as a man who

    (A) is fair and just
    (B) is strict but kindly
    (C) is not to be argued with
    (D) disapproves of his son's friends
    (E) expects his son to become a steamboatman

9. The information presented in lines 5–14 ("but the desire ... possibilities.") suggests that the author viewed working on a steamboat

    (A) as an unattainable vocation
    (B) with passing interest
    (C) as an escape from his father
    (D) with guarded enthusiasm
    (E) with a certain disdain

GO ON TO THE NEXT PAGE

10. The statement that "This thing shook the bottom out of all my Sunday-school teachings" (lines 17–18), primarily suggests that the author

    (A) felt guilty for wishing the "cub"-engineer ill will
    (B) knew it was wrong to be envious of the "cub"-engineer
    (C) felt it increasingly difficult to maintain good-will toward the "cub"-engineer
    (D) was incredulous that something good could happen to someone bad
    (E) was in disbelief over his jealousy of the "cub"-engineer

11. In line 19, the author uses the words "notoriously worldly" to suggest that the other boy is

    (A) extremely wealthy
    (B) reasonably generous
    (C) well known
    (D) highly respected
    (E) somewhat unprincipled

12. The statement that "There was nothing generous about this fellow in his greatness," (lines 21–22) suggests that the author

    (A) exaggerated many of the claims he made about the young steamboatman
    (B) disliked the young steamboatman because of his stinginess
    (C) was disappointed that he had failed to forge a stronger friendship with the young steamboatman
    (D) would have been willing to help the young steamboatman with his tasks
    (E) viewed the young steamboatman as ungrateful toward his good fortune

13. As used in line 28, "swell" most nearly means

    (A) show up
    (B) stretch out
    (C) meander
    (D) swagger
    (E) roam

14. The author's overall tone in this passage is best described as

    (A) serious
    (B) humorous
    (C) angry
    (D) enthusiastic
    (E) uncertain

15. The author and his friends regard the young steamboatman with both

    (A) fear and jealousy
    (B) anger and delight
    (C) pride and appreciation
    (D) respect and hostility
    (E) envy and apprehension

16. In creating an impression of the young steamboatman, the author makes use of

    (A) comparison to the other young boys in town
    (B) contrast to other steamboatmen
    (C) description of the young steamboatman's speech and dress
    (D) evocation of life aboard a steamboat
    (E) dialogue between the author and the steamboatman

17. The author's judgment of the young steamboatman is colored by

    (A) the young steamboatman's character flaws
    (B) the author's obvious jealousy
    (C) the young steamboatman's habit of wearing "the blackest and greasiest clothes"
    (D) the way the young steamboatman speaks
    (E) the author's fear of the young steamboatman

18. The last sentence ("But . . . criticism.") primarily indicates that the author

    (A) knew that the young steamboatman was only pretending to be hurt
    (B) believed that the young steamboatman did not deserve his good fortune
    (C) assumed that the young steamboatman had gone to St. Louis
    (D) was well aware that the young steamboatman had been generous to the other young boys
    (E) thought that the young steamboatman should be admired for his bravery

19. The passage as a whole suggests that as a child, what the author wanted most was

    (A) to be famous
    (B) to travel
    (C) to stand out
    (D) to have power
    (E) to not feel envy

END OF SECTION

IF YOU FINISH BEFORE TIME IS UP, CHECK YOUR WORK ON THIS SECTION ONLY.

ANSWER KEY

Section 1

1. E	7. D	13. D	19. B
2. C	8. E	14. E	20. D
3. B	9. D	15. E	21. D
4. C	10. E	16. B	22. C
5. D	11. E	17. A	23. B
6. A	12. B	18. C	24. A

Section 2

1. B	7. C	13. A	19. B
2. E	8. C	14. C	20. D
3. D	9. A	15. C	21. E
4. C	10. B	16. D	22. A
5. A	11. E	17. C	23. B
6. D	12. D	18. C	24. D

Section 3

1. B	6. D	11. E	16. C
2. A	7. A	12. D	17. B
3. C	8. C	13. D	18. B
4. B	9. A	14. B	19. C
5. A	10. D	15. D	

ANSWERS AND EXPLANATIONS

Section 1

1. **E is correct.** Following the logic of this sentence, you can see that there is little that would be considered *sensible* (A) or *justified* (D) about Marian's writing a critique before she has read the book. Whether or not the review was *benevolent* (meaning "kindly" or "good") is not really the issue, either. A case could perhaps be made for *recalcitrant* (meaning "stubbornly resistant" or "unruly"), although it is not the best answer choice of the five. Rather, it would be considered *premature* (meaning "too early" or "ahead of time") for Marian to have written a critique of a book before having read it in its entirety. Thus, (E) is the best answer.

2. **C is correct.** The key to this vocabulary-in-context question is the phrase "visible throughout the northern hemisphere." Since Orion is "visible" you can eliminate *imperceptible* (A), meaning "impossible or difficult to perceive by the mind or senses," and *audible* (B), meaning "able to be heard." In addition, *diminished* (D) is incorrect because it means "to make smaller or less." *Subjugate* (E), which means "bring under control or conquer," makes no sense in the context of a constellation. The correct answer is *discernible* (C), which means "perceptible" or "recognizable."

3. **B is correct.** In this sentence you are looking for two words that describe the candidate. Because both words are explained later in the sentence, the first word has to mean "unwilling to compromise," while the second word must mean "prone to dividing the sides." Focusing on the first blank, you will see that neither *reticent* (A) nor *reserved* (C) is applicable when describing someone "unwilling to compromise." *Taciturn* (D) means "silent" or "habitually untalkative" and can be discounted, as well. While both *intransigent* (B) and *opinionated* (E) work in the first blank, only one of the words is paired with a compatible match for the second blank. *Conciliatory* (E) means "able to overcome the distrust or animosity by pleas-

ant behavior," and clearly, this description does not fit the candidate. *Intransigent . . . factious* (B) is the correct answer.

4. **C is correct.** "After" is a key word in the first clause of the sentence, as it sets up the logic that after the senator did that, he then did this. (A) and (D) can be discounted because a senator is not likely to deny accusations of impropriety *listlessly* (meaning "with a disinclination to exert an effort") or *apathetically* (meaning "with a lack of interest or concern"). Now, focus on the second blank and the word "sheepishly." To do something sheepishly is to do it "embarrassedly, as if conscious of a fault." Both *repudiate* (meaning "to reject" or "refuse to have anything to do with") and *dispute* (meaning "to argue" or "quarrel") are strong verbs that do not go with the word sheepishly. *Vehemently . . . conceded* (C) is the correct answer.

5. **D is correct.** Many SAT sentence completion questions make use of two clauses that contrast with one another. These contrasting clauses are typically introduced with the words "despite," "although," "however," "rather," or "yet" or the phrases "on the contrary" or "even though." With no such phrases in this particular sentence, consider the idea that the two clauses might complement one another. That is, rather than looking for a pair of words among the answer choices that create a contrast, you want to look for a pair that complement one another. *Disparage . . . derided* (D) is the only answer choice that offers a pair of words that fit this criteria. To *disparage* (meaning "lower in esteem" or "belittle") the lawyer the judge *derided* (meaning "ridiculed") him for arriving unprepared.

6. **A is correct.** By focusing on the first blank, you can almost immediately discount (D) and (E), by logically inferring that a product manufacturer would likely want a consumer to achieve better than *median* or *conventional* results with its product. Turning your attention to the second blank, you'll find that one of the three remaining answer

choices clearly makes more sense than the other two. *Optimum . . . comprehensive* (A) is the correct answer.

7. **D is correct.** Answering this question correctly depends largely on knowing the definitions of the answer choices. You might try to predict an appropriate answer to the question based on the interpretation that the meal was seemingly meant to be eaten long before Abe sat down to it. Perhaps you came up with an answer along the lines of "thickened" or "solidified" to describe the gravy. Although neither of these words is available to you as answer options, you may find one that has connotations similar to them. *Protruded* (A), which means "pushed or thrust outward," and *debilitated* (B), which means "sapped of strength or energy" have nothing to do with *thickened,* so both can be discounted. *Disintegrated* (C), which means "broken up" or "decayed" and *eviscerated* (E), which means "to have taken away a vital or essential part" are not words generally associated with cold gravy. *Coagulated* (D), which means "transformed into a soft, semi-solid, or solid mass," is the correct answer.

8. **E is correct.** *Pragmatists* (E) are defined as "people who take a practical approach to problems and are concerned primarily with the success or failure of their actions." This is the correct answer as well as an apt description of Julia and Marie, who when faced with the problem of not having any water, set out to look for the nearest stream. *Ingénues* (A) are "innocent or naïve young women," and *prodigies* are people "with exceptional talents or powers." Neither of the choices is the best answer. *Thespians* (C) are actors, and had Julia and Marie been *prognosticators* (people who make predictions of the future on the basis of special knowledge), they could have foreseen a lack of water long before they needed to go in search of it.

9. **D is correct.** The passage explains how the northern lights reach Earth.

(A) and (B) are wrong because the passage neither *elicits support for* nor *encourages* any action.

(C) is wrong because the occurrence of the phenomenon is presented not as a theory but rather as fact.

(E) is wrong because there is not enough descriptive language to support this choice.

10. **E is correct.** As stated in the passage, "attempts to pinpoint when and where the phenomenon will appear are largely futile."

(A) is wrong because it is not supported by the passage.

(B) is patently false because aurora borealis and the northern lights are the same thing.

(C) is wrong because the passage explains how the northern lights occur.

(D) is wrong because the passage does not mention how often the lights are seen.

11. **E is correct.** The beginning of the quote, "All the earth colors," is used synonymously with *a wide spectrum of color.*

(A) is wrong because the passage contains no information describing how O'Keeffe *once thought* the desert looked.

(B) is wrong because there is no evidence provided that O'Keeffe made her paints with materials found in the desert.

(C) is wrong because her use of the term *badlands* is not a description of the terrain.

(D) is wrong because it is beyond the scope of the passage.

12. **B is correct.** The term "To date," is a time reference used to modify the description of O'Keeffe that distinguishes her as "the most famous and successful American woman artist."

(A) and (C) are wrong because there are no comparisons made between O'Keeffe and women artists from other countries.

(D) is too general, and (E) focuses on information that is not contained in the passage.

13. **D is correct.** Each of the answer choices is a meaning of the word *engaged*. However, only *participated* makes sense in place of the word *engaged* in this sentence: "I was asked not long ago to tell something about the sports and pastimes that I engaged in during my youth."

14. **E is correct.** The author's "trouble" was not being strong enough to get the corn back up on the horse once it had fallen off. Thus, he was forced to wait until someone older and stronger came along to help before he could continue on his way to the mill.

(A) is wrong because the author does eventually get the corn to the mill to be ground.

(B) is wrong because although the author mentions being afraid to travel at night, this is not the trouble referred to in line 25.

(C) is wrong because the passage does not mention the author's not knowing the way through the woods.

(D) is wrong because the mention of flogging comes later in the passage.

15. **E is correct.** There is no mention of kidnapping in the passage.

(A) is wrong because the passage states "the road was a lonely one," and this contributed to the author's fear.

(B) is wrong because the passage says "the woods were said to be full of soldiers who had deserted from the army," another reason for his fear.

(C) is wrong because the author had been told that "the first thing a deserter did to a Negro boy when he found him alone was to cut off his ears."

(D) is wrong because the author knew that when he was late he would "always get a severe scolding or a flogging."

16. **B is correct.** The author states that until he was asked about which sports and pastimes he participated in as a child, it never occurred to him "that there was no period of my life devoted to play." Thus,

through the memory, the author gained the perspective as an adult in the realization that he "would now be a more useful man if I had had time for sports."

(A) is wrong as the author seemingly has no problem focusing on childhood recollections that appear to be far from what most would consider positive. By mentioning fearful journeys alone in the wilderness at night there is little evidence that the author would agree with this choice.

(C) is wrong because there is no evidence in this passage that the author's childhood memories were a source of optimism. In fact, the reader would expect just the opposite to be true.

(D) is wrong because not a single memory from this melancholic passage would appear to be happy. Rather, the only mentions of emotion involve fear and distress.

(E) is wrong because as unpleasant as the memories in this passage are, the author, in his candor, seems to have no aversion to revisiting them.

17. **A is correct.** The author states that "I was always frightened. The woods were said to be full of soldiers who had deserted from the army, and I had been told that the first thing a deserter did to a Negro boy when he found him alone was to cut off his ears." Clearly, when the author traveled alone to the mill, one of his greatest fears was that he might come upon a deserter.

(B) is wrong because there is no evidence that the author of the passage is trying to pass along lessons from his childhood to a new generation of young people. Rather, he is simply relating some of the experiences of his youth.

(C) is wrong because the statement does not sum up the author's overall view of growing up a slave. Instead, the statement recounts one of the more harrowing memories the author has from his childhood.

(D) is wrong because the statement does not
describe a specific situation the author
encountered. Rather, the statement describes one of the author's greatest fears
he had as a child traveling alone back
and forth to the mill.

(E) is wrong because the author does not
provide any descriptions of good times
he experienced growing up a slave.

18. **C is correct.** Most of the passage is devoted to a description of the "enthralling
pleasures" of life in the country.

(A) is wrong because there is no description
of working on a farm.

(B) is wrong because the author does not describe a particular summer home.

(D) is wrong because Thanksgiving and
Christmas celebrations are only one
small part of the passage. Most of the
passage concerns the sheer joy of spending summers in the country.

(E) is wrong because telling the story of the
pony's name is only one small part of the
passage, not its main purpose.

19. **B is correct.** The tone of Passage 2 is
one of carefree joy and happiness. Making
fun of his sister for not knowing that General Grant was a real person is just one example of the light-heartedness of the entire
passage.

(A) is wrong because the story of the pony's
name does nothing to show a love of
animals.

(C) is wrong because the story of the pony's
name has nothing to do with raising
a pony.

(D) is wrong because the story does not
show anything about the author's love
for his children.

(E) is wrong because there is no mention of
any friendship between the Roosevelt
and Grant families.

20. **D is correct.** Although the author states
that "summers we spent in the country" and
we children "loved the country beyond any-

thing," he never specifically mentions
where the family stays while in the country.
The only reference to where they stayed is
the very vague "now at one place, now at
another."

(A) is wrong because the author states that
"We were always wildly eager to get to
the country when spring came, and very
sad when in the late fall the family
moved back to town."

(B) is wrong because the passage lists many
of the pets the author and his siblings
had in the country, including "cats,
dogs, rabbits, a coon, and a sorrel
Shetland pony named General Grant."

(C) is wrong because the passage states they
spent their time in the country "supervising haying and harvesting, picking ap-
ples, hunting frogs successfully and
woodchucks unsuccessfully. . . ."

(E) is wrong because the author states
that "Thanksgiving was an appreciated
festival, but it in no way came up to
Christmas."

21. **D is correct.** The statement primarily
suggests that the author recreated the
Christmases of his youth primarily because
he enjoyed them so much. When the author
states that he "never knew any one else
have what seemed to me such attractive
Christmases," he is implying that his childhood Christmases were so grand, he carried
on the tradition rather than seeking to improve it. Thus, because he enjoyed them so
much as a child, he thought his children
would, as well.

(A) is wrong because there is no mention
made that the author was setting an
example that he wanted his children to
follow.

(B) is wrong because the author never states
that he misses the Christmases of his
youth. Rather, he is reminiscing about
some of his favorite childhood memories.

(C) is wrong because the passage does not
state or imply that the author had to go
to "great lengths" to reproduce the

Christmases of his youth. From the information presented in the passage, the reader learns that children in his family opened stockings on their parents' bed and have their larger, individual gifts arranged for them on tables. A reader would be hard-pressed to defend these two traditions as going to great lengths.

(E) is wrong because there is no evidence that the author wanted his children to know the value of carrying on traditions.

22. **C is correct.** Passage 1 describes a young boy who does nothing but work and who is often alone and frightened. In contrast Passage 2 describes a youth whose life is full of "uninterrupted and enthralling pleasures."

(A) is wrong because neither passage is fantasy; both describe real-life situations.

(B) is wrong because neither passage evidences rejection of the situation.

(D) is wrong because neither passage depicts humility or pride.

(E) is wrong because neither passage is concerned with fame or fortune.

23. **B is correct.** Both passages are concerned with childhood memories. Passage 1 tells of the early life of a slave, and Passage 2 describes the early life of the son of a privileged family.

(A) is wrong because slavery is mentioned only in Passage 1.

(C) is wrong because holiday celebrations are mentioned only in Passage 2.

(D) is wrong because the pet pony is mentioned only in Passage 2. The horse in Passage 1 is neither a pet nor a pony.

(E) is wrong because haying and harvesting are mentioned only in Passage 2. The chores mentioned in Passage 1 are "cleaning the yards, carrying water to the men in the fields, or going to the mill."

24. **A is correct.** Both passages are told by adults looking back on their very different childhood experiences. In the first sentence,

the author of Passage 1 states that he was asked to tell "something about the sports and pastimes that I engaged in during my youth." The author of Passage 2 tells of wonderful summers spent in the country. He also mentions something that happens "thirty years later" when he has children of his own. These clues are enough to determine that both passages were written by adults.

(B) and (D) are wrong because both passages are written from the point of view of adults, not children.

(C) is wrong because each passage is written in the first person. The use of first person pronouns such as *I* and *me* generally indicates that a passage is autobiographical.

(E) is wrong because knowing that the author of Passage 1 was born a slave (see lines 9–11: "During the period that I spent in slavery I was not large enough to be of much service . . .") and that he has spent almost every day of his life "occupied in some kind of labour" makes it unlikely that he regards his childhood with nostalgia.

Section 2

1. **B is correct.** If the student is staying up all night, he likely has a significant amount of work to accomplish for the project. That means you can eliminate (A) and (E), because the first word in each choice denotes working sporadically. Now focus on the second blank. It makes no sense to *refute* (meaning "to prove to be false or erroneous") sleep or to *dissent* (meaning "to differ in opinion" or "to withhold approval") sleep. After a night of working *interminably* (meaning "endlessly") the student *succumbed* (meaning "gave in to") sleep.

2. **E is correct.** The key to this sentence is the phrase "there would be no turning back." In order to correctly answer this question, you need to find the word that can be most closely defined by this phrase. Although the decision to go whitewater rafting may have ultimately been *misguided* (A),

contextually there is no evidence to support this answer. *Didactic* (B), meaning "inclined to teach or moralize excessively," *ponderous* (C), meaning "labored and dull," and *inculpable* (D), meaning "free of guilt" or "blameless" also lack contextual certainty. Only *irrevocable* (E), meaning "impossible to retract," is correctly restated by the phrase "there would be no turning back."

3. **D is correct.** This question provides a good example of first focusing on the second blank. Because the sentence contains the words "without acknowledgment," you can logically infer that Warhol did something with "other people's images" without giving credit to those other people for their work. Ignoring, bestowing, and mocking have nothing to do with taking something without acknowledgment, so you can eliminate choices (A), (B), and (E). With two possible answers remaining, turn your attention to the first blank. An artist might be considered *controversial* (capable of stirring up debate) for *appropriating* (taking without permission) other people's work in his own, but an artist is not likely to be considered *conciliatory* (able to overcome distrust or animosity) for *allocating* (designating for a special purpose) other people's images without acknowledgment. Choice (D) is the correct answer.

4. **C is correct.** A clue to figuring out this sentence are the phrases "raising taxes" and "new stadium." Most homeowners (and the populace in general) are likely to be opposed to a tax hike so the second blank needs a word with a negative connotation. This eliminates choices (A) and (E). Now look at the phrase "new stadium." Ask yourself: does it make sense to *eradicate* (meaning "to wipe out") a new stadium? The most logical answer is that it does not. So, even though the second word in choice (B) *desiccate* (meaning "lacking spirit or animation") may work in the second blank, this answer can be discounted. Raising property taxes in order to *suppress* a new stadium (meaning "to crush it" or "put it down by force") is illogical, so (D) can also be eliminated. That leaves only (C), Raising taxes to *subsidize* (support) a

new stadium was met with an *ambivalent* (ambiguous or contradictory) response.

5. **A is correct.** Getting the correct answer to this question depends largely on knowing the definitions of the answer choices. *Repulsion* (B) means "an extreme aversion," and *consortium* (C) means "a cooperative arrangement among groups or institutions." Both are incorrect. To have a *knack* (D) is to have a "clever or expedient way of doing something," and a *perspective* (E) is a "mental view or outlook." Without knowing that *propensity* (A) means "an innate inclination" or "a tendency," you may be tempted to select *knack* (D). *Propensity* (A), however, is the best answer.

6. **D is correct.** The author of Passage 1 praises hybrid-electric vehicles for their fuel economy and because they are "environmentally friendly." Thus, it is likely this author will favor the use of renewable energy sources such as wind and solar energy as more environmentally friendly ways to produce power as well.

(A) is wrong because there is nothing to support the idea that wind and solar energy are impractical energy sources.

(B) is wrong because the author of Passage 1 is interested in saving fuel, not finding more of it.

(C) is wrong because there is nothing to support the idea that the development of wind and solar energy is in any way inconsistent with sound energy policy.

(E) is wrong because wind and solar energy are mentioned only in connection with electricity generation, not with increasing the fuel economy of hybrid cars.

7. **C is correct.** As stated in lines 24–27, it is the use of fossil or nuclear fuels for power generation that can be harmful to human health and the environment.

(A) and (B) are wrong because they are mentioned in lines 31–33: "These renewable sources are continuously replenished by nature and significantly reduce the environmental impacts of electricity generation."

(D) and (E) are wrong because they are mentioned in lines 34–37: "Currently, less than 2% of the nation's energy supply is generated from non-hydro renewable resources. The majority of our nation's electricity is generated from fossil fuels."

8. **C is correct.** Both authors suggest alternatives that can save energy and reduce environmental impacts. In the case of Passage 1, the author suggests the use of hybrid vehicles that "improve fuel economy" and are "environmentally friendly, emitting less global warming and smog-forming emissions than most conventional vehicles." In Passage 2, the author suggests the use of renewable energy sources in place of fossil or nuclear fuels to "significantly reduce the environmental impacts of electricity generation."

(A) is wrong because neither passage includes a study.

(B) is wrong because neither passage includes a quotation from an authority.

(D) is wrong because neither passage takes one side of an argument.

(E) is wrong because neither passage presents both sides of an issue.

9. **A is correct.** Both passages encourage actions that reduce the reliance on conventional energy sources. Passage 1 encourages the use of fuel-efficient hybrid cars, and Passage 2 encourages switching from fossil fuels to renewable energy resources to produce electricity.

(B) is wrong because both passages encourage the development of new energy sources.

(C) is wrong because both passages seem to favor investing in new technologies that are less harmful to human health and to the environment.

(D) is wrong because neither passage supports the idea of decreasing energy production.

(E) is wrong because internal combustion engines are discussed only in Passage 1.

10. **B is correct.** The entire passage is concerned with how allergic reactions work.

(A) is wrong because the foods that cause allergies are mentioned only in the final three paragraphs of the passage.

(C) is wrong because the differences between allergic reactions in children and adults is discussed only in paragraphs 6 and 7.

(D) is wrong because the production of immunoglobulin E is only one part of an allergic reaction.

(E) is wrong because the definition of an allergen is mentioned only in paragraph 4.

11. **E is correct.** *Predisposition* means "inclination," "tendency," or "susceptibility." Only choice E could be substituted for predisposition without changing the meaning of the sentence. "The ability of a given individual to form IgE against something as benign as food is an inherited predisposition."

(A) is wrong because an antibody is a protein produced in the body to neutralize an antigen.

(B) is wrong because an allergen is a substance that induces an allergic reaction.

(C) is wrong because a prediction is a foretelling of a future event.

(D) is wrong because a reaction is a response to a stimulus.

12. **D is correct.** Mast cells are cells found in connective tissue throughout the body that release substances such as histamine in response to injury or inflammation of bodily tissues. Although they are involved in an allergic reaction, their presence is not an allergic reaction.

(A), (B), (C), and (E) are all specifically mentioned as allergic reactions.

13. **A is correct.** As stated in lines 10–15, "The ability of a given individual to form IgE against something as benign as food is an inherited predisposition. Generally, such people come from families in which allergies are common—not necessarily food allergies but perhaps hay fever, asthma, or hives."

(B) and (C) are wrong because there is nothing in the passage to support either choice.

(D) is wrong because food proteins may cause an allergic reaction, but they are not the determining factor in an individual's ability to produce IgE.

(E) is wrong because mast cells are the cells to which IgE attaches, but they do not determine an individual's ability to produce IgE.

14. **C is correct.** As stated in lines 24–26, during an allergic reaction. the food "interacts with specific IgE on the surface of the mast cells and triggers the cells to release chemicals such as histamine."

(A) is wrong because a substance that alleviates an allergic reaction is an antihistamine.

(B) is wrong because the proteins within the food that are not broken down by heat or stomach acids are food allergens, not histamines.

(D) is wrong because histamine is not a food fragment. The food fragment that is responsible for an allergic reaction is an allergen.

(E) is wrong because food allergens are the substances that trigger cells to produce IgE in large amounts.

15. **C is correct.** As stated in lines 66–68, "Adults usually do not lose their allergies, but children can sometimes outgrow them."

(A) is wrong because shellfish is listed as one of the most common foods to cause allergic reactions in adults. Eggs, milk, and peanuts are listed as the most common food allergens for children.

(B) is wrong because there is nothing in the passage to support this statement.

(D) is wrong because the passage states only that "the foods that adults or children react to are those foods they eat often." There is nothing to indicate that children are more or less likely than adults to react to such foods.

(E) is wrong because there is nothing in the passage to support this statement.

16. **D is correct.** IgE is produced in response to a food allergen. This IgE attaches to the surface of mast cells. The next time the person eats that food, the food interacts with the specific IgE on the mast cells and triggers the cells to release chemicals that cause any of the various symptoms of food allergy. Therefore, a person must have been exposed to the allergen at least once before in order for an allergic reaction to take place.

17. **C is correct.** The quotation shows that the President has a duty to report to Congress on the State of the Union and to recommend necessary and expedient measures. This annual message to Congress came to be known as the State of the Union.

(A) is wrong because the use of the quotation does not necessarily indicate that the author is knowledgeable about the Constitution, but only about this particular provision.

(B) is wrong because although the quotation does illustrate the actual wording of this section of the Constitution, it is not intended to illustrate the wording of the entire Constitution.

(D) is wrong because there is no demonstration of different interpretations of this provision. The differences cited are in the form, content and delivery method of the message, not in the need to report to Congress.

(E) is wrong because the passage does not distinguish between constitutional duty and custom. The report on the State of the Union is mandated by the Constitution.

18. **C is correct.** The Constitution required the President to give Congress information on the state of the union "from time to time." Throughout the passage (for example, lines 27, 36, and 38), the State of the Union message is referred to as the President's "annual message." Clearly, the phrase "time to time" has come to mean "annually."

19. **B is correct.** This information is found in the opening quote from the U.S. Constitution, which says that Presidents have a constitutional duty to "give to Congress information of the State of the Union."

(A) is wrong because the passage states that George Washington delivered his message because "he was aware of his constitutional duty" to do so.

(C) and (D) are wrong because the State of the Union address is not primarily a means of fulfilling campaign promises or thanking supporters.

(E) is wrong because although attempting to unify opposing factions may be a goal of the message, the primary reason for giving the message at all is the fact that it is required by the Constitution.

20. **D is correct.** Thomas Jefferson thought Washington's oral presentation was "too kingly for the new republic." so Jefferson "detailed his priorities in his first annual message in 1801 and sent copies of the written message to each house of Congress."

(A) is wrong because there is no mention of Jefferson's speaking first to the Senate and then to the House.

(B) is wrong because the passage refers to the State of the Union as an "annual message."

(C) is wrong because it was not until Calvin Coolidge's speech in 1923 that a State of the Union speech was broadcast on radio.

(E) is wrong because Jefferson thought Washington's speech "too kingly" and the subsequent personal reply "too formal" for the new republic.

21. **E is correct.** As stated in the third paragraph, Washington was aware of the need to show the unity of the states. To accomplish this he included a significant detail in his speech. "Instead of datelining his message with the name of the nation's capital, New York, Washington emphasized unity by writing 'United States' on the speech's dateline."

(A), (B), (C) and (D) are all true; however, only (E) emphasizes the idea of unity.

22. **A is correct.** "With the advent of radio and television, the President's annual message has become not only a conversation between the President and Congress but also an opportunity for the President to communicate with the American people at the same time."

(B) is wrong because the Monroe Doctrine was discussed in James Monroe's address in 1823.

(C) is wrong because Wilson is mentioned only as the first modern President to revert to the spoken message originally used by Washington.

(D) is wrong because Roosevelt's four freedoms speech, delivered in 1941, was part of his plea for increased preparedness to protect the United States from any attempt to take away the freedoms to which he believed everyone is entitled.

(E) is wrong because newspapers printed all or part of the President's annual message before the start of the twentieth century.

23. **B is correct.** The word *medium* is used in the following sentence: "Whatever the form, content, delivery method or broadcast medium, the President's annual address is a backdrop for national unity." In this context, "means of communication" is best.

24. **D is correct.** As stated in the passage, "The annual message or 'State of the Union' message's length, frequency, and method of delivery have varied from President to President and era to era." And latter, "Most annual messages outline the President's legislative agenda and national priorities in general or specific terms." Both statements support the generalization stated in choice D.

(A) is wrong because the passage states that the address varies from President to President and from era to era.

(B) is wrong because after Jefferson, the annual message "was not spoken by the President for the next 112 years."

(C) is wrong because the primary purpose of the State of the Union address is to "outline the President's legislative agenda and national priorities." It gives the President "an opportunity to reflect on the past while presenting his hopes for the future to Congress, the American people and the world." Enhancing his own popularity is secondary to promoting his agenda.

(E) is wrong because the Constitution requires that the President report on the State of the Union "from time to time."

Section 3

1. **B is correct.** Neither a *legitimate* (meaning "lawful") nor a *substantiated* (meaning "confirmed") certificate of authenticity would lead an art historian to declare a painting a forgery; rather, either of these certificates would lead the art historian to declare the painting to be authentic. Thus (A) and (D) can be eliminated. *Perfunctory* (C), meaning "done routinely and with little interest or care," and *incantational* (E), meaning "ritualistically recited (as in a charm or a spell)" are also incorrect. *Spurious* (B), meaning "lacking authenticity or validity in essence or origin," is the correct answer.

2. **A is correct.** Getting the correct answer to this question is largely dependent on being familiar with the definitions of the words you have to choose from. Looking only at the first blank, you can eliminate (B) because *abjure* means "to renounce under oath." You can also eliminate both (D) and (E) as they convey similar meanings, with *forgo* meaning "to abstain from," and *eschew* meaning "to avoid or shun." Choice (A) and (C) both work well in the first blank, with *emulate* meaning "imitate" and *capture* meaning "catch" or "represent." However, it makes no sense for Hughes to represent music he *doubted* to be the true expression of his spirit. It is far more reasonable to ex-

pect him to try to capture music he *believed* to be the true expression of his spirit. Thus, (A) is the best answer.

3. **C is correct.** This question asks you to find a word to describe a raincoat that has kept Sheila "dry" during "torrential" rains. A raincoat that was *susceptible* (A) to water would not be the best choice to keep her dry because *susceptible* means "easily influenced or affected by." Neither *elliptical* (B), meaning "of, relating to, or having the shape of an ellipses" nor *salient* (D), meaning "conspicuous" or "prominent" makes sense in the context of the sentence. *Ostensible* (E), meaning "represented or appearing as such" is incorrect as well. *Impervious* (C), meaning "incapable of being penetrated" is the correct answer.

4. **B is correct.** The key to this sentence is the phrase "often working late into the night." Now, while focusing on the first-blank choices, ask yourself: would a curator who was either *negligent* (C) or *unscrupulous* (D) be the best choice for someone for someone who could be found "often working late into the night"? A *vituperative* curator would be harshly critical, which does not make sense in relation to *care*. Because none of these answers seems to fit the description of the curator, you can eliminate all three choices from contention. This curator is most likely to be *fastidious* (A) meaning "displaying careful attention to detail," or she may be *meticulous* (B) meaning "extremely careful and precise." *Fastidious*, however, is paired with *imprudent* (meaning "unwise or indiscreet") and is incorrect. (B) *meticulous . . . impeccable* (meaning "having no flaws" or "perfect") is the correct answer.

5. **A is correct.** This question asks you to choose the word that suitably describes several "rebel factions" becoming "a single army." *Coalesce* (A), meaning "to come together to form one whole" or "unite" is the correct answer. *Diffused* (B), meaning "spread out" or "dispersed," is incorrect, as is *assuaged* (C), meaning "made less intense or severe." *Importuned* (D) means "entreated" or "begged," and makes no sense in the context of the sentence. *Supplicated* (E), meaning

"asked for humbly or earnestly, as by praying," is incorrect as well.

6. **D is correct.** The words "initially" and "later" are important clues that some aspect of the situation presented will likely change from the first clause to the second clause. Beginning with the first blank, you can logically infer that if the suspect's alibi was *solid* (B) or *unshakable* (C), then he would not agree to cooperate with the prosecution. *Improbable* (A), *tenuous* (D), and *dubious* (E) all work well in the first blank, so you will need to turn your attention to the second blank to see which of these remaining three choices you are able to eliminate. Saying that the suspect *relented* his alibi makes little sense because *relented* means that he "became more lenient, compassionate or forgiving." *Abated* means "reduced in amount, degree, or intensity" and is also incorrect. *Tenuous . . . recanted* (D) is the correct answer: At first he stood by his *tenuous* (meaning "flimsy") alibi, but later he *recanted* (meaning retracted) it and agreed to cooperate with the prosecution.

7. **A is correct.** When speaking of his father, the author states that "he was a justice of the peace, and I supposed he possessed the power of life and death over all men and could hang anybody that offended him." Clearly, as a boy, the author displayed a naïveté that many children have with regard to their parents as he marveled at the powers of life and death his father seemed to wield over "all men."

(B) is wrong because there is no sense of sadness or depression in the author's description of his father.

(C) is wrong because *resigned* means "having accepted as inevitable," and this is not appropriate in the context of the author's statement.

(D) is wrong because the author's description is not *somber* (meaning "dark" or "gloomy").

(E) is wrong because the author does not look back at his father in a *wistful* manner (meaning "full of wishful yearning").

8. **C is correct.** Because he believed that his father "possessed the power of life and death over all men and could hang anybody that offended him," it is reasonable to assume that the author would not be likely to argue with his father.

(A), (B), (D), and (E) are all wrong because the author's father is mentioned only in the first sentence and, therefore, all that is known about the man is that he could hang anybody that offended him. There is nothing in the passage to support any of the other answer choices.

9. **A is correct.** The author states that his daydreams of working on a steamboat were "too heavenly to be contemplated as real possibilities": meaning that the thought of ever actually working on a steamboat was too good to be true. Thus, working on a steamboat was an unattainable vocation.

(B) is wrong because the author spends the entire article envying the young man from his town who does find work on a steamboat. From the information presented, there is no way of knowing whether the author had a lifelong interest in steamboat work, but it is most certainly the focus of the article.

(C) is wrong because there is no evidence that the author was trying to escape life with his father. Indeed, there is no evidence suggesting there was anything amiss in the author's relationship with his father.

(D) is wrong because the author seems to have no reservations in his enthusiasm for steamboat work. While his enthusiasm may be interpreted as naïve, it is never in doubt.

(E) is wrong because the author clearly has the highest regard for men who work on a steamboat. In fact, the young man he knows who works on the steamboat is "exalted," while the author languishes in "obscurity and misery."

10. **D is correct.** The author goes on to state that the boy "had been notoriously worldly, and I just the reverse; yet he was

exalted to this eminence, and I left in obscurity and misery." To the author, the boy had been honored and given a position of great distinction despite what the author felt were the boy's less than sacred ways.

(A) is wrong as there is no evidence that the author ever felt guilty at any time throughout the passage. In fact, even when he thought the "cub"-engineer may have perished in a steamboat explosion, he experiences a "tranquil contentment."

(B) is wrong because no mention is made in the passage that the author knew it was wrong to feel envy. In addition, the author never specifically admits to feeling envy, rather he seems comfortable in his description of the boy as "cordially admired and hated."

(C) is wrong because the article never states that the author was at odds maintaining goodwill toward the "cub"-engineer. In fact, although the author implies that he despises the boy, he also makes numerous references to the subjects the boy spoke of, as well as how he spoke of them, leading the reader to believe he spent a fair amount of time listening intently to any story the boy might be willing to share.

(E) is wrong because the author never acknowledges his feelings of jealousy toward the "cub"-engineer. Instead, the author cloaks his jealousy of the boy in unfavorable descriptions such as "ruthless" and disparaging references, including his being an "undeserving reptile." As well, the only disbelief the author exhibits is the disbelief that such a "notoriously worldly" boy could obtain such an "exalted" position.

11. **E is correct.** As stated in lines 17–18, "This thing shook the bottom out of all my Sunday school teachings." The author is distressed to discover that a boy who was widely known to be lacking in spirituality or principles should be rewarded with the very job the author himself, a regular at Sunday school, so longs for.

(A) is wrong because *worldly* has nothing to do with *wealth*.

(B) is wrong because *worldly* has nothing to do with *generosity*.

(C) is wrong because *worldly* has nothing to do with *fame*.

(D) is wrong because *worldly* does not mean *respected*.

12. **D is correct.** The author makes a point of stating that when the boat made temporary stopovers in the author's town, the young steamboatman sat on the inside guard to scrub bolts "where we could all see him and envy him and loathe him," but, presumably, not where they could join him.

(A) is wrong because the passage contains no evidence that the author exaggerated any of the claims he made about the young steamboatman. In fact, it would seem that the author was more likely to downplay the young steamboatman's accomplishments rather than exaggerate them.

(B) is wrong because although the author mentions that "this fellow had money," he does not indicate that he finds the young steamboatman stingy.

(C) is wrong because the passage gives no indication that the author was trying to become friends with the young steamboatman.

(E) is wrong because the passage does not include any information that states that the author viewed the young steamboatman as ungrateful toward his good fortune.

13. **D is correct.** Swell is used in the following sentence: "And whenever his boat was laid up he would come home and swell around the town in his blackest and greasiest clothes, so that nobody could help remembering that he was a steamboatman." The implication is that he wanted everyone to notice him and be aware of his status as a steamboatman. The verb that best conveys this meaning is swagger, which means to strut or walk with a bold or arrogant stride.

(A) is wrong because *show up* does not convey a sense of arrogance.

(B) is wrong because the sentence indicates *moving about,* not *stretching out.*

(C) is wrong because *meander* means to wander aimlessly, not to make people take notice.

(E) is wrong because *roam,* like *meander,* conveys a sense of aimlessness.

14. **B is correct.** Tone is the expression of an author's attitude to the subject. It is created through the author's choice of details and language. In this passage, Twain uses exaggeration or overstatement to create a humorous tone as shown in these examples: the idea that his father could "hang anybody that offended him," that the notoriously worldly young man was "exalted to this eminence" while the much more worthy author was "left in obscurity and misery," that the young steamboatman used all sorts of steamboat technicalities in his talk "as if he were so used to them that he forgot common people could not understand them."

(A) is wrong because the tone is not serious.

(C) is wrong because the author is not really angry. His choice of words indicates that he is actually poking fun at himself and his boyhood friends.

(D) is wrong because the word choice does not indicate enthusiasm.

(E) is wrong because the passage does not show uncertainty on the part of the author.

15. **D is correct.** As stated in lines 52–54, "If ever a youth was cordially admired and hated by his comrades, this one was." Respect and hostility offer the best synonyms for cordial admiration and hatred.

(A) is wrong because the author and his friends did not fear the steamboatman.

(B) is wrong because the author and his friends were not delighted by the actions of the steamboatman.

(C) is wrong because the author and his friends do not show pride in the accomplishments of the steamboatman.

(E) is wrong because the author and his friends do not show apprehension toward the steamboatman.

16. **C is correct.** The author creates an impression of the young steamboatman primarily by describing how he speaks and dresses. Of his speech the author says: ". . . he used all sorts of steamboat technicalities in his talk, as if he were so used to them that he forgot common people could not understand them. He would speak of the 'labboard' side of a horse in an easy, natural way that would make one wish he was dead. And he was always talking about 'St. Looy' like an old citizen." Of his dress the author says: "And whenever his boat was laid up he would come home and swell around the town in his blackest and greasiest clothes, so that nobody could help remembering that he was a steamboatman."

(A) is wrong because there is no comparison drawn between the young steamboatman and the other boys.

(B) is wrong because the author shows no contrast to other steamboatmen.

(D) is wrong because the author does not picture daily life aboard a steamboat.

(E) is wrong because there is no dialogue between the author and the steamboatman.

17. **B is correct.** It is difficult for the reader seriously to assess the author's judgment of the young steamboatman because the author is so blatantly envious of the steamboatman's good fortune. The young man works on a steamboat, which the author describes as a job that is "too heavenly to be contemplated" as a real possibility. As well, the author seems annoyed at the easy manner in which the young man speaks, although he repeats many of the young man's phrases, such as "St. Looy," "labboard," and "cub"-engineer.

(A), (C), and (D) are wrong because pointing out the steamboatman's character flaws, his habit of wearing greasy clothes and the way he speaks are all things the author mentions as part of his assessment

CHAPTER 7 / SAT CRITICAL READING PRACTICE EXAM II

of the young steamboatman. Yet, all of these assessments are colored by the fact that the author so obviously envies the young man.

(E) is wrong because there is nothing to suggest that the author is afraid of the young steamboatman.

18. **B is correct.** The fact that the young steamboatman survived the accident on his boat and came home a hero made the author question why fate should be so kind to someone who obviously does not deserve it.

(A) is wrong because the passage does not suggest that he is only pretending to be hurt.

(C) is wrong because the passage states that the boat had blown up and the author thought the cub engineer went down with the boat, not that he had gone to St. Louis.

(D) is wrong because the author specifically states that "there was nothing generous about this fellow in his greatness."

(E) is wrong because there is nothing to suggest that the author thought the young steamboatman should be admired for his bravery.

19. **C is correct.** Clearly what the author wanted as a boy was to be noticed as by standing apart from the crowd. The passage

indicates that he wanted to be a deckhand, because a deckhand was "particularly conspicuous." As well, the author remarks that the young steamboatman would come home and "swell around the town in his blackest and greasiest clothes, so that nobody could help remembering that he was a steamboat man." Last, the author mentions the young steamboatman coming to church after his boat blew up ". . . renowned . . . battered up and bandaged, a shining hero, stared at and wondered over by everybody. . . ."

(A) is wrong because even though the author acknowledges that the young steamboatman had "money," "hair oil," and an "ignorant silver watch with a showy brass chain" it is clear that these are secondary rewards that come with working on a steamboat. Throughout the article, it is the renown that the author comes back to.

(B) is wrong because although the author mentions a couple of boys who had been to St. Louis, traveling is just one other way boys are able to stand out.

(D) is wrong as there is no evidence that power is the object of the author's desire.

(E) is wrong because although the author clearly envies the young steamboatman, no mention is made that he wishes he did not.

CHAPTER 8

SAT CRITICAL READING PRACTICE EXAM III

ANSWER SHEET

Directions

- Remove this Answer Sheet from the book and use it to record your answers to this test.
- This test will require 1 hour and 10 minutes to complete. Take this test in one sitting.
- The times for each section are indicated at the start of the section. Sections 1 and 2 are each 25 minutes long, and Section 3 is 20 minutes long.
- Work on only one section at a time. If you finish a section before time has run out, check your work on that section only.

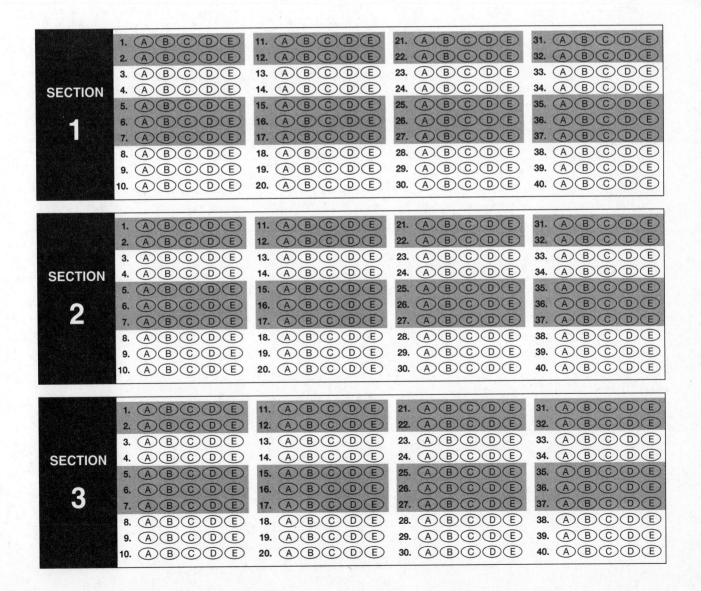

SECTION 1 QUESTIONS

Time—25 Minutes

24 Questions

Directions: This section consists of sentence completion questions and questions based on reading passages. For each question, select the answer you think is best and record your choice by filling in the corresponding oval on the answer sheet.

Directions: Each sentence below has one or two blanks. Each blank indicates that something is missing. Following each sentence are five words or sets of words labeled A, B, C, D, and E. You are to select the word or set of words that, when inserted in the sentence, best fits the meaning of the sentence as a whole.

EXAMPLE:

1. Despite our best efforts to protect the environment and keep it safe, until the problems of pollution are _____, the future of our environment seems, at best, _____.

   (A) created . . . gloomy
   (B) revoked . . . secure
   (C) solved . . . uncertain
   (D) replaced . . . revered
   (E) increased . . . unknown

   Correct Answer: C

1. The Consumer Electronics Association forecasts that in 2011, _____ sales of personal electronic equipment will surpass the $180 billion mark for the first time.

   (A) insurgent
   (B) electoral
   (C) dissipate
   (D) aggregate
   (E) feasible

2. With the vote split evenly, the commissioners waited for the mayor to stop _____ and decide the outcome of the proposal.

   (A) deliberating
   (B) ruminating
   (C) vacillating
   (D) ameliorating
   (E) circumscribing

3. Although she has a _____ voice, Nina had to be _____ by her friend Marco to join the choir.

   (A) mellifluous . . . permitted
   (B) reprehensible . . . coerced
   (C) prosaic . . . begged
   (D) commanding . . . immured
   (E) sublime . . . compelled

4. Arguably the modern world's most infamous dictator, Fidel Castro's _____ to power began in 1959 when he helped _____ the opposition government of Fulgencio Batista.

   (A) rise . . . institute
   (B) addiction . . . depose
   (C) quest . . . authorize
   (D) ascent . . . subvert
   (E) claim . . . affirm

5. After the band failed to _____ the audience or sell many tickets, the offer for an extended engagement was _____.

   (A) overcome . . . negated
   (B) impress . . . rescinded
   (C) accept . . . approved
   (D) inspire . . . established
   (E) rouse . . . protracted

6. After losing for the sixth time in a row, the basketball team hoped it had reached the _____ of its season.

   (A) penultimate
   (B) nadir
   (C) apex
   (D) pinnacle
   (E) conclusion

GO ON TO THE NEXT PAGE

7. The lavish project, really a vanity project dreamed up by the developer, was marked by _____ spending and a _____ waste of resources.

   (A) profligate . . . reckless
   (B) miserly . . . wanton
   (C) moderate . . . licentious
   (D) austere . . . nefarious
   (E) extravagant . . . virtuous

8. Although Martin had made several practice runs through the driving course without incident, he could not help but feel a sense of _____ when he went to take the test.

   (A) ebullience
   (B) deference
   (C) trepidation
   (D) approbation
   (E) vituperation

Directions: The passages below are followed by questions based on their content. Questions that follow a pair of related passages may also ask about the relationship between the paired passages. Answer each question on the basis of what is stated or implied in the passages and any introductory material provided.

Questions 9–12 are based on the following passages.

Passage 1.

Manatees and dugongs, also known as sea cows, belong to the scientific order Sirenia. In ancient
Line mythology, "siren" was a term used for monsters or sea nymphs who lured sailors and their ships to
5 treacherous rocks and shipwreck with mesmerizing songs. Throughout history, sailors sometimes thought they were seeing mermaids when they were probably seeing manatees or dugongs. With a little imagination, manatees have an uncanny resem-
10 blance to human form that could only increase after long months at sea. In fact, manatees and dugongs may have helped to perpetuate the myth of mermaids. Like the mythological creatures for which they were named, all sirenians living on Earth today
15 are vulnerable to extinction.

Passage 2.

Manatees and dugongs are the only completely aquatic mammals that are herbivores. Unlike the other marine mammals (dolphins, whales, seals, sea lions, sea otters, walruses, and polar bears) sirenians
20 eat only seagrasses and other aquatic vegetation. Unlike other marine mammals, sirenians have an extremely low metabolism and zero tolerance for cold water. Like dolphins and whales, manatees and dugongs are totally aquatic mammals that never
25 leave the water—not even to give birth. The combination of these factors means that sirenians are restricted to warm shallow coastal waters, estuaries, and rivers, with healthy ecosystems that support large amounts of seagrass and other vegetation. By
30 far, the largest population of West Indian manatees is found in the United States, primarily in Florida. Manatees, like all other sirenian species, are listed as endangered.

9. Passage 1 is primarily concerned with

   (A) the origin of the scientific classification Sirenia
   (B) the similarities between manatees and mermaids
   (C) how manatees cause shipwrecks
   (D) a comparison between manatees and dugongs
   (E) the imagination of manatees

10. As used in lines 5–6, "mesmerizing" most nearly means

   (A) discordant
   (B) mellifluous
   (C) high pitched
   (D) hypnotic
   (E) mysterious

11. Both passages support which of the following conclusions?

   (A) Manatees live primarily in Florida.
   (B) All sirenians are endangered.
   (C) Only sailors have seen manatees and dugongs.
   (D) Sirenians are mythological creatures.
   (E) Manatees eat only seagrasses.

12. The author develops Passage 2 by presenting

   (A) two sides of an issue
   (B) a thesis followed by specific examples
   (C) a description of similarities and differences
   (D) an opinion and reasons why it is held
   (E) a hypothesis and data to prove it

GO ON TO THE NEXT PAGE

Questions 13–24 are based on the following passage.

The Homestead Act of 1862 has been called one the most important pieces of Legislation in the history of the United States. This Act turned over vast amounts of the public domain to private citizens.

On January 1, 1863, Daniel Freeman, a Union Army scout, was scheduled to leave Gage County, Ne-
Line braska Territory, to report for duty in St. Louis. At a New Year's Eve party the night before, Freeman
5   met some local Land Office officials and con-vinced a clerk to open the office shortly after mid-night in order to file a land claim. In doing so, Freeman became one of the first to take advantage of the opportunities provided by the Homestead
10   Act, a law signed by President Abraham Lincoln on May 20, 1862.

The distribution of Government lands had been an issue since the Revolutionary War. Early meth-ods for allocating unsettled land outside the origi-
15   nal 13 colonies were arbitrary and chaotic, resulting in many overlapping claims and border disputes. The Land Ordinance of 1785 finally implemented a standardized system of Federal land surveys that eased boundary conflicts; however, because the sale
20   of public land was viewed as a means to generate revenue for the Government rather than as a way to encourage settlement, land ownership was finan-cially unattainable for most would-be homesteaders.

In the mid-1800s, popular pressure to change
25   policy led to increased legislative efforts to im-prove homesteading laws. These efforts, however, faced opposition on multiple fronts. Northern fac-tory owners feared a mass departure of their cheap labor force, and Southern states worried that rapid
30   settlement of western territories would give rise to new states populated by small farmers opposed to slavery. Between 1852 and 1860 four bills were proposed and defeated. With the secession of Southern states from the Union and, therefore, re-
35   moval of the slavery issue, finally, in 1862, the Homestead Act was passed and signed into law.

The new law established a three-fold home-stead acquisition process: filing an application, im-proving the land, and filing for deed of title. Any
40   U.S. citizen, or intended citizen, who had never borne arms against the U.S. Government could file an application and lay claim to 160 acres of sur-veyed Government land. For the next 5 years, the homesteader had to live on the land and improve it
45   by building a 12-by-14 dwelling and growing crops. After 5 years, the homesteader could file for a patent (or deed of title) by submitting proof of residency and the required improvements to a local land office.

50   Local land offices forwarded the paperwork to the General Land Office in Washington, DC, along with a final certificate of eligibility. The case file was examined, and valid claims were granted patent to the land free and clear, except for a small
55   registration fee. Title could also be acquired after a 6-month residency and trivial improvements, provided the claimant paid the government $1.25 per acre. After the Civil War, Union soldiers could deduct the time they served from the residency
60   requirements.

Some land speculators took advantage of a leg-islative loophole caused when those drafting the law failed to specify whether the 12-by-14 dwelling was to be built in feet or inches. Others hired
65   phony claimants or bought abandoned land. The General Land Office was underfunded and unable to hire sufficient numbers of investigators for its widely scattered local offices. As a result, over-worked and underpaid investigators were often
70   susceptible to bribery.

Physical conditions on the frontier presented even greater challenges. Wind, blizzards, and plagues of insects threatened crops. Open plains meant few trees for building, forcing many to build
75   homes out of sod. Limited fuel and water supplies could turn simple cooking and heating chores into difficult trials. Even the size of sections took its own toll. While 160 acres may have been sufficient for an eastern farmer, it was simply not enough to
80   sustain agriculture on the dry plains, and scarce natural vegetation made raising livestock on the prairie difficult. As a result, in many areas, the original homesteader did not stay on the land long enough to fulfill the claim.

85   Homesteaders who persevered were rewarded with opportunities as rapid changes in transporta-tion eased some of the hardships. Six months after the Homestead Act was passed, the Railroad Act was signed, and by May 1869, a transcontinental
90   railroad stretched across the frontier. The new rail-roads provided easy transportation for homestead-ers, and new immigrants were lured westward by railroad companies eager to sell off excess land at inflated prices. The new rail lines provided ready
95   access to manufactured goods and catalog houses like Montgomery Ward offered farm tools, barbed wire, linens, weapons, and even houses delivered via the rails.

GO ON TO THE NEXT PAGE

On January 1, 1863, Daniel Freeman and 417
100 others filed claims. Over the next 70 years, many
more pioneers followed, populating the land, building towns and schools and creating new states
from the territories. By the time the Act was repealed in 1934, 1.6 million applications had been
105 processed and more than 270 million acres—10
percent of all U.S. lands—had passed into the
hands of individuals.

13. The primary purpose of the passage is to

    (A) probe the reasons for success in settling the
        American West
    (B) present the history of an important piece of
        legislation
    (C) point out the injustices of the Homestead Act
    (D) argue in favor of repealing the Homestead Act
    (E) explain the importance of the life of Daniel
        Freeman

14. The author characterizes the method by which unset-
    tled lands were acquired following the Revolutionary
    War as

    (A) confusing and overly complex
    (B) impossible to enforce
    (C) difficult to understand
    (D) inconsistent and disorganized
    (E) inefficient and expensive

15. The factor most responsible for getting the Home-
    stead Act passed was

    (A) pressure from Northern factory owners
    (B) secession of the Southern states
    (C) lower land prices
    (D) reduced residency requirements
    (E) increasing claim size to 160 acres

16. In line 7, "file" most nearly means

    (A) arrange in order
    (B) classify
    (C) sharpen
    (D) record
    (E) finish

17. In order to acquire land under the Homestead Act,
    claimants had to satisfy which of the following
    requirements?
    I. be a native-born U.S. citizen
    II. file a claim at the local land office
    III. improve the land

        (A) I only
        (B) II only
        (C) I and II only

    (D) I and III only
    (E) II and III only

18. According to the Homestead Act, all of the follow-
    ing were required in order to obtain a deed of title to
    a claim EXCEPT:

    (A) proof of residency
    (B) building a dwelling
    (C) growing crops on the land
    (D) paying a small registration fee
    (E) proof of service during the Civil War

19. The statement that "Union soldiers could deduct the
    time served from the residency requirements" pri-
    marily suggests that the Government

    (A) thought it best to deny Southerners the right
        to own land
    (B) sought to penalize Southern soldiers for fight-
        ing against the Union
    (C) was providing an incentive for soldiers to
        enlist in the Army
    (D) wanted well-trained troops to occupy the new
        frontier
    (E) knew soldiers would be unable to afford
        $1.25 per acre

20. The "legislative loophole" in lines 61–62 refers to

    (A) the cost of the land
    (B) the use of phony claimants
    (C) the size of the required dwelling
    (D) underpaid investigators who were susceptible
        to bribes
    (E) payment of the registration fee

21. Lines 71–84 ("Physical conditions . . . claim.") serve
    mainly to describe

    (A) weather conditions on the plains
    (B) the hardships endured by early homesteaders
    (C) a typical homestead dwelling
    (D) geographical features of an early homestead
    (E) the difficulty of raising livestock on the prairie

22. In the context of lines 85–98, which of the follow-
    ing was most responsible for making life easier for
    homesteaders?

    (A) new rail lines
    (B) more favorable weather conditions
    (C) more fuel to heat homes
    (D) the arrival of additional settlers
    (E) the availability of more land

GO ON TO THE NEXT PAGE

23. How much U.S. land was transferred to individuals while the Homestead Act was in force?

    (A) 160 acres
    (B) 417 acres
    (C) 1.6 million acres
    (D) 270 million acres
    (E) 30 percent of all U.S. land

24. All of the following questions can be explicitly answered by this passage EXCEPT:

    (A) How was land allocated before the Revolutionary War?
    (B) What led to increased legislative efforts to improve homesteading laws in the mid-19th century?
    (C) Why was land allocation so disorganized before the late 18th century?
    (D) How did speculators take advantage of government oversights after the Civil War?
    (E) Why was it so difficult for people to settle on the frontier?

END OF SECTION

IF YOU FINISH BEFORE TIME IS UP, CHECK YOUR WORK ON THIS SECTION ONLY.

SECTION 2 QUESTIONS

Time—25 Minutes

24 Questions

Directions: This section consists of sentence completion questions and questions based on reading passages. For each question, select the answer you think is best and record your choice by filling in the corresponding oval on the answer sheet.

Directions: Each sentence below has one or two blanks. Each blank indicates that something is missing. Following each sentence are five words or sets of words labeled A, B, C, D, and E. You are to select the word or set of words that, when inserted in the sentence, best fits the meaning of the sentence as a whole.

EXAMPLE:

1. Despite our best efforts to protect the environment and keep it safe, until the problems of pollution are _____, the future of our environment seems, at best, _____.

    (A) created . . . gloomy
    (B) revoked . . . secure
    (C) solved . . . uncertain
    (D) replaced . . . revered
    (E) increased . . . unknown

    Correct Answer: C

---

1. While searching for his library card in a jacket he had not worn since last spring, Alex made the _____ discovery of a $20 bill in one of the pockets.

    (A) deliberate
    (B) serendipitous
    (C) lachrymose
    (D) blithe
    (E) disconsolate

2. The high point of the debate came when the challenger delivered an _____ attack on the incumbent, blasting him for being soft on corporate crime.

    (A) exiguous
    (B) affable
    (C) unwitting
    (D) ambrosial
    (E) excoriating

3. Alfred Hitchcock was the _____ director: an auteur that retained creative control and left his _____ mark on more than fifty feature films.

    (A) foreign . . . enduring
    (B) definitive . . . ambiguous
    (C) famous . . . desultory
    (D) consummate . . . indelible
    (E) inimitable . . . cryptic

4. Despite being mistakenly _____ for leaving the gate open, Derrick was _____ once the puppy crawled out from underneath the couch.

    (A) lectured . . . responsible
    (B) punished . . . amended
    (C) chastised . . . exonerated
    (D) criticized . . . atoned
    (E) absolved . . . forgiven

5. While the logging companies have invaded the state like a _____ army over the last hundred years, the developers have not been far behind.

    (A) munificent
    (B) vanquished
    (C) despondent
    (D) rapacious
    (E) tactile

GO ON TO THE NEXT PAGE

Directions: The passages below are followed by questions based on their content. Answer each question on the basis of what is stated or implied in the passages and any introductory material provided.

Questions 6 and 7 are based on the following passage.

So far, I had not opened my eyes. I felt that I lay upon my back, unbound. I reached out my hand,
Line and it fell heavily upon something damp and hard. There I suffered it to remain for many minutes,
5 while I strove to imagine where and what I could be. I longed, yet dared not to employ my vision. I dreaded the first glance at objects around me. It was not that I feared to look upon things horrible, but that I grew aghast lest there should be nothing to
10 see. At length, with a wild desperation at heart, I quickly unclosed my eyes. My worst thoughts, then, were confirmed.

6. In the context of the passage, which descriptions best characterize the narrator?

   (A) brave and purposeful
   (B) somber and resourceful
   (C) restless and imaginative
   (D) wounded and tired
   (E) puzzled and unsettled

7. The tone employed by the narrator seems to suggest that he

   (A) will soon confront those who have brought him to this place
   (B) is certain this day will be his last
   (C) will most likely be moved from his present location
   (D) is being held captive in some unknown place
   (E) is most certainly about to escape his captors

Questions 8 and 9 are based on the following passage.

Moton High was typical of the all-black schools in the central Virginia county. It was built in 1939 to
Line hold half as many students as it did by the early 1950s; its teachers were paid substantially less than
5 teachers at the all-white high school; and it had no gymnasium, cafeteria, or auditorium with fixed seats like the nearby white Farmville High had. Repeated attempts made by Moton's principal and PTA to convince the school board to erect a new
10 black high school were fruitless. So, in the spring of 1951, the students, led by 16-year-old Barbara Johns, took matters into their own hands. They went on strike and asked for help from the NAACP's special counsel for the Southeastern region of the
15 United States.

8. This passage primarily serves to

   (A) draw attention to a civil-rights issue by questioning it
   (B) provide an overview of the challenges Moton High faced
   (C) advocate the specific course of action that the students took
   (D) inform the reader by personalizing the perspective of Ms Johns
   (E) arouse sympathy by comparing Moton High to Farmville High

9. The author's description of the shortcomings of Moton High's facilities (lines 2–7) might best be described as

   (A) objective
   (B) biased
   (C) impassioned
   (D) empowering
   (E) emphatic

Questions 10–19 are based on the following passage.

Frontierswoman and fighter Calamity Jane tells about her life and adventures in the days of the Wild West.

My maiden name was Marthy Cannary. I was born in Princeton, Missouri, May 1st, 1852. Father and
Line mother were natives of Ohio. I had two brothers and three sisters, I being the oldest of the children. As a
5 child I always had a fondness for adventure and out-door exercise and especial fondness for horses which I began to ride at an early age and continued to do so until I became an expert rider being able to ride the most vicious and stubborn of horses, in fact
10 the greater portion of my life in early times was spent in this manner.

   In 1865 we emigrated from our homes in Missouri by the overland route to Virginia City, Montana, taking five months to make the journey. While
15 on the way the greater portion of my time was spent in hunting along with the men and hunters of the party, in fact I was at all times with the men when there was excitement and adventures to be had. By the time we reached Virginia City I was considered

GO ON TO THE NEXT PAGE

20 a remarkable good shot and a fearless rider for a girl
    of my age . . .
        Mother died at Black Foot, Montana, 1866,
    where we buried her. I left Montana in Spring of
    1866, for Utah, arriving at Salt Lake city during the
25 summer. Remained in Utah until 1867, where my
    father died, then went to Fort Bridger, Wyoming
    Territory, where we arrived May 1, 1868, then went
    to Piedmont, Wyoming, with UP Railway. Joined
    General Custer as a scout at Fort Russell, Wyoming,
30 in 1870, and started for Arizona for the Indian
    Campaign. Up to this time I had always worn the
    costume of my sex. When I joined Custer I donned
    the uniform of a soldier. It was a bit awkward at
    first but I soon got to be perfectly at home in men's
35 clothes.
        Was in Arizona up to the winter of 1871 and dur-
    ing that time I had a great many adventures with the
    Indians, for as a scout I had a great many dangerous
    missions to perform and while I was in many close
40 places always succeeded in getting away safely for
    by this time I was considered the most reckless and
    daring rider and one of the best shots in the western
    country.
        After that campaign I returned to Fort Sanders,
45 Wyoming, remained there until spring of 1872,
    when we were ordered out to the Muscle Shell or
    Nursey Pursey Indian outbreak. In that war Gener-
    als Custer, Miles, Terry and Crook were all en-
    gaged. This campaign lasted until fall of 1873. It
50 was during this campaign that I was christened
    Calamity Jane. It was on Goose Creek, Wyoming,
    where the town of Sheridan is now located. Capt
    Egan was in command of the Post. We were or-
    dered out to quell an uprising of the Indians, and
55 were out for several days, had numerous skirmishes
    during which six of the soldiers were killed and
    several severely wounded. When on returning to
    the Post we were ambushed about a mile and a half
    from our destination. When fired upon Capt Egan
60 was shot. I was riding in advance and on hearing
    the firing turned in my saddle and saw the Captain
    reeling in his saddle as though about to fall. I turned
    my horse and galloped back with all haste to his
    side and got there in time to catch him as he was
65 falling. I lifted him onto my horse in front of me
    and succeeded in getting him safely to the Fort.
    Capt Egan on recovering, laughingly said: "I name
    you Calamity Jane, the heroine of the plains." I
    have borne that name up to the present time.

10. The author could best be described as
    (A) bold and cynical
    (B) fearless and unconventional
    (C) vengeful and sneaky
    (D) ambitious and clever
    (E) tough and inhibited

11. In lines 31–35 ("Up to . . . . . clothes.") the author
    suggests that
    (A) women needed a costume to ride
    (B) women of the time did not wear pants
    (C) Calamity Jane was awkward
    (D) no one knew Calamity Jane was a woman
    (E) the soldiers did not have proper uniforms

12. In line 34, "at home" most nearly means
    (A) in the family
    (B) in the house
    (C) at hand
    (D) at ease
    (E) in a familiar place

13. In line 68, Captain Egan refers to the author as "the
    heroine of the plains" because she
    (A) had traveled from Missouri to Montana
    (B) was one of the best shots in the West
    (C) went on many dangerous missions
    (D) became a scout for General Custer
    (E) had rescued the Captain after he was shot

14. As used in line 69, "borne" most nearly means
    (A) transported
    (B) showed
    (C) carried
    (D) transferred
    (E) gave birth to

15. The main purpose of the final paragraph is to
    (A) tell the story of the author's life
    (B) reveal the dangers of living in the West
    (C) describe how the author dressed at the time
    (D) explain how Calamity Jane got her name
    (E) make a case for using women as scouts

GO ON TO THE NEXT PAGE ➤

16. With which of the following would the author most likely agree?

    (A) Individuals who are different seldom find happiness in life.
    (B) Men have more opportunities for excitement and adventure than women do.
    (C) Traditional social practices must be strictly followed.
    (D) Dangerous work is not for women.
    (E) Children should model their behavior on the behavior of their parents.

17. All of the following questions can be explicitly answered by this passage EXCEPT:

    (A) What activities consumed the majority of Calamity Jane's time before her family left Missouri?
    (B) How did Calamity Jane become such a remarkably good shot?
    (C) How did Calamity Jane save Capt. Egan?
    (D) What role did Calamity Jane serve upon joining General Custer?
    (E) What event led to Marthy Cannary being known as Calamity Jane?

18. Which information is most likely to be included in the next paragraph of this passage?

    (A) a biographical sketch of Captain Egan
    (B) a childhood escapade of Calamity Jane
    (C) an explanation of how Calamity Jane got her reputation as one of the best shots in the West
    (D) an anecdote from the trip west
    (E) an event in the life of Calamity Jane after 1873

19. The primary purpose of this passage is to

    (A) present a first-hand account of how the West was settled
    (B) provide an historical perspective of the battles Western settlers fought
    (C) provide a detailed explanation of how Calamity Jane got her name
    (D) entertain readers with imaginative stories of the "Wild West"
    (E) describe the early life of a well-known, 19th century American

Questions 20–24 are based on the following passage.

In this excerpt from his address to the American Historical Association in 1912, Theodore Roosevelt discusses the qualities that define great works of literature and great works of history.

Literature may be defined as that which has permanent interest because both of its substance and
Line its form, aside from the mere technical value that inheres in a special treatise for specialists. For a
5 great work of literature there is the same demand now that there always has been; and in any great work of literature the first element is great imaginative power. The imaginative power demanded for a great historian is different from that demanded
10 for a great poet; but it is no less marked. Such imaginative power is in no sense incompatible with minute accuracy. On the contrary, very accurate, very real and vivid, presentation of the past can come only from one in whom the imaginative gift is
15 strong. The industrious collector of dead facts bears to such a man precisely the relation that a photographer bears to Rembrandt. There are innumerable books, that is, innumerable volumes of printed matter between covers, which are excellent for their
20 own purposes, but in which imagination would be as wholly out of place as in the blue prints of a sewer system or in the photographs taken to illustrate a work on comparative osteology. But the vitally necessary sewer system does not take the place of the
25 cathedral of Rheims or of the Parthenon; no quantity of photographs will ever be equivalent to one Rembrandt; and the greatest mass of data, although indispensable to the work of a great historian, is in no shape or way a substitute for that work.

30   History, taught for a directly and immediately useful purpose to pupils and the teachers of pupils, is one of the necessary features of a sound education in democratic citizenship. A book containing such sound teaching, even if without any literary
35 quality, may be as useful to the student and as creditable to the writer as a similar book on medicine. I am not slighting such a book when I say that, once it has achieved its worthy purpose, it can be permitted to lapse from human memory as a good
40 book on medicine, which has outlived its usefulness, lapses from memory. But the historical work which does possess literary quality may be a permanent contribution to the sum of man's wisdom, enjoyment, and inspiration. The writer of such a
45 book must add wisdom to knowledge, and the gift of expression to the gift of imagination.

GO ON TO THE NEXT PAGE

20. According to Roosevelt, the defining quality of great literature is

    (A) poetic language
    (B) vivid descriptions
    (C) great imagination
    (D) meaningful content
    (E) lasting interest

21. In line 4, "inheres in" most nearly means

    (A) is made from
    (B) takes place in
    (C) is incompatible with
    (D) resides with
    (E) is inherent to

22. With which of the following statements is the author most likely to agree?

    (A) There is a basic incompatibility between imagination and historical accuracy.
    (B) The primary purpose of a great work of history is to present masses of data.
    (C) The major difference between a work of history and a great work of history is the soundness of the teaching it contains.
    (D) Imagination is as essential to the historian as it is to the poet.
    (E) A work of history cannot outlive its usefulness.

23. The comparison in lines 15–17 ("The industrious. . . Rembrandt.") is intended to illustrate how

    (A) essential art is to history
    (B) important creativity is in a work of history
    (C) necessary illustrations are to a work of history
    (D) difficult it is for historians to collect accurate data
    (E) famous Rembrandt's work is

24. The author believes that a great work of history does all of the following EXCEPT:

    (A) add to knowledge
    (B) contribute to enjoyment and inspiration
    (C) include many photos
    (D) contain minutely accurate data
    (E) create vivid pictures of the past

END OF SECTION

IF YOU FINISH BEFORE TIME IS UP, CHECK YOUR WORK ON THIS SECTION ONLY.

■ SECTION 3 QUESTIONS

Time—20 Minutes

19 Questions

Directions: This section consists of sentence completion questions and questions based on reading passages. For each question, select the answer you think is best and record your choice by filling in the corresponding oval on the answer sheet.

Directions: Each sentence below has one or two blanks. Each blank indicates that something is missing. Following each sentence are five words or sets of words labeled A, B, C, D, and E. You are to select the word or set of words that, when inserted in the sentence, best fits the meaning of the sentence as a whole.

EXAMPLE:

1. Despite our best efforts to protect the environment and keep it safe, until the problems of pollution are _____, the future of our environment seems, at best, _____.

    (A) created . . . gloomy
    (B) revoked . . . secure
    (C) solved . . . uncertain
    (D) replaced . . . revered
    (E) increased . . . unknown

    Correct Answer: C

---

1. On the last weekend of summer break at the seashore, the roads were jammed with traffic and the beach _____ with vacationers.

    (A) dispersed
    (B) proscribed
    (C) deprecated
    (D) inveighed
    (E) teemed

2. Stock market analysts have advised investors to examine leading economic indicators that _____ a recession before making any financial decisions.

    (A) portend
    (B) encumber
    (C) condone
    (D) vindicate
    (E) impede

3. Though in _____ disrepair, the investors saw the value in buying the _____ building solely for the land it was built on.

    (A) absolute . . . exquisite
    (B) palatial . . . vacant
    (C) opulent . . . worthless
    (D) complete . . . dissipated
    (E) utter . . . dilapidated

4. Although the cyclist had to overcome obstacles that most people would consider _____, he was _____ in his determination to qualify for the prestigious Tour de France.

    (A) devastating . . . resistant
    (B) insurmountable . . . resolute
    (C) undeniable . . . irreverent
    (D) indomitable . . . irreplaceable
    (E) elusive . . . unwavering

5. Considering that the author spent only 4 seconds signing her book, Micah decided that 8 hours was an _____ amount of time to have waited in line.

    (A) evanescent
    (B) incumbent
    (C) ephemeral
    (D) inordinate
    (E) imponderable

6. By noon, the newspaper staff had been _____ with phone calls about the power outage, and by evening, it seemed as though the _____ would continue.

    (A) inundated . . . deluge
    (B) overwhelmed . . . dearth
    (C) besieged . . . abatement
    (D) harassed . . . spate
    (E) depleted . . . barrage

GO ON TO THE NEXT PAGE

<u>Directions:</u> The passages below are followed by questions based on their content and on the relationship between the passages. Answer each question on the basis of what is stated or implied in the passages and any introductory material provided.

<u>Questions 7–19 are based on the following passages.</u>

Both of the passages that follow discuss the San Francisco earthquake of 1906. Passage 1 was excerpted from an account by novelist and short story writer Jack London. Passage 2 was written by Emma M. Burke, who lived with her husband and son in an apartment near Golden Gate Park at the time of the earthquake.

Passage 1.

The earthquake shook down in San Francisco hundreds of thousands of dollars worth of walls and
Line chimneys. But the conflagration that followed burned up hundreds of millions of dollars' worth of
5   property. There is no estimating within hundreds of millions the actual damage wrought. Not in history has a modern imperial city been so completely destroyed. San Francisco is gone. Nothing remains of it but memories and a fringe of dwelling-houses on
10   its outskirts. Its industrial section is wiped out. Its business section is wiped out. Its social and residential section is wiped out. The factories and warehouses, the great stores and newspaper buildings, the hotels and the palaces of the nabobs, are all
15   gone. Remains only the fringe of dwelling houses on the outskirts of what was once San Francisco.

Within an hour after the earthquake shock the smoke of San Francisco's burning was a lurid tower visible a hundred miles away. And for three days
20   and nights this lurid tower swayed in the sky, reddening the sun, darkening the day, and filling the land with smoke.

On Wednesday morning at a quarter past five came the earthquake. A minute later the flames were
25   leaping upward. In a dozen different quarters south of Market Street, in the working-class ghetto, and in the factories, fires started. There was no opposing the flames. There was no organization, no communication. All the cunning adjustments of a twentieth
30   century city had been smashed by the earthquake. The streets were humped into ridges and depressions, and piled with the debris of fallen walls. The steel rails were twisted into perpendicular and horizontal angles. The telephone and telegraph systems
35   were disrupted. And the great water-mains had burst. All the shrewd contrivances and safeguards of man had been thrown out of gear by thirty seconds' twitching of the earth-crust.

By Wednesday afternoon, inside of twelve
40   hours, half the heart of the city was gone. At that

time I watched the vast conflagration from out on the bay. It was dead calm. Not a flicker of wind stirred. Yet from every side wind was pouring in upon the city. East, west, north, and south, strong
45   winds were blowing upon the doomed city. The heated air rising made an enormous suck. Thus did the fire of itself build its own colossal chimney through the atmosphere. Day and night this dead calm continued, and yet, near to the flames, the
50   wind was often half a gale, so mighty was the suck.

Wednesday night saw the destruction of the very heart of the city. Dynamite was lavishly used, and many of San Francisco's proudest structures were crumbled by man himself into ruins, but there
55   was no withstanding the onrush of the flames. Time and again successful stands were made by the firefighters, and every time the flames flanked around on either side or came up from the rear, and turned to defeat the hard-won victory.

Passage 2.

60   No one can comprehend the calamity to San Francisco in its entirety. The individual experience can probably give the general public the clearest idea. I was one of the fortunate ones, for neither personal injury nor death visited my household; but what I
65   saw and felt I will try to give to you.

It was 5:13 a.m., and my husband had arisen and lit the gas stove, and put on the water to heat. He had closed our bedroom door that I might enjoy one more nap. We were in a fourth-story apartment
70   flat, said to be built with unusual care.

Twelve flats, so constructed, occupied a corner one block from Golden Gate Park. All our rooms, six in number, opened into a square reception hall, from which the stairs descended.

75   The shock came, and hurled my bed against an opposite wall. I sprang up, and, holding firmly to the foot-board managed to keep on my feet to the door. The shock was constantly growing heavier; rumbles, crackling noises, and falling objects al-
80   ready commenced the din.

The door refused to open. The earthquake had wedged it in the door-frame. My husband was pushing on the opposite side and I pulled with all

GO ON TO THE NEXT PAGE ➜

my strength, when a twist of the building released
85   it, and the door sprang open. We braced ourselves
in the doorway, clinging to the casing. Our son appeared across the reception room, and my husband
motioned to him to stand in his door also, for fear
of the chimney.

90   It grew constantly worse, the noise deafening;
the crash of dishes, falling pictures, the rattle of the
flat tin roof, bookcases being overturned, the piano
hurled across the parlor, the groaning and straining
of the building itself, broken glass and falling plas-
95   ter, made such a roar that no one noise could be
distinguished.

We never knew when the chimney came tearing
through; we never knew when a great marine picture weighing one hundred and twenty-five pounds
100 crashed down, not eight feet away from us; we were
frequently shaken loose from our hold on the door,
and only kept our feet by mutual help and our
utmost efforts, the floor moved like short, choppy
waves of the sea, crisscrossed by a tide as mighty
105 as themselves. The ceiling responded to all the angles of the floor. I never expected to come out alive.
I looked across the reception room at the white face
of our son, and thought to see the floors give way
with him momentarily. How a building could stand
110 such motion and keep its frame intact is still a mystery to me.

7.   The first paragraph of Passage 1 establishes a mood of

(A) awe and disbelief
(B) desperate longing
(C) uncontrolled outrage
(D) cautious optimism
(E) heartfelt pity

8.   The author of Passage 1 describes the effects of the
earthquake by relying on

(A) scientific knowledge
(B) comparisons to similar events in history
(C) confirmed statistical data
(D) vivid images appealing primarily to the sense
of sight
(E) insights based largely on interviews with
residents

9.   In Passage 1, line 14 "nabob" most nearly means

(A) knave
(B) wealthy person
(C) elected official
(D) native son
(E) descendant of royalty

10. The statement from Passage 1 that "All the cunning
adjustments of a twentieth century city had been
smashed by the earthquake" (lines 29–30) suggests
primarily that

(A) the city had been reduced to a primitive existence
(B) the earthquake destroyed many of the city's
newest buildings
(C) numerous irreplaceable mechanisms were lost
during the earthquake
(D) only necessities such as plumbing and electricity remained intact
(E) many people died as a result of the earthquake

11. Which best describes the overall organization of
Passage 1?

(A) a discussion of opposing viewpoints
(B) a description of events in spatial order
(C) a description of events in chronological order
(D) an enumeration of facts supported by statistical
data
(E) a statement of opinion backed up by reasons

12. The primary purpose of Passage 1 is to

(A) present a scientific explanation of the San
Francisco earthquake
(B) provide an eyewitness report of the San Fran-
cisco earthquake
(C) convey the despair of San Francisco residents
as they watched the destruction of their city
(D) describe the conditions that allowed the fires
to spread
(E) praise the efforts of fire fighters who battled
bravely to put out the fires

13. In Passage 2, line 60, "calamity" most nearly means

(A) cacophony
(B) gratuity
(C) disaster
(D) ferocity
(E) rectitude

14. The author of Passage 2 regards herself as

(A) lucky
(B) clever
(C) strong-willed
(D) easily frightened
(E) wealthy

GO ON TO THE NEXT PAGE

15. The author of Passage 2 never knew when the chimney came crashing down because

   (A) the windows were broken, and she could not see out
   (B) there was so much noise that she could not tell one sound from another
   (C) the bedroom door refused to open, and she could not get out
   (D) the building was well built, and no one expected it to be damaged
   (E) the floor moved like waves, and she could not get across it

16. In the last paragraph of Passage 2, (lines 97–111) the author uses a simile to describe

   (A) the destruction she saw all around her
   (B) the challenge of remaining upright
   (C) the cacophonous sounds of her possessions being displaced
   (D) the momentous feeling of loss
   (E) the relief she felt because her family survived

17. Unlike the author of Passage 1, the author of Passage 2 tells about the earthquake from the point of view of

   (A) a participant
   (B) an observer
   (C) a scientist
   (D) one who suffered great losses
   (E) a visitor to the city

18. The authors of both passages directly support the idea that

   (A) fire caused more damage than the earthquake itself
   (B) some people escaped with no injuries or deaths in their families
   (C) many buildings were destroyed by dynamite
   (D) the San Francisco earthquake was a disaster of epic proportions
   (E) the noise caused by breaking glass, groaning buildings, falling plaster, and crashing chimneys was deafening

19. Which of the following best describes the primary difference between the two passages?

   (A) Passage 1 is purely scientific, whereas Passage 2 is overly emotional.
   (B) Passage 1 is primarily concerned with the fate of the fire fighters, whereas Passage 2 is primarily concerned with the fate of one family.
   (C) Passage 1 focuses on the city itself, while Passage 2 focuses on individuals.
   (D) Passage 1 describes actual events, whereas Passage 2 presents a fictionalized version of events.
   (E) Passage 1 consists primarily of facts, while Passage 2 consists primarily of opinions.

END OF SECTION

IF YOU FINISH BEFORE TIME IS UP, CHECK YOUR WORK ON THIS SECTION ONLY.

ANSWER KEY

Section 1

1. D	7. A	13. B	19. B
2. C	8. C	14. D	20. C
3. E	9. A	15. B	21. B
4. D	10. D	16. D	22. A
5. B	11. B	17. E	23. D
6. B	12. C	18. E	24. A

Section 2

1. B	7. D	13. E	19. E
2. E	8. B	14. C	20. C
3. D	9. A	15. D	21. E
4. C	10. B	16. B	22. D
5. D	11. B	17. B	23. B
6. E	12. D	18. E	24. C

Section 3

1. E	6. A	11. C	16. B
2. A	7. A	12. B	17. A
3. E	8. D	13. C	18. D
4. B	9. B	14. A	19. C
5. D	10. A	15. B	

ANSWERS AND EXPLANATIONS

Section 1

1. **D is correct.** Knowing the definitions of the words you have to choose from will help you select the correct answer for this question. *Insurgent* (A), meaning "rising in revolt against established authority" makes no sense in the context of the sentence. *Electoral* (B), meaning "of, related to, or composed of electors" is also incorrect. *Dissipate* (C), is a verb, not an adjective, and means "to drive away or disperse." Perhaps a case could be made for *feasible* (E), meaning, "possible" or "capable of being accomplished or brought about," but the word "forecast" and the phrase "for the first time" should give you reason to reconsider this choice. After all, in a parallel situation, a meteorologist is unlikely to forecast "possible" record temperatures "for the first time." *Aggregate* (D), meaning "total" and "constituting or amounting to a whole" is the correct answer.

2. **C is correct.** This question asks you to find a word to describe a mayor who is faced with a "vote that is split evenly" and whose actions "will decide the outcome of the proposal." *Vacillating* (C), which means "swinging indecisively from one course of action or opinion to another," is the best answer. *Deliberating* (A) and *ruminating* (B) both make sense in context; however, because both words carry the same meaning ("thinking something over" or "considering something carefully"), neither one can be the best answer. *Ameliorating* (D), which means "improving" or "making or becoming better," is obviously wrong, as is *circumscribing* (E), which means "drawing a line around" or "limiting narrowly."

3. **E is correct.** The logic of the sentence requires that the two clauses contrast with each other. Thus, if Nina's voice sounds good, her friend would encourage her to sing and if her voice sounds bad, her friend would most likely discourage her from singing. Applying this logic, both (B) and (C) can be eliminated, for if Nina's voice was *reprehensible* (meaning "deplorable" or "wretched"),

Marco would not be likely to *coerce* (meaning "force") her to sing in the choir, and if her voice was *prosaic* (meaning "ordinary") he is not likely to *beg* her to sing. *Mellifluous* (meaning "sweet" or "pleasing to the ear") is a good first-blank choice, however the fact that Nina would have to be "*permitted* by her friend Marco to join the choir" is unreasonable, so (A) can also be eliminated. As for choice (D), although *commanding* works in the first blank, *immured* (meaning "imprisoned" or "confined") is clearly incorrect for the second blank. That leaves choice (E), which is correct. If Nina's voice is *sublime* (meaning "inspiring awe" or "splendid") it is likely Marco would want to *compel* (meaning "force") her to join the choir.

4. **D is correct.** Try filling in the blanks on this question before you look at the answers, as this may help you establish the context of it. The word "opposition" provides a clue to the correct answer, and should help you eliminate some of the incorrect choices for the second blank. Logically, you can infer that Castro would not *institute* (A), *authorize* (C), or *affirm* (E) the opposition's government. This leaves you with a choice between *depose* (B), meaning to "remove from office or power," and *subvert* (D), meaning "to overthrow completely." Both work well within the context, however choice (D) offers a better first-blank choice with *ascent*, meaning "the act of going upward or rising." Choice (D), *ascent . . . subvert*, is the correct answer.

5. **B is correct.** Knowing that the band failed to sell many tickets is the clue that will help you find the correct answer to this sentence completion question. Focusing on the second blank, you can eliminate choices (C), (D), and (E) because a band that failed to sell many tickets would not likely have an offer to extend the engagement *approved, established,* or *protracted* (meaning "drawn out" or "lengthened in time"). Now, turning your attention to the first blank you can logically determine that a band need not *overcome* its audience in order to be considered a success. Choice (B) is the correct answer.

A band that failed to *impress* the audience is likely to have the offer for an extended engagement *rescinded* (meaning "voided" or "repealed").

6. **B is correct.** Knowing the definitions of the choices will help you answer this question correctly, although, by focusing on the phrase "after losing for the sixth time in a row," you can eliminate some of the obviously wrong options. Clearly, a team suffering through a losing streak is not at the high point of its season; therefore, you can discount *apex* (C) and *pinnacle* (D) as they are synonyms and both refer to "the highest point." *Penultimate* (A) means "next to last," and can be eliminated as it makes little sense in this sentence. *Conclusion* (E) may seem correct, though a team would know when it has reached the end of its season; it likely would not have to "hope" it has reached the end of its season. *Nadir* (B) meaning "the lowest point" or "the time of greatest depression or adversity" is the correct answer.

7. **A is correct.** The clue to this sentence completion question is the word "lavish." Both (B) and (C) can be discounted because neither *miserly* nor *moderate* is likely to be used to in reference to spending on a "lavish" project. Choice (D) can also be eliminated because *austere* meaning "severe" or "very plain," is not consistent with the idea of a lavish project. Both (A) and (E) provide good first-blank choices in *profligate* (meaning "wasteful") and *extravagant* (meaning "excessive"), but you would be hard pressed to find an instance involving a "waste of resources" being considered *virtuous* (meaning "having or showing moral excellence"). *Profligate . . . reckless* (A) is the correct answer.

8. **C is correct.** This sentence asks you to find a word to describe a sense that overcame Martin as he went to take his driving test, despite having done well on his practice runs. Try thinking of a word to describe this sense before you look at the answer choices. Perhaps you came up with words like "nervousness" or "apprehension." However, because neither of these words is an option, you will have to look for the choice that comes closest in meaning. *Ebullience* (A) denotes "zestful enthusiasm," and *deference* (B) means "courteous yielding to the opinion, wishes, or judgment of another"; both are incorrect. *Approbation* (D) is "an expression of warm approval or praise" and *vituperation* means "sustained, harshly abusive language." Neither is synonymous with "nervousness" or "apprehension." *Trepidation* (C) meaning "a state of alarm or dread" is the correct answer.

9. **A is correct.** The passage tells how manatees and dugongs came to be called sirenians because of their resemblance to the sirens, or sea nymphs, of Greek mythology.

(B) is wrong because although the passage mentions that sailors—particularly those who have spent many months at sea—may have mistaken a manatee for a mermaid, it does not provide specific similarities between manatees and mermaids.

(C) is wrong because it was the sirens of mythology who are said to have caused shipwrecks.

(D) is wrong because the passage does not compare manatees and dugongs, except to say that both are sirenians.

(E) is wrong because it is the observer of the manatee, not the manatee itself, who might imagine that the manatee looks like a mermaid.

10. **D is correct.** The second sentence of Passage 1 tells how the sirens "lured sailors and their ships to treacherous rocks and shipwreck with mesmerizing songs." *Mesmerizing* means "captivating," "spellbinding," or "hypnotic."

(A) is wrong because *discordant* means "clashing" or "not in harmony." Such a song is unlikely to attract sailors to the singer.

(B) is wrong because *mellifluous* means "sweet" or "smooth." While sweet singing might attract sailors, it is not likely to cause them to smash their ships on the rocks.

(C) is wrong because pitch has nothing to do with how irresistible a song is.

(E) is wrong because a mysterious song is not likely to be so irresistible as to lure sailors into the rocks.

11. **B is correct.** The last sentence of Passage 1 ("Like the mythological creatures for which they were named, all sirenians living on Earth today are vulnerable to extinction.") and the last sentence of Passage 2 ("Manatees, like all other sirenian species, are listed as endangered.") each support the idea that all sirenians are endangered.

(A) is wrong because the fact that manatees live primarily in Florida is mentioned only in Passage 2.

(C) is wrong because neither passage supports the idea that only sailors have seen manatees and dugongs.

(D) is wrong because sirenians are not mythical creatures. The sirens, from whom manatees and dugongs got their scientific name, come from Greek mythology.

(E) is wrong because the fact that manatees eat seagrasses is mentioned only in Passage 2.

12. **C is correct.** Lines 17–25 ("Unlike . . . birth.") of the passage are devoted to listing the ways in which sirenians are different from and similar to other marine mammals.

(A) is wrong because the passage does not present opposing sides of an issue.

(B) is wrong because the passage does not state a thesis and give specific examples.

(D) is wrong because the passage presents an opinion and reasons for it.

(E) is wrong because the passage does not provide a hypothesis and data to prove it.

13. **B is correct.** This informative passage tells about the Homestead Act of 1862, including the provisions of the Act and the part it played in the settling of the American West.

(A) is wrong because the passage focuses on the Homestead Act, not on the settling of the West.

(C) is wrong because although the passage briefly discusses some of the ways in which unscrupulous individuals took advantage of the Homestead Act, this is not the primary purpose of the entire passage.

(D) is wrong because the passage does not argue for the repeal of the Act.

(E) is wrong because Daniel Freeman is mentioned only as one of the first homesteaders, not as the subject of the entire passage.

14. **D is correct.** As stated in lines 13–15, "Early methods for allocating unsettled land outside the original 13 colonies were arbitrary and chaotic." *Inconsistent* and *disorganized* means most nearly the same as *arbitrary* and *chaotic.*

(A) is wrong because the passage does not mention complexity as an issue.

(B) is wrong because there is no mention of enforcement.

(C) is wrong because the author does not mention that the method was particularly difficult to understand. Only that it was *arbitrary* (inconsistent or capricious) and *chaotic* (disorganized or uncontrolled).

(E) is wrong because the author says nothing about the earliest method being expensive.

15. **B is correct.** Despite popular pressure to improve homesteading laws, each new bill met opposition on multiple fronts. "Northern factory owners feared a mass departure of their cheap labor force and Southern states worried that rapid settlement of western territories would give rise to new states populated by small farmers opposed to slavery. . . . With the secession of Southern states from the Union and, therefore, removal of the slavery issue, finally, in 1862, the Homestead Act was passed and signed into law."

(A) is wrong because Northern factory owners were opposed to the Homestead Act.

(C) is wrong because there is no mention of the price of land having anything to do with passage of the Act.

(D) is wrong because residency requirement are not mentioned as a stumbling block to passage of the Act.

(E) is wrong because there is no mention of the size of the claim affecting passage of the Act.

16. **D is correct.** *File* is used in the following sentence: "At a New Year's Eve party the night before, Freeman met some local Land Office officials and convinced a clerk to open the office shortly after midnight in order to file a land claim." Although each of the choices is a possible meaning for the word *file*, the one that makes sense in the context of this sentence is *record* (choice D).

17. **E is correct.** As stated in lines 39–46: "Any U.S. citizen, or intended citizen, who had never borne arms against the U.S. Government could file an application and lay claim to 160 acres of surveyed Government land. For the next 5 years, the homesteader had to live on the land and improve it by building a 12-by-14 dwelling and growing crops."

(A), (C), and (D) are wrong because the passage does not state that applicants had to be native-born U.S. citizens.

(B) is wrong because in order to acquire land under the Homestead Act, claimants had to both file a claim and improve the land.

18. **E is correct.** The only mention of the Civil War concerns the ability of Union soldiers to deduct the time they served from the residency requirements. There is no mention of a requirement that homesteaders have served in the Civil War. In fact, the requirement that a claimant never have borne arms against the U.S. government would make Confederate soldiers ineligible to claim land under the Homestead Act.

(A) is wrong because it is specifically mentioned as a requirement in lines 47–48.

(B) is wrong because it is specifically mentioned as a requirement in line 45.

(C) is wrong because it is specifically mentioned as a requirement in lines 45–46.

(D) is wrong because it is specifically mentioned as a requirement in lines 54–55.

19. **B is correct.** The Homestead Act was passed in 1862 during the Civil War. At the time, the Government recognized only Union soldiers as serving the interests of the United States. Thus, the implication is that the Government sought to penalize the Southern soldiers and make it more difficult for them to acquire land in the new West. Moreover, the reader can infer that the Government was seeking to curb the spread of Southerners' proslavery ideology.

(A) is wrong because the passage does not indicate that Southern landowners suffered any consequences for land they already owned in the South. Thus, the Government was not trying to deny Southerners the right to own land.

(C) is wrong because the passage states that Union soldiers could deduct the time served from the residency requirements after the Civil War. No mention is made of the Government providing this as an incentive to boost enlistment.

(D) is wrong as the passage provides no information about the Government's wanting well-trained troops occupying the new frontier.

(E) is wrong because the passage provides no support for this statement. Rather, the passage implies that Union soldiers were granted leniency as a type of bonus after the Civil War.

20. **C is correct.** The "legislative loophole" is the failure of the Act to specify whether the size of the dwelling is measured in feet or inches. As stated in lines 62–64, the legislative loophole was caused "when those drafting the law failed to specify whether the 12-by-14 dwelling was to be built in feet or inches."

(A) is wrong because the cost was stated in the Act. Valid claims were granted title to the land at no cost except for a small registration fee. Title could also be granted after only 6 months' residency and trivial improvements, provided the claimant paid the government $1.25 per acre.

(B) is wrong because although some land speculators hired phony claimants to acquire land, the claimants had nothing to do with the legislative loophole.

(D) is wrong because although the passage mentions that underpaid investigators where susceptible to bribes, the investigators are not a legislative loophole.

(E) is wrong because the payment of a registration fee was required of all claimants.

21. **B is correct.** The paragraph describes the hardships endured by homesteaders, including harsh weather, insects, lack of trees for building, limited fuel and water, and scarce vegetation.

(A) is wrong because it is only one of many hardships described.

(C) is wrong because the paragraph does not describe a typical dwelling, except to say that some were built out of sod because of the lack of wood for building.

(D) is wrong because the paragraph does not discuss the geographical features of a particular homestead.

(E) is wrong because the difficult of raising livestock on the prairie is only one of the many hardships described.

22. **A is correct.** The arrival of rail lines eased some of the hardships of the settlers. The new rail lines provided "easy transportation for homesteaders" as well as "ready access to manufactured goods." Homesteaders could order farm tools, barbed wire, linens, and even houses to be delivered by rail.

(B) is wrong because weather conditions do not change much from year to year.

(C) and (D) are wrong because the rail lines brought the additional fuel and settlers.

(E) is wrong because there is no mention of a change in the availability of land.

23. **D is correct.** As stated in the last sentence, "By the time the Act was repealed in 1934 . . . more than 270 million acres . . . had passed into the hands of individuals."

(A) is wrong because each applicant could lay claim to 160 acres.

(B) is wrong because 417 is the number of applicants who filed claims for land on January 1, 1863.

(C) is wrong because 1.6 million is the number of applications that were processed while the Act was in force.

(E) is wrong because the passage states that 10 percent, not 30 percent, of all U.S. lands passed into the hands of individuals.

24. **A is correct.** Although the passage mentions that "The distribution of Government land had been an issue since the Revolutionary War," no mention is made of how the Government went about allocating land before this time.

(B) is wrong because the passage states that "In the mid-1800s, popular pressure to change policy led to increased legislative efforts to improve homesteading laws."

(C) is wrong because the passage states that "Early methods for allocating unsettled land outside the original 13 colonies were arbitrary and chaotic, resulting in overlapping claims and border disputes."

(D) is wrong because the passage states that "Some land speculators took advantage of a legislative loophole caused when those drafting the law failed to specify whether the 12-by-14 dwelling was to be built in feet or inches."

(E) is wrong because the passage explicitly states that "Physical conditions on the frontier presented even greater challenges. Wind, blizzards, and plagues of insects threatened crops. Open plains meant fewer trees for building, forcing many to build homes out of sod. Limited fuel and water supplies could turn simple cooking and heating chores into difficult trials. Even the size of sections took its own toll."

Section 2

1. **B is correct.** It is unlikely that Alex's discovery of a $20 bill, found in the pocket of a jacket that he had not worn since last spring, would have been *deliberate* (meaning "premeditated" or "on purpose"), *lachrymose* (meaning "tearful"), or *disconsolate* (meaning "cheerless" or "gloomy"), so (A), (C), and (E) can be eliminated. A case could perhaps be made for *blithe* (D), which means "carefree" or "lighthearted," but the best choice is *serendipitous* (B), which means "fortuitous" or "accidental."

2. **E is correct.** For the challenger to deliver an *exiguous* (A) attack would not make sense, because *exiguous* means "scanty" or "meager." In addition, an *affable* (B) attack would be unlikely because *affable* means "gentle and gracious." *Unwitting* (C) means "unintentional," and *ambrosial* (D) means "delicious" or "divine"; both are incorrect. It is most likely that the challenger delivered an *excoriating* (E) attack on the incumbent, a scathing attack that censured the incumbent strongly for being soft on corporate crime. *Excoriating* (E) is the correct answer.

3. **D is correct.** The key to figuring out this question is finding a first-blank choice that restates "an auteur that retained creative control," as well as a second-blank choice that modifies the "mark" Hitchcock left on "more than fifty feature films." As will often be the case on the SAT, you may want to start with the second-blank options. *Ambiguous* and *cryptic* hardly seem like appropriate words to describe the mark left by an "auteur" (meaning "a filmmaker, usually a director, who exercises creative control over his works and has a strong personal style"), and both can be eliminated. As well, *desultory* (C), meaning "disconnected" or "jumping from one thing to another," does not fit the context of the sentence. Faced with a choice between (A) and (D), you should recognize that (D) is better because *consummate* (meaning "having or revealing supreme mastery or skill") offers a better restatement of the context clue "auteur" than *foreign* does.

4. **C is correct.** "Despite" is the key word in this sentence, and it is often used in sen-tence completion questions to signal a contrast between the correct answers in two-blank questions. The structure of the sentence is designed to stress one character-istic of the subject in the first clause and then to contrast this characteristic with an-other characteristic in the second clause. *Lectured . . . responsible* (A), *punished . . . amended* (B), and *criticized . . . atoned* (D) lack the contrast needed for this type of sen-tence. Although all of the first-blank choices seem to fit, the meaning of the sentence be-comes unclear once the second-blank choices are inserted. *Absolved . . . forgiven* (E) is incorrect as well because the two words are synonymous. Only *chastised . . . exonerated* (C) has the requisite conflicting meanings to effectively convey the logic of this sentence. He was *chastised* (meaning "scolded" or "punished") for leaving the gate open, but *exonerated* (meaning "absolved" or "freed from blame") once the puppy reappeared from under the couch.

5. **D is correct.** This sentence provides the key word "invaded" and asks you to find the appropriate adjective that can describe how both an army and a logging company oper-ate. *Rapacious* (D), meaning "predatory" or "taking by force" is the only correct answer. (A) is wrong because *munificent* means "very liberal in giving" and "generous," which is an antonym of the word you are looking for. (B) is wrong because *vanquished* (B) means "defeated" or "conquered," which does not describe what the logging companies or the army are like. (C) is wrong because *despon-dent* means "without hope," and (E) is wrong because *tactile* means "perceptible to the sense of touch" or "tangible."

6. **E is correct.** The information that the narrator's hand "fell heavily upon something damp and hard" and that he lay for awhile with a "wild desperation" point to (E) as the best answer choice.

(A) is wrong because of the use of words such as *suffered*, *dreaded*, and *aghast*.

(B) is wrong because there is not enough in-formation in the passage to draw such a conclusion.

(C) is wrong because the passage states that the narrator was content to rest a bit and gather his wits.

(D) is wrong because it is not supported by information in the passage.

7. **D is correct.** This is the only answer choice that does not contain language about what is likely to happen next.

(A) and (C) are wrong because they make predictions about the narrator's fate, though it is clear from the passage that the narrator has little idea of where he is or what his future may hold.

(B) and (E) are wrong because they use either *certain* or *certainly* to foreshadow a situation that is far from absolute. These choices lead the reader to believe that the narrator has an idea of what may happen next, when in fact he does not.

8. **B is correct.** The passage presents a brief description of the conditions that existed at Moton High in the early 1950s.

(A) is wrong because the passage does not pose any questions.

(C) is wrong because the passage does not take any particular stance on the student strike.

(D) is wrong because although Ms Johns is mentioned by name, her story is not personalized.

(E) is wrong because the comparisons between Moton High and Farmville High are statements of fact, rather than a bid for sympathy.

9. **A is correct.** The author is merely presenting a fact-based account of Moton High School in the early 1950s.

(B) is wrong because there is no evidence of bias in the author's description of the school.

(C) is wrong because the passage lacks the powerful language that could be used to describe it as impassioned.

(D) is wrong because the passage does not take an authoritative enough stance to call it empowering.

(E) is wrong because the passage does not place enough emphasis on any of the school's shortcomings to label it as emphatic.

10. **B is correct.** Calamity describes herself as "a fearless rider" (line 20) and "one of the best shots in the western country" (lines 42–43). She also tells of becoming a scout for General Custer and donning the uniform of a soldier (lines 28–33). Her actions are best described as both *fearless* and *unconventional*.

(A) is wrong because the author is not cynical.

(C) is wrong because the author is not sneaky.

(D) is wrong because the author is motivated by adventure, not ambition.

(E) is wrong because the author is not inhibited.

11. **B is correct.** Calamity Jane says, "Up to this time I had always worn the costume of my sex. When I joined Custer I donned the uniform of a soldier. It was a bit awkward at first but I soon got to be perfectly at home in men's clothes." In other words, prior to becoming a scout, she had worn dresses like the other women of that time. Once she joined Custer, she started wearing a soldier's uniform. Because she had not worn men's pants before, the uniform seemed strange to her at first, but soon she got used to it and felt quite comfortable in the uniform.

(A) is wrong because the "costume of my sex" refers to a woman's dress, not a riding costume.

(C) is wrong because it is the uniform that felt awkward. The passage never refers to Calamity Jane as being awkward.

(D) is wrong because there is no mention in the passage of using the uniform to disguise the fact that Calamity Jane is a woman.

(E) is wrong because there is no mention of the soldiers not having proper uniforms.

12. **D is correct.** *At home* is used in the following sentence: "It was a bit awkward at first but I soon got to be perfectly at home in

men's clothes." The phrase *at home* can mean "in one's own house, neighborhood or country"; or it can mean "familiar, comfortable, or at ease." In this context the second meaning is best.

13. **E is correct.** Seeing that the Captain was about to fall from his horse, Calamity Jane galloped back to catch him and brought the injured Captain safely back to the fort. As a result of this action, Captain Egan referred to Calamity as "the heroine of the plains."

(A) is wrong because the family traveled to Montana long before the author met Captain Egan.

(B) is wrong because Egan is referring to her bravery in coming back to rescue him, not her shooting ability.

(C) is wrong because the dangerous missions mentioned in the passage did not involve Egan.

(D) is wrong because the author became a scout before the incident with Egan.

14. **C is correct.** The word *borne* appears in the last sentence of the passage: "I have borne that name up to the present time." In this context, *carried* is the best fit.

15. **D is correct.** The entire paragraph explains the events that led up to the author's being christened Calamity Jane.

(A) is wrong because this paragraph concerns only one event in the author's life.

(B) is wrong because the point of the paragraph is not to show the dangers of living in the West, but rather to explain how Calamity Jane got her name.

(C) is wrong because the description of how the author dressed is provided earlier in the passage, in paragraph 3.

(E) is wrong because the passage makes no attempt to suggest that women should be used as scouts.

16. **B is correct.** The author's attitude is made clear in the second paragraph: "While on the way the greater portion of my time was spent in hunting along with the men and hunters of the party, in fact I was at all times with the men when there was excitement and adventures to be had." Becoming a scout for Custer and going out on dangerous missions are still other examples of the author's love of excitement and adventure, which she is able to satisfy in the company of men, not women.

(A) is wrong because the author is herself different from most women of her day and yet she seems to be happy in what she does.

(C) is wrong because the author does not follow traditional social practices.

(D) is wrong because the author indulges in dangerous work.

(E) is wrong because the author did not model her behavior on the behavior of her parents.

17. **B is correct.** Although the passage states that "By the time we reached Virginia City I was considered a remarkable good shot . . ." no mention is made of how she became one. Was it because she practiced incessantly? Was it because she was born with some innate ability? The reader does not know, because the passage does not say.

(A) is wrong because the passage explicitly states that "the greater portion" of her life before she left Missouri was spent on "adventure and out-door exercise." As well, this is the period of time when she became an "expert rider being able to ride the most vicious and stubborn of horses."

(C) is wrong because the passage clearly states that she saved Capt Egan by galloping back to him "with all haste" and getting there "in time to catch him as he was falling" after he had been shot.

(D) is wrong because the passage states that she "joined General Custer as a scout."

(E) is wrong because the passage states that Capt Egan christened Cannary "Calamity Jane" after he was shot, and she saved him.

18. **E is correct.** The entire passage is organized chronologically. Paragraph 1 covers the author's birth in 1852 and events in her childhood. Paragraph 2 concerns the move to Montana in 1865. Paragraph 3 deals with events from 1866 to 1870. Paragraph 4 covers adventures in the winter of 1871. Paragraph 5 covers the time from the spring of 1872 until the fall of 1873. Logically, the next paragraph will cover events after the fall of 1873.

(A) is wrong because the passage concerns the life of Calamity Jane, not Captain Egan.

(B) is wrong because childhood escapades were covered in paragraph 1.

(C) is wrong because the fact that Calamity Jane had the reputation of being "one of the best shots in the western country" was covered in paragraph 4.

(D) is wrong because the events of the trip west were covered in paragraphs 2 and 3.

19. **E is correct.** The passage is an autobiographical account of Marthy Cannary, better known as Calamity Jane. The information she presents describes her childhood, her family, how she got her nickname, and other events covering the first 21 years of her life.

(A) is wrong because the first two paragraphs of the passage present information that has nothing to do with how the West was settled. Rather, these paragraphs describe Cannary's early years in Missouri and a brief history of her family.

(B) is wrong because too much other information is presented in the passage for this choice to be seen as the primary purpose. Although the passage includes first-hand accounts of several battles fought by people settling the West, these are events that occurred in the early life of Calamity Jane. Thus, the reason she is describing these events is because she experienced them.

(C) is wrong because although the passage includes the story of how Marthy Cannary came to be known as Calamity

Jane, this is only one detail of the passage, not its primary focus.

(D) is wrong because the details provided by Cannary are factual accounts, not imaginative stories. Moreover, given the historical perspective, the passage is meant to inform, rather than entertain.

20. **C is correct.** As stated in lines 6–8, "in any great work of literature the first element is great imaginative power."

(A), (B), (D), and (E) are all characteristics of great literature, but not the defining, or most important, characteristic.

21. **E is correct.** "Inheres in" occurs in the first sentence of the passage: "Literature may be defined as that which has permanent interest because both of its substance and its form, aside from the mere technical value that inheres in a special treatise for specialists." The technical value is an essential quality of or inherent to the treatise.

(A) and (C) are wrong because they change the meaning of the original sentence.

(B) and (D) are possible answers, but (E) is best.

22. **D is correct.** This statement is a rephrasing of the author's statement in lines 8–10: "The imaginative power demanded for a great historian is different from that demanded for a great poet; but it is no less marked."

(A) is wrong because the author says just the opposite in lines 10–15: "Such imaginative power is in no sense incompatible with minute accuracy. On the contrary, very accurate, very real and vivid, presentation of the past can come only from one in whom the imaginative gift is strong."

(B) is wrong because the author says that the greatest mass of data, although indispensable to the work of the historian, is in no way a substitute for imaginative power.

(C) is wrong because imagination, not soundness of the teaching, distinguishes a work of history from a great work of history.

(E) is wrong because the author states that once it has achieved its purpose, a book that contains sound teaching but lacks literary quality "can be permitted to lapse from human memory as a good book on medicine, which has outlived its usefulness, lapses from memory."

23. **B is correct.** The author is saying that the historian who merely collects facts can be compared to the historian of great imaginative powers in the same way that the photographer who merely snaps pictures can be compared to Rembrandt. Obviously, the element of creativity is important in both instances.

(A) is wrong because the comparison says nothing about art being essential to history.

(C) is wrong because the comparison says nothing about the role of illustrations in a work of history.

(D) is wrong because the comparison has nothing to do with the ease or difficulty of collecting data.

(E) is wrong because the comparison has nothing to do with the issue of fame.

24. **C is correct.** The author never mentions the need for a large number of photos as a requirement for a great work of history

(A) is wrong because it is mentioned in line 34.

(B) is wrong because it is mentioned in line 44.

(D) is wrong because it is mentioned in line 12.

(E) is wrong because it is mentioned in line 13.

Section 3

1. **E is correct.** Logically, you can infer from this sentence that if the roads were "jammed with traffic," then the beach must have been "packed with vacationers." This question asks you to find a word that is synonymous with "packed." *Teemed* (E), meaning "abounded" or "swarmed" is the answer you are looking for. *Dispersed* (A) means "driven off or scattered in different directions," and *proscribed* (B) means "denounced or condemned." *Deprecated* (C) means "expressed disapproval of," and *inveighed* (D) means "protested vehemently."

2. **A is correct.** The only way to arrive at the correct answer to this question is to know the definitions of the choices you are given. When you encounter this type of question, you may want to come up with an answer of your own before looking at the choices. Doing this can help you to get an idea of the word you are looking for and eliminate those that do not match your choice. Perhaps you came up with "predict" or "indicate." *Encumber* (B) and *impede* (E) are synonyms, which mean "to hinder the action or performance of." Neither one has anything to do with predicting, so you can eliminate both of these choices. To *condone* (C) is to "excuse, overlook, or make allowances for," and to *vindicate* (D) is to "clear of accusation, blame, suspicion, or doubt with supporting arguments or proof." Only *portend* (A), which means "to serve as an omen or a warning of," conveys the proper meaning of this sentence.

3. **E is correct.** The word "disrepair" and the phrase "solely for the land it was built on" offer two clues to help you discern the correct answer to this question. *Absolute, complete,* and *utter* are all synonyms and all are suitable first-blank choices. *Palatial* (B), meaning "of or suitable for a palace," and *opulent* (C), meaning "possessing or exhibiting great wealth" do not describe a state of "disrepair" and should be discounted. Once you are able to eliminate possible choices for one blank of a two-blank question, some of the plausible answer for the remaining blank will be eliminated as well. Such is the case with this question whereby knowing the definitions of *palatial* and *opulent* allow you to discount the seemingly correct choices *vacant* and *worthless*. Turning your

attention to the second blank, you can eliminate *exquisite* (A) because developers are unlikely to buy an *exquisite* building solely for the land it sits on. Finally, you can eliminate (D) because *dissipated* means "dispersed" or "scattered," which is not a likely description of a building. *Dilapidated* (E), which means "fallen into a state of disrepair," correctly repeats the description of the building given in the first part of the sentence.

4. **B is correct.** The logic of the sentence indicates that if most people thought the cyclist could not overcome the obstacles they must have been big ones. Thus, you can eliminate (E) because *elusive* (meaning "fleeting" or "difficult to describe") does not describe a great obstacle. Now consider the second blank. If the cyclist overcame great obstacles he must have really wanted to qualify for the race. This allows you to eliminate (A) because he would not be *resistant* (meaning "actively opposing") in his determination. Likewise you can eliminate (C) and (D) because neither *irreverent* (meaning "disrespectful") nor *irreplaceable* (meaning "not able to be replaced") makes sense in relation to his determination. The correct choice is (B). The cyclist overcame seemingly *insurmountable* (meaning "unbeatable") obstacles because he was *resolute* (meaning "steadfast" or "firm") in his determination to qualify for the race.

5. **D is correct.** The key to this sentence is the irony that Micah spent eight hours in line for an autograph that the author spent four seconds giving. This question asks you to find a word to suitably describe this imbalance of time. *Evanescent* (A), which means "vanishing or likely to vanish like vapor," and *incumbent* (B), which means "imposed as an obligation or duty" are both incorrect in the context of the sentence. *Ephemeral* (C), which means "lasting for a markedly brief time," could be used to describe the amount of time it took the author to give the autograph, but not the amount of time Micah spent waiting for the autograph. *Imponderable* (E), which means "incalculable," is incorrect because Micah knows precisely how much time she spent waiting for

the autograph. *Inordinate* (D), which means "exceeding reasonable limits," is the correct answer.

6. **A is correct.** Notice the absence of words such as "although," "but," "however," "yet," and "despite" in this sentence. Because it does not have these words that set up a contrast, this sentence probably requires two words that complement each other. The word "continue" offers a clue to the answer of this question. Logically, you can infer that whatever happened "by noon" at the newspaper "continued" through the evening. Choices (B), (C), and (E) all offer contrasting pairs of words and are incorrect. Choice (D), offers a viable choice, but is it really the best answer? *Spate* (meaning "flood" or "outpouring") could work in the second blank, but has the newspaper staff really been *harassed* (meaning "irritated or tormented persistently") by the calls? Choice (A) is the best choice. The staff was *inundated* (meaning "engulfed" or "flooded") with calls, and it seemed as through the *deluge* (meaning "overwhelming rush"), would continue.

7. **A is correct.** The constant repetition of "gone" and "wiped out" in lines 8–15 serves to emphasize the author's inability to believe that such devastation could possibly occur. "San Francisco is *gone*. . . . Its industrial section is *wiped out*. Its business section is *wiped out*. Its social and residential section is *wiped out*. The factories and warehouses, the great stores and newspaper buildings, the hotels and the palaces of the nabobs, are all *gone*."

(B), (D), and (E) are wrong because there are no words in the paragraph that support a mood of desperate longing, cautious optimism, or heartfelt pity.

(E) is possible; however, the mood of the paragraph is much closer to awe and disbelief than it is to uncontrolled outrage, so (A) is a better choice.

8. **D is correct.** Here are just a few examples of the vivid images provided by the author: ". . . the smoke of San Francisco's burning was a lurid tower visible a hundred miles away . . ." "The streets were humped into ridges and depressions, and piled with

the debris of fallen walls." "The steel rails were twisted into perpendicular and horizontal angles."

(A) is wrong because the passage contains no scientific facts.

(B) is wrong because the author does not compare the San Francisco earthquake to earthquakes of the past.

(C) is wrong because there is no statistical data provided.

(E) is wrong because the author does not provide any direct quotes that could have resulted from interviews with residents.

9. **B is correct.** A *nabob* is "a rich and important person."

(A) is wrong because a *knave* is "a rascal" or "a rogue."

(C) and (D) are wrong because a *nabob* is neither an elected official nor a native son (a native of a particular geographic area).

(E) is wrong because although the passage mentions "the palaces of nabobs," a nabob does not have to be of royal blood.

10. **A is correct.** The passage tells mainly of the massive destruction the San Francisco earthquake caused; roads and rail systems were destroyed, telephone and telegraph systems were "disrupted," and "the water-mains had burst." Thus, the statement conveys the idea that all modern conveniences had been lost, and the city had been reduced to living without twentieth century amenities.

(B) is wrong because the passage never specifies that many of the city's newer buildings were destroyed by the earthquake. Rather, the passage states that nearly every building in San Francisco was "wiped out" except "the fringe of dwelling houses on the outskirts" of the city.

(C) is wrong because the passage does not mention that "irreplaceable mechanisms were lost during the earthquake."

(D) is wrong because the passage explicitly states that "the great water-mains had

burst," and makes no mention of electricity being available.

(E) is wrong because the passage does not discuss how many people died in the earthquake.

11. **C is correct.** The passage is arranged in chronological order. This is evident in the first few words of paragraphs 3, 4, and 5. Paragraph 3 starts with the words "On Wednesday morning," paragraph 4 starts with "By Wednesday afternoon," and paragraph 5 starts with "Wednesday night."

(A) is wrong because there are no opposing points of view in this passage.

(B) is wrong because events are not described as happening from left to right or from top to bottom.

(D) is wrong because there are no statistics given.

(E) is wrong because the passage describes the devastation of the earthquake as seen by the author over the course of time. It is not a statement of opinions and reasons.

12. **B is correct.** As evidenced by lines 40–41 ("At that time I watched the vast conflagration from out on the bay."), the author was an eyewitness to the earthquake. His primary purpose for writing this passage was to report what he saw during that terrible time.

(A) is wrong because the passage provides no scientific explanation telling how earthquakes occur.

(C) is wrong because the passage describes the events of the earthquake, but does not go into the feelings of the residents.

(D) is wrong because only one paragraph of the account is devoted to the winds that helped the fire spread.

(E) is wrong because the author's praise for fire fighters' efforts is only one small part of the account, not its entire focus.

13. **C is correct.** *Calamity* means "grave misfortune" or "disaster."

(A) is wrong because *cacophony* means "discord" or "noise."

(B) is wrong because *gratuity* means "donation" or "tip."

(D) is wrong because *ferocity* means "fierceness" or "brutality."

(E) is wrong because *rectitude* means "integrity" or "honesty."

14. **A is correct.** As stated in the first paragraph of Passage 2, "I was one of the fortunate ones, for neither personal injury nor death visited my household."

(B), (C), (D), and (E) are all wrong because there is nothing in the passage that supports any of these choices.

15. **B is correct.** The last two paragraphs of Passage 2 describe the deafening noise of crashing dishes, falling pictures, breaking glass, and falling plaster, "which made such a roar that no one noise could be distinguished."

(A) is wrong because there is no mention of not being able to see out the windows.

(C) is wrong because the bedroom door sprang open once "a twist of the building released it," and so the author was not trapped in the bedroom.

(D) is wrong because the fact that the building was said to be "built with unusual care," has nothing to do with not being able to tell when the chimney crashed down.

(E) is wrong because the movement of the floor has nothing to do with knowing when the chimney fell.

16. **B is correct.** The author uses the simile that "the floor moved like short, choppy waves of the sea, crisscrossed by a tide as mighty as themselves," to describe the difficulty she and her family had in standing throughout the earthquake. Thus, she is comparing how her family "kept our feet" in the midst of an earthquake with trying to stand in the crosscurrents of the sea.

(A), (C), (D), and (E) are incorrect because the comparison is specifically about the challenge the family members faced as they tried to remain standing in the doorways of their home throughout the earthquake.

17. **A is correct.** The author of Passage 2 was a wife and mother living in San Francisco at the time of the earthquake. As stated in the first paragraph, she describes what she thought and felt as the quake began. The author of Passage 1 paints vivid word pictures of what he sees at the scene, but does not tell how the events affected him personally.

(B) is wrong because the author of Passage 2 is clearly involved in the action she describes.

(C) is wrong because the author of Passage 2 does not describe the scene in scientific terms.

(D) is wrong because the first paragraph states that the author is "one of the fortunate ones, for neither personal injury nor death visited my household."

(E) is wrong because the author lives in the city with her husband and son.

18. **D is correct.** This is the only statement that can be verified by information in both passages.

(A) is supported by Passage 1, but is not mentioned in Passage 2.

(B) is mentioned in Passage 2, but not in Passage 1.

(C) is stated in Passage 1, but not in Passage 2.

(E) is mentioned in Passage 2, but not in Passage 1.

19. **C is correct.** Passage 1 describes the effects of the earthquake on the city—the smoke that reddened the sun and darkened the day, the fires that raged, the streets that were humped into ridges and depressions, the water mains that burst, and the buildings that crashed and burned. Passage 2 describes the effects of the earthquake on one

family in their apartment near Golden Gate Park.

(A) is wrong because Passage 1 does not describe the earthquake from a scientific point of view.

(B) is wrong because the fate of the fire fighters is just one small part of the account rendered in Passage 1, not the main focus of the account.

(D) is wrong because both the introduction to the passages and the first paragraph of Passage 2 make it clear that this passage is an actual account of the effects of the earthquake on the author and her family, not a fictionalized version of events.

(E) is wrong because both passages are primarily factual.

CHAPTER 9

SAT CRITICAL READING PRACTICE EXAM IV

ANSWER SHEET

Directions

- Remove this Answer Sheet from the book and use it to record your answers to this test.
- This test will require 1 hour and 10 minutes to complete. Take this test in one sitting.
- The times for each section are indicated at the start of the section. Sections 1 and 2 are each 25 minutes long, and Section 3 is 20 minutes long.
- Work on only one section at a time. If you finish a section before time has run out, check your work on that section only.

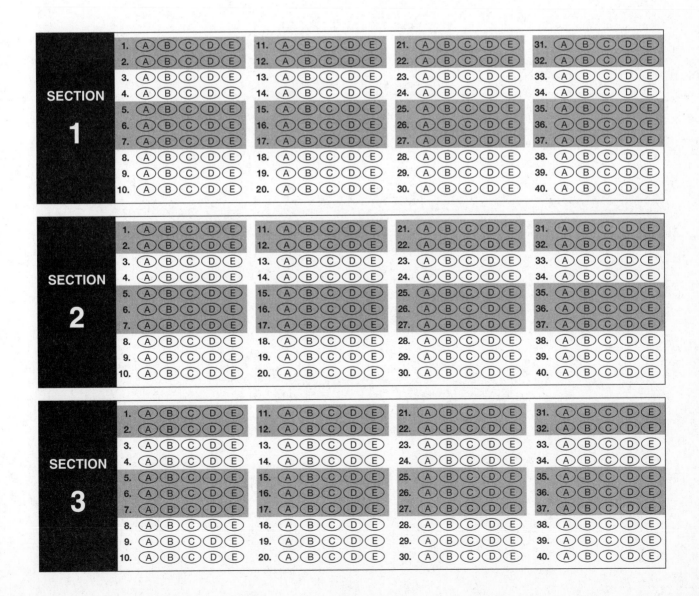

▨ SECTION 1 QUESTIONS

Time—25 Minutes

24 Questions

Directions: This section consists of sentence completion questions and questions based on reading passages. For each question, select the answer you think is best and record your choice by filling in the corresponding oval on the answer sheet.

Directions: Each sentence below has one or two blanks. Each blank indicates that something is missing. Following each sentence are five words or sets of words labeled A, B, C, D, and E. You are to select the word or set of words that, when inserted in the sentence, best fits the meaning of the sentence as a whole.

EXAMPLE:

1. Despite our best efforts to protect the environment and keep it safe, until the problems of pollution are _____, the future of our environment seems, at best, _____.

   (A) created . . . gloomy
   (B) revoked . . . secure
   (C) solved . . . uncertain
   (D) replaced . . . revered
   (E) increased . . . unknown

   Correct Answer: C

---

1. Giving preference to his brother's son for the job smacked of _____ to all the other employees of the company.

   (A) chauvinism
   (B) sycophancy
   (C) nepotism
   (D) nihilism
   (E) solipsism

2. The compromise bill is _____; both Democrats and Republicans can live with it.

   (A) friable
   (B) tenable
   (C) reprehensible
   (D) trenchant
   (E) frangible

3. During the Revolutionary War, Hessian troops fought on the British side not as _____, but as_____. They were paid in money, not glory.

   (A) infantry . . . mutineers
   (B) orderlies . . . traitors
   (C) renegades . . . assassins
   (D) friends . . . warriors
   (E) allies . . . mercenaries

4. A week of sun and exercise had a _____ effect; when Dawn returned, the tired look on her face had disappeared.

   (A) peremptory
   (B) salutary
   (C) sentient
   (D) contentious
   (E) fulsome

5. Whenever the press pursued her, the film star sought _____ in her palatial home.

   (A) refuge
   (B) repute
   (C) reserve
   (D) renown
   (E) reference

6. She was known for her _____; in short, no one was more _____ than she.

   (A) altruism . . . selfless
   (B) economy . . . profligate
   (C) virtue . . . wanton
   (D) conservatism . . . leftist
   (E) communism . . . democratic

GO ON TO THE NEXT PAGE ▶

7. Snakebites are not _____ fatal, but they can sometimes cause death if not _____ immediately.

   (A) inevitably . . . treated
   (B) occasionally . . . remedied
   (C) ever . . . acknowledged
   (D) indubitably . . . cured
   (E) especially . . . clarified

8. Ancient Greek authors believed that literature should contain a perfect balance between the social and the personal, objectivity and _____, _____ and emotion.

   (A) selectivity . . . passion
   (B) subjectivity . . . reason
   (C) subjection . . . rationality
   (D) passion . . . socialism
   (E) personality . . . sociability

Directions: The passages below are followed by questions based on their content. Questions that follow a pair of related passages may also ask about the relationship between the paired passages. Answer each question on the basis of what is stated or implied in the passages and any introductory material provided.

Questions 9–12 are based on the following passages.

Passage 1.

Testing on animals has helped develop vaccines for many life-threatening diseases such as hepatitis, polio, rabies, malaria, mumps, and viruses related
Line to organ transplantation rejection. In addition to
5 this, animal testing has also helped refine procedures involved in measuring blood pressure, implanting pacemakers, and perfecting the treatment of heart and lung diseases. You will be surprised to read that anesthesia which is used to numb the body
10 from acute pain during surgery is available today only because it was successfully tested on animals first. The fact of the matter is that to make advances in the field of medicine, animal testing is a necessary evil. A recent survey conducted by the Amer-
15 ican Medical Association indicates that 97% to 99% of all active physicians in the United States believe that animal research has resulted in medical advancements. The real goal of medical researchers should not be to abandon animal testing, but rather
20 to ensure that this research is carried out in a safe, ethical manner causing as little pain and discomfort as possible to the animal.

Passage 2.

There is a rapidly growing movement of professionals including medical researchers, practicing
25 doctors, and animal rights advocates who oppose using animals in medical testing, specifically on scientific and medical grounds. These professionals believe that animal testing and research are based on false premises and that the results ob-
30 tained cannot be applied to humans. Animals react differently than humans where drug experiments and vaccines are concerned. Perhaps the most famous example of the dangers of animal-based medical testing is the thalidomide tragedy of the 1960s
35 and 1970s. Thalidomide was marketed as a wonder drug, an amazing sedative for pregnant mothers that could not harm either the mother or the child. Despite this "safety testing," tens of thousands of children were born with severe physical deformi-
40 ties. Likewise, Clioquinol, an animal-tested drug for relieving diarrhea, caused thousand of cases of paralysis and blindness as well as several thousand deaths. Clearly, if we are looking to make any progress in medicine, an entirely new approach is
45 required. Human medicine should no longer be dependent on the suffering of animals. It is dangerous and fraudulent to apply data retrieved from one species to another entirely different species.

9. Like Passage 1, Passage 2 does which of the following?

   (A) explains the negative medical results of research based on animal testing
   (B) presents data from authorities on the efficacy of animal testing
   (C) presents both sides of the issue concerning the use of animals in medical research
   (D) argues for a particular point of view and action to be taken concerning the use of animal testing
   (E) offers only opinions and almost no factual evidence to support the author's point of view

10. Unlike the author of Passage 2, the author of Passage 1 believes that

   (A) the results of animal testing cannot be applied to expected results among humans
   (B) animal testing has never been successful in creating new treatments for important medical problems
   (C) animal suffering during medical testing is not worth the few new cures and vaccines it has produced
   (D) medical researchers should not be prevented from using animal testing in their work
   (E) no one understands the pain and suffering that animals endure during medical testing procedures

11. Both authors would most likely agree with which of the following statements?

   (A) No other research procedures have proved to be as successful as animal testing.
   (B) Animal medical testing is expensive and inhumane, and the results are meaningless.
   (C) Doctors should make the final decision whether to proceed with animal testing in medical research.
   (D) Results from animal testing can never be applied to humans because they are not the same species.
   (E) Animals used as subjects in current medical research undergo undeserved suffering.

12. Which best expresses a true relationship between Passage 2 and Passage 1?

   (A) A change in policy on using animals in medical research is necessary.
   (B) Animal testing in medical research often produces inaccurate results.
   (C) The harm caused to humans by inaccurate results of animal research is the most important issue to consider.
   (D) Using animals in medical research is a controversial subject among medical and health professionals.
   (E) Animals are living things that should never be subjected to painful experimentation.

Questions 13–24 are based on the following passage.

This passage is excerpted from Sarah Orne Jewett's story, "The Hilton's Holiday," published in 1896.

An hour later the best wagon was ready and the great expedition set forth. The little dog sat apart,
Line and barked as if it fell entirely upon him to voice the general excitement. Both seats were in the
5 wagon, but the empty place testified to Mrs. Hilton's unyielding disposition. She had wondered why one broad seat would not do, but John Hilton meekly suggested that the wagon looked better with both. The little girls sat on the back seat
10 dressed alike in their Sunday hats of straw with blue ribbons, and their little plaid shawls pinned neatly about their small shoulders. They wore gray threaded gloves, and sat very straight. Susan Ellen was half a head the taller, but otherwise, from be-
15 hind, they looked much alike. As for their father, he was in his Sunday best—a plain black coat, and a winter hat of felt, which was heavy and rusty-looking for that warm early summer day. He had it in mind to buy a new straw hat at Topham, so that
20 this with the turnip seed and the hoe made three important reasons for going.

   "Remember an' lay off your shawls when you get there, an' carry them over your arms," said the mother, clucking like an excited hen to her chick-
25 ens. "They'll do to keep the dust off your new dresses goin' and comin'. An' when you eat your dinners don't get spots on you, an' don't point at folks as you ride by, an' stare, or they'll know you come from the country. An' John, you call into
30 Cousin Ad'line Marlowe's an' see how they all be, an' tell her I expect her over certain to stop awhile before hayin'. It always eases her phthisic to git up here on the highland, an' I've got a new notion about doin' over her best-room carpet sense I see
35 her that'll save rippin' one breadth. An' don't come home all wore out; an', John, don't you go buy me no kick-shaws to fetch home. I ain't a child, an' you ain't got no money to waste. I expect you'll go, like's not, an' buy you some kind of a
40 foolish boy's hat; do look an' see if it's reasonable good straw, an' won't splinter all off round the edge. An' you mind, John"—

   "Yes, yes, hold on!" cried John impatiently; then he cast a last affectionate, reassuring look at
45 her face, flushed with the hurry and responsibility of starting them off in proper shape. "I wish you was goin' too," he said, smiling. "I do so!" Then the horse started, and they went out at the bars, and began the careful long descent of the hill. The
50 young dog, tethered to the lilac bush, was frantic with piteous appeals; the little girls piped their

eager goodbys again and again, and their father turned many times to look back and wave his hand. As for their mother, she stood alone and watched
55 them out of sight.

There was one place far out on the high-road where she could catch a last glimpse of the wagon, and she waited what seemed a very long time until it appeared and then was lost to sight again behind
60 a low hill. "They're nothin' but a pack o' child'n together," she said aloud; and then felt lonelier than she expected. She even stooped and patted the unresigned little dog as she passed him, going into the house.

13. According to the passage, Mrs. Hilton's "unyielding disposition" is the reason

(A) the little girls are dressed alike
(B) there is an empty place in the wagon
(C) her husband seems so meek
(D) the rest of the family is leaving
(E) there is only one broad seat in the wagon

14. The mother is compared to a hen in terms of her

(A) brooding nature
(B) attitude toward the dog
(C) concern over her children
(D) lazy but kind temperament
(E) constant talking

15. The mother is worried that her children might do all of the following EXCEPT

(A) spill food on their best clothes
(B) point and stare at people passing by
(C) misbehave in their cousin's house
(D) get their dresses dusty while riding
(E) forget to remove their shawls while in town

16. The word "kick-shaws" (line 37) apparently refers to

(A) money
(B) parasols
(C) a kind of hat
(D) odds and ends
(E) plaid shawls

17. The main point of the third paragraph (lines 43–55) is to

(A) highlight the parents' loving relationship
(B) emphasize the mother's stubbornness
(C) stress how anxious John is to begin the trip
(D) show the dog's distress at being left behind
(E) indicate the girls' wish not to leave their mother alone

18. In general, the family could be described as

(A) dysfunctional
(B) quite sophisticated
(C) fairly wealthy
(D) relatively poor
(E) new residents

19. When compared to her husband, the mother is probably

(A) the more impulsive of the two
(B) the lazier of the two
(C) the more practical of the two
(D) the more frightened of the two
(E) the older of the two

20. It's obvious from the passage that the family's visits to Topham are

(A) unnecessary excursions
(B) regular occurrences
(C) unplanned incidents
(D) sad family events
(E) rare shopping trips

21. The mother stoops to pat the dog (lines 62–64) because

(A) she can't stand his incessant barking
(B) she wants to untie him from the lilac bush
(C) she is afraid he will run after the wagon
(D) she wants to reward him for doing something good
(E) she shares his feelings of loneliness

22. The author's attitude toward her characters can be summed up as

(A) uncaring
(B) affectionate
(C) troubled
(D) confused
(E) benevolent

GO ON TO THE NEXT PAGE

23. The author's use of colloquial dialogue serves primarily to suggest
    (A) the longtime country roots of the family
    (B) the status of the family members as strangers to the community
    (C) the differences between the daughters and their parents
    (D) the excessive concern of the mother toward her children and husband
    (E) the impractical behavior of the husband, John

24. The fact that the mother finds two opportunities to view the wagon as it leaves indicates that
    (A) the mother is extremely concerned with her family's well-being
    (B) the father and daughters are more concerned with the trip than with the mother's feelings
    (C) the mother will miss the family and wants to keep them within her view as long as possible
    (D) poor weather might prove dangerous to the traveling family members
    (E) the mother is concerned about what may happen to her when she is alone

END OF SECTION

IF YOU FINISH BEFORE TIME IS UP, CHECK YOUR WORK ON THIS SECTION ONLY.

■ SECTION 2 QUESTIONS

Time—25 Minutes

24 Questions

Directions: This section consists of sentence completion questions and questions based on reading passages. For each question, select the answer you think is best and record your choice by filling in the corresponding oval on the answer sheet.

Directions: Each sentence below has one or two blanks. Each blank indicates that something is missing. Following each sentence are five words or sets of words labeled A, B, C, D, and E. You are to select the word or set of words that, when inserted in the sentence, best fits the meaning of the sentence as a whole.

EXAMPLE:

1. Despite our best efforts to protect the environment and keep it safe, until the problems of pollution are _____, the future of our environment seems, at best, _____.

   (A) created . . . gloomy
   (B) revoked . . . secure
   (C) solved . . . uncertain
   (D) replaced . . . revered
   (E) increased . . . unknown

   Correct Answer: C

1. The astute attorney asked many _____ questions of the witness in an attempt to _____ the truth.

   (A) pretentious . . . prolong
   (B) loquacious . . . contradict
   (C) vague . . . mitigate
   (D) probing . . . elicit
   (E) spurious . . . verify

2. It is easy to see the difference between the two photographs when they are placed in _____.

   (A) disarray
   (B) juxtaposition
   (C) composition
   (D) jeopardy
   (E) collaboration

3. The beggar smiled _____ as he threw back the nickel, saying, "Here! You need it more than I do."

   (A) kindly
   (B) indifferently
   (C) impulsively
   (D) sardonically
   (E) inappropriately

4. Although she had _____ about the storm, she had _____ about her ability to navigate safely through it.

   (A) doubts . . . certainty
   (B) foresight . . . misunderstandings
   (C) qualms . . . confidence
   (D) misgivings . . . knowledge
   (E) doubts . . . evidence

5. Being a stickler for promptness is just one of Aaron's many _____.

   (A) aversions
   (B) peccadilloes
   (C) skills
   (D) weaknesses
   (E) assertions

GO ON TO THE NEXT PAGE ➤

Directions: The passages below are followed by questions based on their content. Questions that follow a pair of related passages may also ask about the relationship between the paired passages. Answer each question on the basis of what is stated or implied in the passages and any introductory material provided.

Questions 6 and 7 are based on the following passage.

Olfaction, the act or process of smelling, is a dog's primary special sense. A dog's sense of smell is
Line said to be a thousand times more sensitive than that of humans. In fact, a dog has more than 220 million
5 olfactory receptors in its nose, whereas humans have only 5 million. Today, people use a dog's keen sense of smell in many ways. Federal, state, and local government agencies employ specially trained dogs in search and rescue missions and in
10 the detection of narcotics and contraband agricultural products. The Federal Emergency Management Agency has national dog-handler teams that respond to disasters worldwide. State and local law enforcement agencies in the United States also
15 have canine units trained to detect drugs and to search for lost individuals, homicide victims, and forensic cadaver materials. U.S. Customs and Border Protection has more than 800 canine teams that work with the U.S. Department of Homeland Se-
20 curity to combat terrorist threats, stop the flow of illegal narcotics, and detect unreported currency, concealed humans, or smuggled agricultural products. Its Canine Enforcement Program (CEP) uses a variety of dogs including Labrador retrievers,
25 golden retrievers, German shepherds, Belgian Malinois, and many mixed breeds. The CEP also uses beagles to detect agricultural contraband. The passively trained Beagle Brigade dogs detect prohibited fruits, plants, and meats in the baggage and
30 vehicles of international travelers as they go through Federal Inspection Service areas. Beagle Brigade teams work at several major border-crossing stations in the United States as well as at many international airports that are ports of entry
35 into the United States.

6. The examples used in this passage are intended to show

(A) the many ways trained dogs use their sense of smell to help government agencies
(B) how dogs' sophisticated sense of smell is developed in training programs
(C) how superior dogs' sense of smell is when compared with humans' olfactory sense
(D) how costly it is to train dogs to use their sense of smell in stopping and solving crimes
(E) the possible uses of dogs' vision and hearing in tracking criminals and contraband

7. This passage primarily serves to

(A) explain why dogs' sense of smell is so much greater than that of humans
(B) discuss the need for more special dog units in the fight against terrorism
(C) describe how dogs' sense of smell can be used to the benefit of citizens
(D) recount examples of the success of special canine units in detecting agricultural contraband
(E) identify organizations that use special canine units to identify illegal aliens

Questions 8 and 9 are based on the following passage.

Who would think that Iceland is one of the world's volcanic hot spots? In fact, Iceland boasts about
Line 130 volcanic mountains, many of which have erupted during the past 500 years. The biggest
5 eruption in modern history occurred in 1783, when the volcano Laki caused widespread devastation locally and in Europe and North America. The dust cloud from this eruption was reported as far away as Asia and Africa. Laki ruined crops, lowered tem-
10 peratures, drenched European forests in acid rain, caused skin lesions in children, killed 9,000 people, and resulted in the death of millions of cattle. Fortunately, the recent eruption of the Icelandic volcano Eyjafjallajokull on April 14, 2010, did not
15 result in any human deaths, but it caused serious economic losses for European air traffic and commerce. This eruption resulted in the cancellation of

GO ON TO THE NEXT PAGE

about 100,000 flights in more than 25 countries, and it left millions of travelers stranded at airports
20 and in neighboring towns and cities. Pilots and airline agencies feared that flying into the volcanic dust would make airplane engines fail and result in crashes. In addition, the eruption affected the transport of hundreds of millions of dollars of produce
25 worldwide. The question that remains is what we can expect next from Icelandic volcanoes. Unfortunately, during the last 2,000 years, every time Eyjafjallajokull has erupted a nearby volcano named Katla has also erupted within the year. Katla is 10
30 times the size Eyjafjallajokull and has resulted in even greater devastation and economic loss than that caused by its smaller neighbor. Is history a prelude to the future? Only time will tell.

8. Based on the passage, which inference would NOT be reasonable?

   (A) Volcanic eruptions always cause some damage.
   (B) Transportation problems are incidental to the loss of human life caused by volcanic eruptions.
   (C) According to historical references, volcanic eruptions sometimes can be expected.
   (D) The timing of volcanic eruptions can never be predicted with certainty.
   (E) The next volcanic eruption will take place somewhere in Iceland.

9. According to this passage, the dust cloud caused by a volcanic eruption

   (A) is only a problem for the localities near the volcano
   (B) is catastrophic for any towns and cities within the country where it takes place
   (C) drifts far away from its original source and can be carried across many continents
   (D) circles around planet Earth forever, causing permanent damage as it continues moving
   (E) leaves Earth's atmosphere within a week or two

Questions 10 and 18 are based on the following passage.

John Muir became the most famous American conservationist of late nineteenth century. His work spurred the modern conservation movement. Shortly after moving to California in 1869, Muir spent the summer in the Sierra mountains, and this was the first of hundreds of trips he

would take to the area. He recorded his first sights and impressions in a diary, from which this passage is excerpted.

Sugar pine cones are cylindrical, slightly tapered at the end and rounded at the base. Found one today
Line nearly twenty-four inches long and six in diameter, the scales being opened. Another specimen nine-
5 teen inches long; the average length of full-grown cones on trees favorably situated is nearly eighteen inches. On the lower edge of the belt at a height of about twenty-five hundred feet above the sea they are smaller, say a foot to fifteen inches long, and at
10 a height of seven thousand feet or more near the upper limits of its growth in the Yosemite region they are about the same size. This noble tree is an inexhaustible study and source of pleasure. I never weary of gazing at its grand tassel cones, its per-
15 fectly round bole one hundred feet or more without a limb, the fine purplish color of its bark, and its magnificent outsweeping, down-curving feathery arms forming a crown always bold and striking and exhilarating. In habit and general port it looks
20 somewhat like a palm, but no palm that I have seen yet displays such majesty of form and behavior either when poised silent and thoughtful in sunshine, or wide-awake waving in storm winds with every needle quivering. When young it is very straight
25 and regular in form like most other conifers; but at the age of fifty to one hundred years it begins to acquire individuality, so that no two are alike in their prime or old age. Every tree calls for special admiration. I have been making many sketches, and re-
30 gret that I cannot draw every needle. It is said to reach a height of three hundred feet, though the tallest I have measured falls short of this stature by sixty feet or more. The diameter of the largest near the ground is about ten feet, though I've heard of
35 some twelve feet thick or even fifteen. The diameter is held to a great height, the taper being almost imperceptibly gradual. Its companion, the yellow pine, is almost as large. The long silvery foliage of the younger specimens forms magnificent cylindri-
40 cal brushes on the top shoots and the ends of the upturned branches, and when the wind sways the needles all one way at a certain angle every tree becomes a tower of white quivering sun-fire. Well may this shining species be called the silver pine.
45 The needles are sometimes more than a foot long, almost as long as those of the long-leaf pine of Florida.

GO ON TO THE NEXT PAGE →

10. The word "scales" (line 4) is used to mean

   (A) measures
   (B) weights
   (C) scrapings
   (D) husks
   (E) balances

11. By "favorably situated" (line 6), Muir probably means

   (A) in an approved site
   (B) positioned pleasantly
   (C) newly planted
   (D) far above the sea
   (E) having suitable sun and water

12. By "general port" (line 19), Muir means

   (A) a place where ships dock
   (B) the manner in which something bears itself
   (C) placement to the left
   (D) an opening for intake
   (E) a hole for firing weapons

13. In comparing the pine to a palm, Muir

   (A) finds the pine less majestic
   (B) assigns the pine human characteristics
   (C) finds the palm less majestic
   (D) both A and B
   (E) both B and C

14. The word "bole" (line 15) means

   (A) trunk
   (B) top
   (C) tree
   (D) leaf
   (E) branch

15. When Muir says that the sugar pine acquires "individuality" at the age of fifty to one hundred years, he means that it

   (A) becomes more irregular in form and stature
   (B) has grown so large that it dwarfs the surrounding trees
   (C) has reached its maximum height
   (D) begins to bend due to age
   (E) changes in its coloration

16. You might reasonably infer from the passage that

   (A) Muir's study of the sugar pine was nearly complete
   (B) Muir would never tire of studying the sugar pine
   (C) Muir's fascination with the sugar pine would eventually wane
   (D) Muir confused the silver pine with the yellow pine
   (E) Muir was a fine artist in addition to being a naturalist

17. Muir's attitude toward the pine might be called

   (A) reverential
   (B) daunting
   (C) imperious
   (D) contrite
   (E) charitable

18. Muir's purpose in writing this passage seems to have been to

   (A) show how all sugar pines are alike
   (B) encourage tourists to visit the Sierras
   (C) recruit others to the field of conservation
   (D) document the characteristics of sugar pines
   (E) draw precisely accurate pictures of sugar pines

Questions 19–24 are based on the following passage.

Ralph Waldo Emerson is one of America's best-known essayists. In 1837 he was called on to give the Phi Beta Kappa address to Harvard students and their guests. He spoke on the subject of "The American Scholar."

It is remarkable, the character of the pleasure we derive from the best books. They impress us with
Line the conviction that one nature wrote and the same reads. We read the verses of one of the great En-
5 glish poets, of Chaucer, of Marvell, of Dryden, with the most modern joy—with a pleasure, I mean, which is in great part caused by the abstraction of all *time* from their verses. There is some awe mixed with the joy of our surprise, when this poet,
10 who lived in some past world, two or three hundred years ago, says that which lies close to my own soul, that which I also had well-nigh thought and said. But for the evidence thence afforded to the philosophical doctrine of the identity of all minds,
15 we should suppose some preestablished harmony,

GO ON TO THE NEXT PAGE

some foresight of souls that were to be, and some
preparation of stores for their future wants, like the
fact observed in insects, who lay up food before
death for the young grub they shall never see.

20   I would not be hurried by any love of system,
by an exaggeration of instincts, to underrate the
Book. We all know, that as the human body can be
nourished on any food, though it were boiled grass
and the broth of shoes, so the human mind can be
25 fed by any knowledge. And great and heroic men
have existed who had almost no other information
than by the printed page. I would only say that it
needs a strong head to bear that diet. One must be
an inventor to read well. As the proverb says, "He
30 that would bring home the wealth of the Indies,
must carry out the wealth of the Indies." There is
then creative reading as well as creative writing.
When the mind is braced by labor and invention,
the page of whatever book we read becomes lumi-
35 nous with manifold allusion. Every sentence is
doubly significant, and the sense of our author is as
broad as the world. We then see, what is always
true, that as the seer's vision is short and rare
among heavy days and months, so is its record, per-
40 chance, the least part of his volume. The discerning
will read, in his Plato or Shakespeare, only that
least part,—only the authentic utterances of the oracle;—all the rest he rejects, were it never so many
times Plato's and Shakespeare's.

45   Of course there is a portion of reading quite indispensable to a wise man. History and exact science he must learn by laborious reading. Colleges,
in like manner, have their indispensable office,—to
teach elements. But they can only highly serve us
50 when they aim not to drill, but to create; when they
gather from far every ray of various genius to their
hospitable halls, and by the concentrated fires, set
the hearts of their youth on flame.

19. By "one nature wrote and the same reads" (lines
     3–4), Emerson means that

     (A) the author is rereading his own work
     (B) nature writing is read by the same people
     (C) author and reader live in the same era
     (D) author and reader are in accord
     (E) the reader does not remember his own writing

20. The word "abstraction" (lines 7–8) is used to mean

     (A) conception
     (B) notion
     (C) preoccupation
     (D) elimination
     (E) inattention

21. Emerson uses the image of insects (lines 17–19) to
     parallel his discussion of

     (A) past writers storing knowledge for future
          readers
     (B) authors working in grubby surroundings
     (C) soulless parents toiling blindly for unknown
          children
     (D) the natural food chain
     (E) the harmony of the natural world

22. A good title for paragraph 2 might be

     (A) "Creative Writing"
     (B) "Creative Reading"
     (C) "Rating Books"
     (D) "The Wealth of the Indies"
     (E) "Visions of the Past"

23. The word "laborious" (line 47) is used to mean

     (A) boring
     (B) ungratifying
     (C) requiring hard work
     (D) amusing
     (E) mandatory

24. When Emerson says, "Colleges, in like manner, have
     their indispensable office,—to teach elements" (lines
     47–49), he means

     (A) Every college should have a large administra-
          tive space.
     (B) Attending college is absolutely necessary to
          be a good reader.
     (C) Every student must study the elements of
          geometry.
     (D) All colleges are made of various departments
          of learning.
     (E) The purpose of a college is to teach students
          basic principles of thinking and analysis.

E N D   O F   S E C T I O N

IF YOU FINISH BEFORE TIME IS UP, CHECK YOUR WORK ON THIS SECTION ONLY.

■ SECTION 3 QUESTIONS

Time—20 Minutes

19 Questions

Directions: This section consists of sentence completion questions and questions based on reading passages. For each question, select the answer you think is best and record your choice by filling in the corresponding oval on the answer sheet.

Directions: Each sentence below has one or two blanks. Each blank indicates that something is missing. Following each sentence are five words or sets of words labeled A, B, C, D, and E. You are to select the word or set of words that, when inserted in the sentence, best fits the meaning of the sentence as a whole.

EXAMPLE:

1. Despite our best efforts to protect the environment and keep it safe, until the problems of pollution are _____, the future of our environment seems, at best, _____.

    (A) created . . . gloomy
    (B) revoked . . . secure
    (C) solved . . . uncertain
    (D) replaced . . . revered
    (E) increased . . . unknown

    Correct Answer: C

1. You cannot be present in fifth-century Britain, but you can experience it _____ by reading Joy Chant's book *The High Kings.*

    (A) directly
    (B) reminiscently
    (C) vicariously
    (D) infinitely
    (E) audibly

2. The general _____ his order; he had his troops _____ rather than advance toward the enemy.

    (A) reinforced . . . march
    (B) rescinded . . . retreat
    (C) reviewed . . . charge
    (D) countermanded . . . encircle
    (E) confirmed . . . attack

3. If you act _____ to other guests, you will not be asked to any other party they give.

    (A) tranquilly
    (B) deferentially
    (C) obligingly
    (D) contritely
    (E) disrespectfully

4. The college draws a very _____ student body; thirty different _____ groups are in the freshman class.

    (A) diverse . . . related
    (B) similar . . . scholarly
    (C) homogeneous . . . language
    (D) heterogeneous . . . ethnic
    (E) intelligent . . . high school

5. After the interview, Eduardo was _____ to learn that the head of human resources said that he was _____ for the job.

    (A) thrilled . . . unqualified
    (B) confused . . . hired
    (C) embarrassed . . . overqualified
    (D) surprised . . . underpaid
    (E) dismayed . . . unsuitable

6. While his partner was furious with the loss of one of their biggest clients, Matthew was _____ and showed no real emotion when he learned of the loss.

    (A) apathetic
    (B) conciliatory
    (C) knowledgeable
    (D) appreciative
    (E) vigilant

GO ON TO THE NEXT PAGE ➤

> Directions: The passages below are followed by questions based on their content. Questions that follow a pair of related passages may also ask about the relationship between the paired passages. Answer each question on the basis of what is stated or implied in the passages and any introductory material provided.

Questions 7–19 are based on the following passage.

Harriet Beecher Stowe became famous for writing a novel called *Uncle Tom's Cabin* in 1852. Citizens who wanted to ban slavery praised the book. In Passage 1, Stowe presents background information about the writing of her popular novel. In Passage 2, Frederick Douglass writes about the eve of his second attempt to escape from slavery. In time, Douglass became a popular lecturer and publisher.

Passage 1—Harriet Beecher Stowe, from a letter to Mrs. Follen (1853)

I had two little curly-headed twin daughters to begin with, and my stock in this line was gradually
Line increased, till I have been the mother of seven children the most beautiful and the most loved of
5   whom lies buried near my Cincinnati residence. It was at his dying bed and at his grave that I learned what a poor slave mother may feel when her child is torn away from her. In those depths of sorrow which seemed to me immeasurable, it was my only
10   prayer to God that such anguish might not be suffered in vain. There were circumstances about his death of such peculiar bitterness, of what seemed almost cruel suffering, that I felt that I could never be consoled for it unless this crushing of my own
15   heart might enable me to work out some great good to others. . . .

I allude to this here because I have often felt that much that is in that book ("Uncle Tom") had its root in the awful scenes and bitter sorrows of
20   that summer. It has left now, I trust, no trace on my mind except a deep compassion for the sorrowful, especially for mothers who are separated from their children. . . .

I am now writing a work which will contain,
25   perhaps, an equal amount of matter with "Uncle Tom's Cabin." It will contain all the facts and documents upon which that story was founded, and an immense body of facts, reports of trial, legal documents, and testimony of people now living South,
30   which will more than confirm every statement in "Uncle Tom's Cabin."

I must confess that till I began the examination of facts in order to write this book, much as I thought I knew before, I had not begun to measure

35   the depth of the abyss. The law records of courts and judicial proceedings are so incredible as to fill me with amazement whenever I think of them. It seems to me that the book cannot but be felt, and, coming upon the sensibility awaked by the other,
40   do something.

I suffer exquisitely in writing these things. It may be truly said that I suffer with my heart's blood. Many times in writing "Uncle Tom's Cabin" I thought my heart would fail utterly, but I prayed
45   earnestly that God would help me till I got through, and still I am pressed beyond measure and above strength. . . .

Passage 2—Recollection of Frederick Douglass (1855)

It is impossible for me to describe my feelings as the time of my contemplated start grew near. I had
50   a number of warm-hearted friends in Baltimore,— friends that I loved almost as I did my life,—and the thought of being separated from them forever was painful beyond expression. It is my opinion that thousands would escape from slavery, who not
55   remain, but for the strong cords of affection that bind them to their friends. The thought of leaving my friends was decidedly the most painful thought with which I had to contend. The love of them was my tender point, and shook my decision more than
60   all things else. Besides the pain of separation, the dread and apprehension of a failure exceeded what I had experienced at my first attempt. The appalling defeat I then sustained returned to torment me. I felt assured that, if I failed in this attempt, my case
65   would be a hopeless one—it would seal my fate as a slave forever. I could not hope to get off with anything less than the severest punishment, and being placed beyond the means of escape. It required no very vivid imagination to depict the most frightful
70   scenes through which I would have to pass, in case I failed. The wretchedness of slavery, and the blessedness of freedom, were perpetually before me. It was life and death with me. But I remained firm and according to my resolution, on the third
75   day of September, 1838, I left my chains, and succeeded in reaching New York without the slightest interruption of any kind.

GO ON TO THE NEXT PAGE

7. The phrase "stock in this line" (line 2) means the number of

    (A) her shares of stock
    (B) her animals
    (C) her relatives
    (D) her sons
    (E) her children

8. What did Stowe learn at her son's "dying bed" and grave (lines 6–8)?

    (A) a mother's pain at being separated from her child
    (B) the importance of having many children
    (C) the horrors of slavery
    (D) that the child lost becomes the most important one
    (E) that there is no substitute for having good medical care, especially for children

9. In paragraph 1, with whom does Stowe have affinity because of her experience with her son?

    (A) mothers of large families
    (B) mothers losing sons
    (C) fathers losing a child
    (D) mothers with twins
    (E) slave mothers whose children are torn from them

10. The phrase "crushing of my own heart" (lines 14–15) means

    (A) a broken rib
    (B) the beginning of a heart attack
    (C) the end of an ability to love
    (D) an almost unbearable heartache
    (E) the end of faith in God

11. What reason does Stowe give for making reference to the death of her son (paragraph 2)?

    (A) to gain readership for *Uncle Tom's Cabin*
    (B) to provide background on the reason for writing *Uncle Tom's Cabin*
    (C) to encourage others experiencing pain
    (D) to make others aware that she herself has experienced pain
    (E) to gain notoriety for her family

12. The purpose of paragraph 3 is to

    (A) announce that Stowe is working on a new book
    (B) show that Stowe is an industrious person
    (C) show that Stowe's new book has been well researched and well documented
    (D) show that Stowe is a prolific writer
    (E) show that Stowe is still committed to her writing projects

13. The phrase "depth of the abyss" (line 35) means

    (A) pain in losing her son
    (B) ignorance of those supporting slavery
    (C) the horrible institution of slavery
    (D) the incompetence of judges
    (E) the incompetence of lawyers

14. To what is Frederick Douglass referring with the words "contemplated start" (Passage 2, line 2)?

    (A) his first day as a slave
    (B) his first day as a free man
    (C) his change in status as a slave
    (D) his first day on a new job
    (E) his flight to freedom

15. Why is Douglass hesitant to leave Baltimore?

    (A) fear of the unknown
    (B) fear about finding a place to live
    (C) fear about not having any money
    (D) pain at being separated from friends
    (E) pain at being separated from family

16. The word "failure" as used in Passage 2, line 61, means

    (A) failure to escape
    (B) failure to reach his goals
    (C) failure to be acknowledged
    (D) failure to be able to leave his friends
    (E) failure to leave what is familiar

17. What pain did Harriet Beecher Stowe suffer that Frederick Douglass did not?

    (A) the struggle to write
    (B) the loss of a child
    (C) years of research
    (D) the loss of a son
    (E) the uncertainty of getting her book published

GO ON TO THE NEXT PAGE

18. What pain did Frederick Douglass suffer that Harriet Beecher Stowe did not?

    (A) never knowing his father
    (B) never knowing his mother
    (C) the state of servitude
    (D) the gaining of friends
    (E) the loss of family

19. Harriet Beecher Stowe and Frederick Douglass have the same opinion about

    (A) life in the South
    (B) the wretchedness of slavery
    (C) the difficulty of being a writer
    (D) the pain of losing a child
    (E) the difficulty of persuading others to support your opinion

END OF SECTION

IF YOU FINISH BEFORE TIME IS UP, CHECK YOUR WORK ON THIS SECTION ONLY.

ANSWER KEY

Section 1

1. C	7. A	13. B	19. C
2. B	8. B	14. C	20. E
3. E	9. D	15. C	21. E
4. B	10. D	16. D	22. B
5. A	11. E	17. A	23. A
6. A	12. D	18. D	24. C

Section 2

1. D	7. C	13. E	19. D
2. B	8. E	14. A	20. D
3. D	9. C	15. A	21. A
4. C	10. D	16. B	22. B
5. B	11. E	17. A	23. C
6. A	12. B	18. D	24. E

Section 3

1. C	6. A	11. B	16. A
2. B	7. E	12. A	17. D
3. E	8. A	13. C	18. C
4. D	9. E	14. E	19. B
5. E	10. D	15. D	

ANSWERS AND EXPLANATIONS

Section 1

1. **C is correct.** Be suspicious of choices that seem linked to the subject matter. If you consider the connotations as well as the denotations of each answer choice, it is clear that you are looking for a word with negative connotations, as you can tell from the phrase "smacks of" and the general negative tone of the speaker's comment. Choice (C), *nepotism*, means "favoring relatives for appointment to office," exactly the definition you need here. The "nep" in *nepotism* is from the same root as the "nep" in *nephew*, which fits the context clue "his brother's son."

(A), *chauvinism*, may at first seem like it might have something to do with preference and granting someone a job; but in fact, *chauvinism* means "exaggerated patriotism" or "partiality to one's race, sex, etc." So (A) is incorrect.

(B), *sycophancy*, makes no sense, since a favor to a father's son is unlikely to involve "servile flattery."

(D), *nihilism*, implies "anarchism" and does not make sense in the sentence.

(E), *solipsism*, implies "extreme preoccupation" and also does not make sense.

2. **B is correct.** This question asks you to find a word to describe a bill that is acceptable to both Democrats and Republicans. *Tenable* means "capable of being held or defended in an attack or argument." (B) is the correct answer choice, since the context clues indicate that the bill is a "compromise" and that members of both parties can reach agreement about it.

(A), *friable*, means "readily crumbled or brittle," and is not the correct choice.

(C), *reprehensible*, means "deserving of blame, rebuke, or censure" and is incorrect because neither party would blame the other if they both "can live with it."

(D), *trenchant*, means "clearly or sharply defined"; therefore, it is a possible correct answer choice. However, *trenchant* car-

ries the connotation of "caustic or critical," which does not fit the context of the sentence.

(E), *frangible*, means "frail, fragile, or easily broken," and this does not fit the idea of a compromise both parties "can live with."

3. **E is correct.** The contrast word *but* tells you that there is a shift from the first part of the sentence. The sentence states that Hessian troops fought "not as _____, *but* as _____." Therefore, you should look for answer choices that are the opposite of each other. The word *allies* is the opposite of *mercenaries*. Even if you didn't know that soldiers who hire themselves out to foreign armies are called *mercenaries*, you can select choice (E) as correct because this pair of words shows a contrast relationship that is implied by the word *but*.

(A), (B), (C), and (D) are incorrect, since none of them shows this contrast.

4. **B is correct.** From the support clues "tired look" and "disappeared," you can infer that the second part reinforces the first part. Now study the sentence itself. From the clues "the tired look on her face had disappeared," you can figure out that the week of sun and exercise must have had a beneficial effect. (Remember, you are dealing with a support word clue in this question.) Therefore, you should look for a word choice that means "good." The only word that fits is *salutary*, choice (B), since the word means "healthful."

(A), *peremptory*, means "arbitrary, autocratic," so it is clearly incorrect for the context.

(C), *sentient*, means "alive, aware," so it does not fit either.

(D), *contentious*, means "argumentative, belligerent," which does not fit the sentence.

(E), *fulsome*, means "sickening, gross, excessive," and is clearly not the word called for here.

5. **A is correct.** Choice (A), *refuge*, means "shelter or safety" and clearly fits the context of the sentence, since the film star wants to get away from the pursuing press. Choice (B), *repute*, means "favorable reputation." While a film star may have a favorable reputation, this wouldn't be the cause of her wanting to get away from the press. Choice (C), *reserve*, means "something kept or stored for future use" and does not fit the structure of the sentence, since "her palatial home" is not kept by her as a "reserve." Choice (D), *renown*, means "fame," which does not make sense here, since it is the film star's fame that is causing her to get away from the pursuing press. Choice (E), *reference*, means "a mention, an act of referring, or a statement about a person's character." None of these meanings of *reference* fits the context of the sentence.

6. **A is correct.** The summary clue "in short" is placed after the first clause. This tells you that anything after the semicolon defines what comes before it. Since the first half of the sentence must define the second half, the two missing words must be synonyms. The only two words that are synonyms are *altruism* and *selfless*, choice (A). *Altruism* means "concern for others," which makes sense when linked to *selfless*.

(B) is wrong because a person known for economy would be the opposite of *profligate* ("wasteful, uneconomical").

(C) can be eliminated because a person known for *virtue* would be the opposite of *wanton* ("immoral or lewd").

(D) is incorrect because a person known for *conservatism* would be a rightist, not a leftist.

(E) is incorrect because a person known for *communism* would not be dubbed democratic.

7. **A is correct.** The word *but* signifies a change in meaning between the two parts of a sentence. Snakebites may sometimes cause death, but they are not *inevitably*, or necessarily, fatal. Snakebites must be *treated* immediately.

(B), *occasionally*, the first word of the pair, does not fit the sentence structure, although *remedied* does fit the second part of the sentence. Remember both words in a pair must fit the sentence.

(C) is incorrect because the statement "snakebites are not *ever* fatal" is patently false.

(D) might seem like a possible correct answer, since *indubitably* means "too apparent to be doubted, unquestionable" and *cured* means "healed or restored to health"; however, the use of *not indubitably* is self-contradictory. Therefore, choice (D) is incorrect.

(E), *clarified*, the second word, does not fit the context of the sentence, making this answer choice incorrect.

8. **B is correct.** The phrase "perfect balance" and the first example, "the social and the personal," indicate that you must supply opposites for *objectivity* and for *emotion*, in that order. Objectivity is the state of mind that views outer reality factually, without reference to personal feelings, in a way that all people could agree on. The opposite is the state of mind that views outer reality in terms of personal emotions and individual need: *subjectivity*. In this context, the opposite of emotion is *reason*. Therefore, choice (B) fits both blanks in the sentence.

(A), *selectivity*, is not the opposite of *objectivity*, and *passion* is a synonym for *emotion*; therefore, this choice is incorrect.

(C), *subjection*, means "the act or fact of being subjected, or made a slave." In addition to not being an opposite of *objectivity*, *subjection* is not parallel in structure to *objectivity*. Therefore, choice (C) is incorrect.

(D), *socialism* is not the opposite of *emotion* and does not fit the context of the sentence.

(E), *personality* and *sociability* are not opposites of *objectivity* and *emotion*.

9. **D is correct.** Choice (D) is the best answer, since each passage argues for only one

point of view—positive or negative—concerning medical animal testing.

(A) is not correct because only Passage 2 presents the negative medical results of animal testing; Passage 1 presents the positive medical results of animal testing.

(B) is incorrect for reasons similar to those cited for choice (A).

(C) is incorrect because each passage presents only one side of the issue of animal medical testing.

(E) is incorrect because both passages do offer facts and opinions about animal testing.

10. **D is correct.** The author of Passage 1 clearly argues that the use of animals in medical testing should be continued, whereas the author of Passage 2 argues that these procedures should be discontinued. Therefore, choice (D) is correct.

(A) is incorrect because this is a position taken by the author of Passage 2, not the author of Passage 1.

(B) is also incorrect because this is a position presented by the author of Passage 2, not the author of Passage 1.

(C) is incorrect, since the author of Passage 1 argues that suffering of animals in medical testing is worth the cures that have been developed, although such suffering should be minimized.

(E) may seem like a possible answer choice; however, it is not clearly the best answer choice.

11. **E is correct.** Both authors seem to agree that animals used in current medical research suffer during the research. Passage 1 indicates this by saying that rather than abandoning animal testing, the testing should be done in an "ethical manner causing as little pain and discomfort as possible to the animal." Passage 2 indicates that the author believes research animals suffer by stating, "Human medicine should no longer be dependent on the suffering of animals." Therefore, choice (E) is the correct answer.

(A) is incorrect. Only the author of Passage 1 argues that no other research procedures have proved as successful as the use of animals in research.

(B) is incorrect. Neither Passage 1 nor Passage 2 mentions the cost associated with animal research; furthermore, only the author of Passage 2 argues that these procedures are inhumane and inapplicable to humans.

(C) is incorrect. Only the author of Passage 1 argues that doctors should make the final decision with respect to the continuation of animal medical testing.

(D) is incorrect because only the author of Passage 2 argues that the results of animal medical testing cannot be applied to another species, such as humans.

12. **D is correct.** Only choice (D) presents a true relationship that can be inferred from Passages 1 and 2. The presentations of both authors make clear that the subject of using animals in medical testing is controversial.

(A), (B), (C), and (E) are incorrect because each is presented by only one of the two authors of the passages.

13. **B is correct.** This question asks you to identify the effect of a cause. In this question, the cause is Mrs. Hilton's "unyielding disposition." You can find the answer clearly stated in the passage's first paragraph, where you are told "Both seats were in the wagon, but the empty place testified to Mrs. Hilton's unyielding disposition."

(A), (C), and (D) are incorrect even though they all did occur. However, there is no indication that any of them was the effect of Mrs. Hilton's disposition.

(E) is contradicted by lines 6–9 of the selection, which reveal that both broad seats were in the wagon.

14. **C is correct.** This question requires you to identify an important detail about a character in the passage. To find the answer, skim through the passage to find the place where the mother is compared to a hen (lines 24–25). Then, from the text given im-

mediately before and after the simile of the hen, you can determine that the correct answer is (C).

(A) is incorrect because, although a hen does *brood,* in that case it means "to protect with wings" or "to sit on eggs until they are hatched." In this sentence, a brooding nature means "a morbid or gloomy nature," a view not supported by the passage.

(B) is incorrect because Mrs. Hilton's attitude toward the dog is represented by a single act of assurance and affection, which does not indicate an excessive concern for the dog.

(D) is incorrect because there is nothing in the selection to indicate that Mrs. Hilton is lazy; to the contrary, she is busily concerned with every detail of the "holiday" even though she herself is not going.

(E) is a possibility, since Mrs. Hilton clearly chatters, but she does not do so incessantly, or all the time. Therefore, choice (E) is not the best choice.

15. **C is correct.** This question also focuses on the mother, but the form of the question has been reversed from question 14. You must find the one detail in the list of five choices that is *not* supported by information from the passage. The answer can be found in the passage's second paragraph, in which the mother gives her children pointers about proper behavior. There is nothing in the passage to indicate that the mother is concerned about her children misbehaving in their cousin's home. Since this answer choice is not evident from the passage, choice (C) is correct.

(A) is not correct because Mrs. Hilton tells the girls not to spill food on their dresses.

(B) is not correct because Mrs. Hilton tells the girls not to "point at folks . . . an' stare."

(D) is not correct because Mrs. Hilton tells the girls not to keep their shawls on while riding in the wagon so as not to get their dresses dusty.

(E) is not correct because Mrs. Hilton tells the girls not take their shawls off when they get to town.

16. **D is correct.** To answer this question, you will need to use the process of elimination. First, go to line 37 and find the sentence in which *kick-shaws* appears. The context will quickly lead you to rule out answer choices (A), (B), (C), and (D).

(A) is incorrect, as the mother tells her husband, "don't you go buy me no kick-shaws," and he wouldn't buy money.

(B) is incorrect because nothing in the passage indicates that kick-shaws might be parasols.

(C) might seem plausible at first because Mrs. Hilton does talk about a hat later in the paragraph. However, the hat Mrs. Hilton discusses here is the one her husband wants for himself, not one he plans to buy for her. Therefore, (C) is incorrect.

(E) might be tempting, since Mrs. Hilton also talks about shawls, but she refers only to her daughter's shawls. Thus, (E) is not the correct answer.

17. **A is correct.** To answer this question, you must carefully read and then evaluate the information in the third paragraph. There are several pieces of evidence that point to (A) as the best answer. John cast an "affectionate" look at this wife, he smiled at her and wished she was going with them, and he turned many times to look back at her and wave.

(B) is incorrect because there is no discussion of the mother's stubbornness in the paragraph.

(C) is incorrect. Although you do learn that John responded "impatiently," it is not clear whether he is impatient with his wife's orders or simply impatient because he wants to get going. Furthermore, this seems like a minor, not a major, point. Therefore, (C) is at best ambiguous, and ambiguous answers on the SAT are never correct.

(D) is incorrect because the dog's distress is not a major point of the paragraph.

(E) is incorrect because the girls are clearly described as being "eager" to go on the trip.

18. **D is correct.** To complete this generalization about the family, you need to consider the information from the entire passage. In lines 36–38, Mrs. Hilton says, "John, don't you go buy me no kick-shaws to fetch home. I ain't a child, an' you ain't got no money to waste." However, the father does plan to buy a few things at Topham's: a hoe, turnip seed, and a hat. From these details, you can reasonably infer that the Hiltons are relatively poor.

(A) is incorrect because there is nothing in the passage to suggest anything other than that the family is normal and quite loving.

(B) is incorrect because the family members are simple country people, as evidenced by their clothing, their language, and their excitement about a trip to town.

(C) is incorrect. We know the family is *not* fairly wealthy because Mr. Hilton had only enough money to buy turnip seed, a hoe, and a straw hat, and because Mrs. Hilton admonished him not to waste money on trinkets for her.

(E) is incorrect because there is nothing in the passage to suggest that the Hiltons are new residents in the area; the fact that Mrs. Hilton's cousin lives in town suggests that the Hiltons probably have lived there for a while.

19. **C is correct.** To answer this question, you need to consider the character traits revealed about Mr. and Mrs. Hilton. Choice (C) fits the details provided in the passage, since it is Mrs. Hilton who is concerned with giving advice to every member of family who is going to town.

(A) is incorrect, as we know that Mrs. Hilton is deliberate about every detail of the trip, which would not be the case with someone who was impulsive.

(B) is incorrect because nothing in the passage suggests that either Mrs. Hilton or her husband is lazy.

(D) is incorrect because there are no details in the passage to indicate that Mrs. Hilton is anything but concerned.

(E) is incorrect because the passage makes no reference to the ages of Mr. and Mrs. Hilton except that they are adults with young children.

20. **E is correct.** To answer this question, you need to find information in the passage that supports at least one of the answer choices. It is apparent from the passage that an aura of excitement surrounds the family as the father and children prepare to leave for town. These clues indicate that the trips are not commonplace.

(A) is incorrect. Mr. Hilton clearly has a reason to go to town: to buy what he needs at needs at Topham's store. Thus, the trips there are not unnecessary excursions.

(B) is incorrect. Mrs. Hilton's numerous comments and advice indicate that she is concerned. If the trips were regular occurrences, her concern would have dissipated, if not disappeared altogether.

(C) is incorrect because the passage makes it clear that the trip to town is not an unplanned incident; to the contrary, Mrs. Hilton's actions make it obvious that there has been plenty of planning.

(D) is incorrect because there is nothing in the passage that indicates the trip involves any sad family event; the excitement of the father and the girls indicates otherwise.

21. **E is correct.** This is a cause-and-effect question that requires you to find the cause of a stated effect. Since the answer is not immediately obvious from the passage, you must synthesize evidence to identify the correct response. Evidence is offered in the passage to support this choice. In the last paragraph, you are told that the woman watched the wagon until it was lost to sight,

and then she felt lonelier than she had expected. This information is immediately followed by "She even stooped and patted the unresigned little dog." The word *even* is a clue word here, as it links the fact that the woman felt lonelier than expected with her act of patting the dog. Thus, these details from the passage support choice (E) as the correct answer.

(A) is incorrect. There is nothing in the passage to indicate that the mother "couldn't stand [the dog's] incessant barking."

(B) is incorrect. As with choice A, there is nothing in the passage to indicate that Mrs. Hilton wanted to untie the dog from the lilac bush, and this is not something that she does.

(C) is incorrect, since the dog is already tied to the lilac bush and can't run after the wagon.

(D) doesn't fit the context of the story, as the dog only barks and whimpers, which is not necessarily something that would be considered good.

22. **B is correct.** In this story, Sarah Orne Jewett gives many clues about her feelings toward her characters. Throughout the passage, the author is warmly affectionate toward her characters and cares about their feelings and interactions with each other. You never get the sense that Jewett is troubled by her characters' words or actions.

(A) is incorrect. The author renders her characters with great care and warmth; these qualities are the opposite of uncaring.

(C) is incorrect because the author never indicates she has a troubled view of any of the characters and nothing in the selection indicates that the characters are troubled about themselves.

(D) is incorrect because there no details in the passage that support the notion that the author or the characters are confused.

(E) is incorrect. Even though *benevolent* implies that the author has kindly feelings for her characters, it also implies that

the author has something to offer them, which is not the case.

23. **A is correct.** From the colloquial language that the characters use to express their thoughts and feelings, you know that they are not sophisticated city dwellers. Mrs. Hilton uses a nonstandard dialect throughout the story, and this fact supports the idea that she and the rest of the family are long-time residents of the country. Also, the author makes it clear that the trip to Topham goes from the country to the town.

(B) is incorrect. The dialogue in the story never mentions that the family members are strangers in the community. Indeed, the presence of the mother's cousin in town indicates the contrary.

(C) is incorrect. This answer choice can be eliminated because the children never speak in the story and there is nothing that supports the idea that they are different from their parents.

(D) is incorrect, since the mother is quite direct in expressing her concerns and advice. The text does not suggest this; it directly states this.

(E) is incorrect. In only one part of the mother's dialogue does she express the idea that the father is impractical: when she tells him not to waste money buying trinkets for her.

24. **(C) is correct.** The fact that the mother goes out of her way to find both opportunities to view the wagon as it leaves indicates her feelings toward the family. She loves them, knows she will miss them, and wants to keep them in her view as long as possible.

(A) is incorrect. The passage indicates that the mother's concern for her family's well-being is related only to the details of their comfort and behavior and not to anything awful that might happen to them.

(B) is incorrect. The passage makes it clear that the father and daughters are excited by the prospect of the trip, but that they also wish the mother was going with them.

(D) is incorrect. Nothing in the story suggests anything about bad weather and resulting difficulties the husband and girls might encounter.

(E) is incorrect. As with choice (D), nothing in the passage supports the idea that the mother is concerned about what might happen to her when she is alone.

Section 2

1. **D is correct.** *Probing* implies being "careful and thoughtful," and *elicit* means "to draw out." Both these words fit the structure and meaning of the sentence.

(A) is incorrect. *Pretentious* means "making an exaggerated show of importance," and *prolong* means "to make longer in time." An *astute* attorney is one who makes "penetrating observations" and is "sharp or keen." An astute attorney is unlikely to need to be pretentious or to draw out an inquiry with questions that "extend the truth."

(B) is incorrect. The word *loquacious* means "long-winded or excessively wordy," whereas *contradict* means "to assert the contrary of." Within the context of the sentence, "contradict the truth" does not make sense.

(C) is incorrect. *Vague* means "not clear or definite," and *mitigate* means "to make less severe or harsh." A sharp attorney would not ask vague questions and "make less severe" does not really fit the context of the sentence.

(E) is incorrect. *Spurious* means "not true or genuine," and *verify* means "to prove the truth." While an astute attorney would be interested in proving the truth, he or she would not use *spurious* questions to do so.

2. **B is correct.** *Juxtaposition* means "placed side by side," which would be the easiest way to see similarities and differences.

(A) is incorrect. *Disarray* means "disorder." Since the item says, "It is easy to see the difference between the two photo-

graphs," they are unlikely to be in disarray; instead, they would be placed side by side to make comparison easy.

(C) is incorrect. *Composition* means "structure, or manner of being composed." Comparing the two photographs would involve looking at the way their compositions are similar and different. However, the photographs would not be "placed in" composition.

(D) is incorrect. *Jeopardy* means "danger" and makes no sense in the context of the sentence.

(E) is incorrect. *Collaboration* means "working together cooperatively to complete a project." There is no clue in the paragraph that indicates that the two photographs were produced by collaboration.

3. **D is correct.** *Sardonically* means "in a mocking, cynical, or sneering manner." The beggar's words, in addition to his action, make it clear that he is mocking the person who gave him the nickel. This fits all the information provided in the sentence.

(A) is incorrect. *Kindly* means "with sympathetic or helpful kindness" and does not fit the context of the sentence, which says that the beggar "threw back the nickel."

(B) is incorrect. *Indifferently* means "without interest or concern, neither good nor bad in character"; therefore, this choice does not make sense in the context of the sentence. Clearly, the beggar threw the coin in anger.

(C) is incorrect. *Impulsively*, meaning "caused by emotional or involuntary impulses," seems a possible answer, since the beggar's action is certainly emotional. However, the beggar makes his feelings clear when he throws back the nickel. Thus, his action is intentional.

(E) is incorrect. *Inappropriately*, meaning "not proper," may seem to accurately apply to the beggar's action and words; however, the placement of the word in the sentence indicates that this adverb is being used to modify "smiled."

4. **C is correct.** Both *qualms* and *confidence* fit the context of the sentence in meaning and structure. This pair of words works perfectly with the clue word *although*.

(A) is incorrect. The words in this pair, *doubts* and *certainty,* seem as if they might be correct. However, the word choice is somewhat awkward, which indicates that this choice is wrong.

(B) is incorrect. *Foresight* and *misunderstandings* do not make sense, since a person is not likely to have "had *misunderstandings* about her ability to navigate safely through [the storm]."

(D) is incorrect. This word pair fits the structure of the sentence; however, these words do not work well with *although,* which requires opposing ideas.

(E) is incorrect. Although the words *doubts* and *evidence* are possible here, they do not fit the sentence nearly as well as the words in choice (C).

5. **B is correct.** The word *peccadilloes* means "minor offenses or indiscretions." This meaning of this word is in accord with the other sentence clues such as "stickler for promptness" and "Aaron's many," which suggest a somewhat demanding nature.

(A) is incorrect. The word *aversions* means "strong dislikes," and this seems an excessive response to being late.

(C) is incorrect because the word *skills* means "abilities" and is not compatible with the idea of Aaron "being a stickler for promptness."

(D) is incorrect because the word *weaknesses* refers to a "lack of strength or firmness," which has nothing to do with the idea of promptness.

(E) is incorrect because *assertions* means "positive statements or declarations," and promptness is neither a statement nor a declaration.

6. **A is correct.** The entire paragraph is focused on various ways dogs are trained to use their sense of smell to help government agencies at every level.

(B) is incorrect. Dogs' superior sense of smell is mentioned in the passage, but there is no detailed information given about the training dogs undergo.

(C) is incorrect. The superiority of dogs' sense of smell to that of humans is mentioned only at the beginning; the remainder of the passage discusses the use of dogs by government agencies.

(D) is incorrect. The cost of training dogs to use their sense of smell in stopping and solving crimes is never mentioned in the passage.

(E) is incorrect, since the use of dogs' vision and hearing are never mentioned in the passage.

7. **C is correct.** The entire paragraph focuses on examples of the successful use of dogs' sense of smell in their work for all levels of government. This choice succinctly describes the primary idea or purpose of the passage.

(A) is incorrect. Although the superiority of dogs' ability to smell is mentioned in the introductory sentences of the passage, this is not its main idea, since the remainder of the paragraph provides examples of successful canine units.

(B) is incorrect. The use of dogs to combat terrorism is mentioned in the passage, but the need for *more* dog units that do this is never mentioned.

(D) is incorrect. The passage does provide examples of the success of special canine units in detecting agricultural contraband, but this is not the main idea of the *entire* paragraph.

(E) is incorrect. The paragraph never specifically mentions using canine units to identify illegal immigrants.

8. **E is correct.** Notice that this question asks you to identify an inference that is *not* reasonable. This requires you to identify inferences that are reasonable and then exclude them. Only choice (E) is an unreasonable inference, since the passage never mentions that the next volcanic erup-

tion will take place in Iceland, only that Katla usually erupts sometime soon after Eyjafjallajokull.

(A) is incorrect. Although not explicitly stated in the passage, it is a truism that something will be damaged as the result of a volcanic eruption, if only a small part of the locale where the eruption occurs.

(B) is incorrect because it is a reasonable inference based on the information presented in the passage; therefore, it cannot be the correct answer.

(C) is incorrect because the passage makes clear that historically Iceland has experienced many eruptions during the past 500 years and that Katla has always erupted within a year of Eyjafjallajokull's eruption during the past 2,000 years.

(D) is incorrect. The passage does mention the fact that Katla has exploded every time Eyjafjallajokull has erupted during the past 2,000 years, but it also says that this is not a guarantee. Furthermore, even if you interpret the text as indicating that Katla will definitely erupt, you cannot infer that a volcano in another location may erupt before Katla.

9. **C is correct.** The passage makes clear that dust clouds caused by large volcanic eruptions can travel to very distant places and cause damage there.

(A) and (B) are incorrect because they conflict with the examples provided in the paragraph about the long-distance effects of volcanic eruptions.

(D) is incorrect. Nothing in the passage suggests that dust clouds from volcanic eruptions circle the globe forever.

(E) is incorrect. Nothing in the passage suggests that dust clouds leave the atmosphere within a few weeks.

10. **D is correct.** In the passage, Muir refers to the "scales" on a pine cone. Scales, or plates, are found on armor and some animals like armadillos. Only answer choice

(D), *husks*, comes closest to this meaning of *scales*.

(A), (B), and (C) are incorrect because they all suggest another word with the same spelling and pronunciation, which refers to an instrument for determining weight. Choice (C), *scrapings*, means "something that is scraped off." While this may seem reasonable at first, because a scale can be scraped off a pine cone, this meaning does not fit the context of this passage, in which the scales are open and thus still on the pine cone.

11. **E is correct.** The passage clearly refers to the average length of pine cones when Muir uses the phrase "favorably situated," meaning those pine cones that have enough water and sun to grow properly to their full capacity.

(A) is incorrect because it makes no sense for someone to approve the site for a tree growing in the wild.

(B) is incorrect because it seems too mild and vague compared to the specificity of choice (E).

(C) is incorrect because the trees are clearly not newly planted, as Muir specifically discusses the height, appearance, and age of the trees and pine cones he is observing.

(D) is incorrect because Muir mentions that full-grown cones are smaller at 2,500 feet above sea level, which does not indicate that this is a more favorably situated location than others.

12. **B is correct.** Occasionally, an unusual meaning of a word will appear in a passage. In this text, the meaning of *port*—"the manner in which something bears itself"—may be unfamiliar. You can usually still figure out these unfamiliar meanings by using the context of the passage. In this case, the phrase "In *habit* and *general* port it looks somewhat like a palm" offers the clues you need.

(A) is incorrect. Although *port* can refer to "a place where ships dock," this meaning of the word does not make sense within the context of this sentence.

(C) is incorrect. *Port* can mean "placement to the left," but this is not the meaning of the word *port* as it is used in the context of this passage.

(D) is incorrect. "An opening for intake" is a legitimate meaning of *port,* but it does not fit the context of the passage.

(E) is incorrect because, although *port* can refer to the way a military rifle is carried, this meaning does not it does not fit the context of the passage.

13. **E is correct.** Muir makes it clear that he finds the pine more majestic than the palm when he refers to "this noble tree" and later says, ". . . no palm that I have seen yet displays such *majesty* of form and behavior." Likewise, Muir assigns the pine the human characteristics "silent and thoughtful" and "wide-awake." Both (B) and (C) are true and included in choice (E), so this is the correct answer.

(A) is incorrect, since Muir clearly states that the pine is more majestic than the palm.

(B) is incorrect because, although the statement is true, it is not the only true statement.

(C) is incorrect because, although the statement is true, it is not the only true statement.

(D) is incorrect because (A) is incorrect and (D) includes (A).

14. **A is correct.** The structure that is mentioned is perfectly round and without a limb; it is also tall, about 100 feet. The trunk is the only part of the tree that satisfies this description.

(B),(C), (D), and (E) are incorrect. *Top, tree, leaf,* and *branch* do not match all the clues given in the description of the bole.

15. **A is correct.** In lines 24–28, Muir contrasts young trees that are "very straight and regular in form" with older trees that have acquired "individuality, so that no two are alike in their prime or old age," suggesting the irregularity of older trees.

(B) is incorrect. While sugar pine trees grow as tall as 250 to 300 feet (lines 30–33), nowhere in the passage does Muir suggest that the pines "dwarf" the surrounding trees.

(C) is incorrect because nothing in the passage says that the tree reaches its maximum height before it shows individuality.

(D) is incorrect. The passage only describes that the branches are "down-curving." Nothing in the passage mentions that the tree itself bends due to age.

(E) is incorrect. The passage describes the coloration of the pines, but does not mention that there is any change in color.

16. **B is correct.** In lines 12–14, Muir states, "This noble tree is an inexhaustible study and source of pleasure. I never weary of gazing at its grand tassel cones . . ." The words "inexhaustible" and "never weary" clearly indicate that Muir would never tire of studying the sugar pine.

(A) and (C) are incorrect because they contradict what Muir says in lines 12–14.

(D) is incorrect. Muir is quite specific in his contrasting descriptions of the sugar pine and the silver pine.

(E) is incorrect. The passage indicates that Muir was making sketches of the trees and their pine cones, but it offers nothing to indicate that Muir was a fine artist.

17. **A is correct.** Muir finds the sugar pine majestic; therefore, it is something he regards with reverence, as citizens might regard the president of their country.

(B) is incorrect. Although Muir finds the sugar pine something to respect, he gives no indication that he finds it *daunting,* which means "something that overcomes him with fear."

(C) is incorrect. This passage does not suggest that Muir finds anything about the sugar pine domineering or dictatorial, which is the meaning of *imperious*.

(D) is incorrect. The word *contrite* means "filled with remorse or guilt" and makes no sense within the context of the passage.

(E) is incorrect. *Charitable* means "generous or kindly," which is meaningless within the context of this passage.

18. **D is correct.** All the details of the passage offer descriptive documentation of the sugar pines—where they grow, their measurements, and their coloration.

(A) is incorrect. Muir speaks of the individuality of the older sugar pines, thereby indicating that all sugar pines are not alike.

(B) is incorrect. Although Muir's conservation efforts no doubt brought tourists to the Sierras, nothing in the passage mentions this or suggests that this was his purpose in writing it.

(C) is incorrect. As a leading exponent of conservation, Muir did influence others to enter the field of conservation; however, nothing in the passage suggests that this had anything to do with his purpose in writing it.

(E) is incorrect. The passage does mention Muir's drawings of sugar pines. However, the drawings are only one part of Muir's attempt to document the characteristics of sugar pines. In addition, Muir regrets that he can't "draw every needle."

19. **D is correct.** If you understand the main idea expressed in the first paragraph of the passage, you can answer this interpretation question at once, without even looking at the quoted sentence. In the passage, Emerson talks about the connection between creative writers and creative readers. He says there is awe mixed with surprise "when this poet, who lived in some past world, two or three hundred years ago, says that which lies close to my own soul, that which I also had well-nigh thought and said."

(A) is incorrect because Emerson is not talking about rereading his own work.

(B) is incorrect because Emerson is not discussing nature writing.

(C) is incorrect. Emerson did not live in the same era as the writers he mentions; one of his points is that modern readers can connect with writers of a different era.

(E) is incorrect. Nothing in the passage suggests that Emerson cannot remember his own writing.

20. **D is correct.** A good strategy for answering this type of vocabulary-in-context question is to plug the meanings into the sentence in which the vocabulary word appears. This often leads you to find clues in the sentence that make it easy to rule out possible answer choices. In this case, *abstraction* appears in the part of the sentence that says: ". . . which is in great part caused by the abstraction of all *time* from their verses." Thus, *abstraction* is paired with the preposition *from*. The only answer choice that makes sense with *from* is *elimination*, as in the *elimination* of something *from*, something else.

(A), (B), (C), and (E) are incorrect. None of these choices fits the structure of the sentence when the word is paired with the preposition *from*.

21. **A is correct.** This question asks you to relate an image of insects to the main idea of the passage. You do not really need to go back to the passage to answer this question. Since choice (A) is the only one that makes reference to both readers and writers, it is the correct answer.

(B) and (C) are incorrect. The meanings of these choices do not support the image the author projects, as well as departing too far from the tone of the selection, which is elevated and positive. There is nothing "grubby" here and certainly nothing so negative as "soulless parents toiling blindly for unknown children."

(D) is incorrect. This choice may seem plausible, but only if you read the sentence in isolation and not in the context of the entire selection.

(E) is incorrect. The idea expressed in this choice is never alluded to in the selected passage.

22. **B is correct.** Questions that ask you to choose a title for the passage are evaluation questions. These questions test your ability to sum up, as exactly as possible, the main idea or subject of the selection. To answer these questions correctly, you must ignore titles that focus on secondary ideas and are too specific, as well as titles that are too general.

(A),(C), (D), and (E) are incorrect. You need only know that the passage is about books and reading, and then you can eliminate any title that does not refer to either, such as choices (D) and (E). Creative writing is mentioned only as it relates to creative reading. Emerson says, "There is then creative reading as well as creative writing." The use of the word "then" suggests that the connection between creative writing and creative reading is based on Emerson's comparison of these two activities, which eliminates choice (A). (C) can be eliminated, since Emerson is not telling you that some books are better than others.

23. **C is correct.** This vocabulary-in-context question requires some care in order to identify the correct answer. In the passage, Emerson writes, "Of course, there is a portion of reading quite indispensable to a wise man. History and exact science he must learn by laborious reading." In other words, a reader must expend significant effort when reading history and science. Therefore, *laborious* in this context means "requiring great effort."

(A) is incorrect. Nothing in the paragraph supports the idea that Emerson finds anything boring to read.

(B) is incorrect. Emerson indicates that all reading, even when it requires hard work, is interesting; therefore, reading is never ungratifying.

(D) is incorrect. Emerson indicates that all reading is satisfying, but he never suggests through his examples that all reading is amusing.

(E) is incorrect. Nothing in the passage mentions that any type of reading is obligatory, which is the meaning of *mandatory*.

24. **E is correct.** Only choice (E) makes sense within the context of the selection. Emerson clearly states that colleges can only achieve their goals if they teach basics and can "highly serve us when they aim not to drill, but to create . . . and set the hearts of their youth on flame."

(A) is incorrect because in this passage *office* refers to "a position of duty or authority," not to "a space where business is conducted."

(B) is incorrect. Nowhere in the passage does Emerson suggest that it is necessary to go to college to be a good reader.

(C) is incorrect. This choice refers to Euclid's famous book *Elements of Geometry*. SAT reading comprehension questions never require test takers to use information not available in the given reading passage, and the passage makes no reference to any study of geometry.

(D) is incorrect. It is true that colleges have many different departments of learning; however, choice (D) is incorrect because this idea is never mentioned in the passage.

Section 3

1. **C is correct.** *Vicariously* means "felt or enjoyed through imagined participation in the experience of others."

(A) is incorrect. To experience it *directly*, you would have to be present when it happened.

(B) is incorrect. To experience it *reminiscently* would require you to have been present at that time in order to think back on it.

(D) is incorrect. To experience something *infinitely* would require you to experience it forever, which is impossible, since no time or person exists forever.

(E) is incorrect. *Audibly* means "capable of being heard." Again, this would require you to have been there at the time the events occurred.

2. **B is correct.** The words in this choice make sense and fit the context of the sentence. *Rescind* means "to revoke or repeal." Thus, the second word would need to mean the opposite of *advance*, which is indeed the meaning of *retreat*.

(A) is incorrect, since the words do not quite fit the context of the sentence. If the general *reinforced* his order, he would want the troops to continue to advance. Notice that the sentence says "rather than advance"; thus, you are looking for a word that stands in opposition to *advance*. Since *march* is not very different from *advance*, (A) cannot be correct.

(C) is incorrect because, like choice (A), this choice only repeats the sense of the general's original order; it does not indicate that the general did something otherwise.

(D) is incorrect. *Countermanded* carries the same meaning as *rescinded*. However, the second word of the pair, *encircle*, does not imply the opposite of *advance*.

(E) is incorrect. *Confirmed* and *attack* do not connote anything that is contradictory to *advance*.

3. **E is correct.** Since the second part of the sentence is negative and says that "you will not be asked to any other party they give," you are looking for a word that would cause the negative result. *Disrespectfully* means "lacking courtesy." If this is how you acted toward other guests, it definitely would influence whether you should be invited to future parties.

(A) is incorrect. *Tranquilly* means "peacefully or calmly" and thus does not make sense with the rest of the sentence.

(B) is incorrect. *Deferentially* means "with respect." If you treat the other guests with respect, you would not expect this to keep you from being invited back.

(C) is incorrect. *Obligingly* means "amiably" or "in a friendly manner," which would not be likely to keep you from being asked to another party they give.

(D) is incorrect. If you acted *contritely*, it means you would have been remorseful or had a sense of guilt before you did anything to cause you not to be invited to another party.

4. **D is correct.** *Heterogeneous* means a group whose members are diverse; different ethnic groups are thus by definition heterogeneous.

(A) is incorrect. *Diverse* makes sense, since the second part of the sentence makes reference to "thirty different . . . groups." However, the second word of the pair, *related*, does not fit the structure of the sentence. It doesn't make sense to say "thirty different *related* groups."

(B) is incorrect. The words *similar* and *scholarly* are incompatible here, since *scholarly* would be preceded by the word *different*, which contradicts the initial premise of the sentence.

(C) is incorrect. A group that is *homogeneous* has members who are similar. It's contradictory to call a freshman class homogeneous when it consists of thirty *different* language groups.

(E) is incorrect. *Intelligent* fits the structural context of the sentence. However, the second clause is premised on the first, and the diversity of 30 different high school groups has nothing to do with intelligence.

5. **E is correct.** Both words in choice (E) fit the context of the sentence. *Dismayed* means "disheartened or disillusioned," a feeling that Eduardo would likely experience if he was thought to be *unsuitable* for the job.

(A) is incorrect. It is unlikely that Eduardo would be thrilled that someone said he was unqualified for the job he had just interviewed for.

(B) is incorrect. Although Eduardo might be surprised that he had been *hired* for the job, it doesn't make sense to say that he was *confused* by the decision.

(C) is incorrect. To be called *overqualified* is not a reason to feel *embarrassed.*

(D) is incorrect. Eduardo has not yet been hired; he has just been interviewed. Therefore, to say that he was *underpaid* for the job does not make sense based on the logical order of events.

6. **A is correct.** *Apathetic* means "indifferent to or unconcerned with." Since Matthew showed no real emotion about the loss of one of the biggest clients, his behavior can be accurately described as apathetic.

(B) is incorrect. *Conciliatory* means "flexible or compromising." There is nothing within the context of the sentence to suggest that there was anything to compromise about with the partner or the client.

(C) is incorrect. *Knowledgeable* does not fit the context of the sentence, since being knowledgeable really has nothing to do with Matthew's emotional state.

(D) is incorrect because there is no reason why Matthew would be *appreciative* about losing a big client.

(E) is incorrect. *Vigilant* means "keenly watchful to detect a danger." While losing a big client might be considered dangerous, there is no indication that Matthew was "keenly watching" for the loss of the client.

7. **E is correct.** To answer this question, you must use context clues provided by the paragraph. The phrase "stock in this line," followed by the statement that Stowe had seven children, indicates that she is referring to the number of children in her family.

(A) is incorrect. The phrase "shares of stock" refers to ownership shares in a corporation available to the public for purchase. This meaning of *stock* has nothing to do with the meaning of the word as it is used in the opening sentence of this passage.

(B) is incorrect. Although the word *stock* can refer to animals, this sense of the

word also has nothing to do with the rest of this passage.

(C) is incorrect because Stowe never mentions relatives other than her children in the letter.

(D) is incorrect. Stowe mentions the death of one of her sons, but this does not qualify as "stock in this line," as it is too specific.

8. **A is correct.** Her son's death caused Stowe to experience the pain of being separated from her child, which helped her understand what a slave mother would feel at losing a child.

(B) is incorrect. "The importance of having many children" may seem like a good answer, but the selection is about the loss of a child, not about having many children, which is mentioned only in passing.

(C) is incorrect. The main reason Stowe wrote her letter was to explain the motivation for writing *Uncle Tom's Cabin.* The novel does describe the horrors of slavery, but Stowe's letter concerns the background of the book, not its contents.

(D) is incorrect. Stowe mentions that she loved her dead son most of all, which might imply that "the child lost becomes the most important one." However, lines 5–8 specifically state that Stowe learned from this experience "what a poor slave mother may feel when her child is torn away from her."

(E) is incorrect because it does not fit the context of the passage nor the time period in which it was written.

9. **E is correct.** In lines 5–8, Stowe clearly indicates that she feels an affinity with slave mothers because of the loss of her own son.

(A) and (B) are incorrect. Although Stowe mentions that she is the mother of a large family and that she has lost a son to death, neither choice indicates what she shares with others.

(C) is incorrect. The selection makes no mention of Stowe's husband or any other father.

(D) is incorrect. The author mentions that she is the mother of twins, but this bears no relation to what she has in common with others.

10. **D is correct.** The phrase "crushing of my own heart" is close in meaning to "an almost unbearable heartache." Other details in the selection also indicate the level of pain Stowe suffered—for example, "the depths of sorrow which seemed to me immeasurable."

(A) is incorrect. A broken rib is too literal an interpretation of the phrase "crushing of my own heart."

(B) is incorrect, The passage makes no reference to a heart attack.

(C) is incorrect. Stowe remains a loving mother to her other children and a sympathetic compatriot of those who endured slavery.

(E) is incorrect. Stowe's love did not end with the death of her son, and she never describes losing her faith in God; to the contrary, she prays "to God that such anguish might not be suffered in vain."

11. **B is correct.** In paragraph 2, Stowe makes it clear that her new book will contain "all the facts and documents upon which that story was founded." In addition, the introduction to the passage makes it clear that Stowe's purpose is to provide background for her writing the book.

(A) is incorrect. Nothing in the passage, either in content or tone, indicates that Stowe's purpose is to gain readership for *Uncle Tom's Cabin*.

(C) is incorrect because there is no indication in the selection that her purpose is to *encourage* others experiencing pain. She saw her pain in the pain and suffering of slave mothers losing their children.

(D) is incorrect. While it is true that Stowe makes readers aware of her own pain, that is not the purpose of the selection. Instead, her intention is to let people

know about the suffering of others, especially slave mothers, caused by the loss of their children.

(E) is incorrect. There is nothing in the passage that supports the idea that Stowe is writing for a selfish reason such as gaining notoriety for her family.

12. **A is correct.** Paragraph 3 deals only with the details indicating that Stowe is writing another book that will present her factual research for *Uncle Tom's Cabin* along with other documents that support the veracity of details in the novel.

(B) is incorrect because it is self-evident that Stowe is industrious if she is busy writing another book.

(C) is incorrect. Paragraph 3 does support the idea that Stowe's new book has been well researched and well documented. However, the goal of the new book is to prove that the details of *Uncle Tom's Cabin* are based on accurate testimony.

(D) is incorrect. It is debatable at what point a writer becomes prolific. The passage mentions only two books—certainly not a prolific output.

(E) is incorrect. Although Stowe is committed to the antislavery cause, we do not know for certain that she is still committed to *all* her writing projects.

13. **C is correct.** At the point Stowe uses the phrase "depth of the abyss," (line 35), she is no longer talking about her own loss of a son but about the horrible institution of slavery. She clearly references slavery in the text before and after this phrase.

(A) is incorrect, as noted above, because she is not referring to her personal loss.

(B) is incorrect. Stowe does not discuss people who support slavery, and she makes only a passing reference to those "living South."

(D) and (E) are incorrect. Although Stowe discusses the "law records of courts and judiciary proceedings" as well as "reports of trial, legal documents, and testimony of people," she does not make reference to the *incompetence* of judges and lawyers.

14. **E is correct.** In the first sentence of the passage, Douglass says, "It is impossible for me to describe my feelings as the time of my contemplated start grew near." He then goes on to mention other failed attempts to escape from slavery.

(A) is incorrect. "First day as a slave" is contradicted by all the details in the passage.

(B) is incorrect. This choice seems as if it might be the correct answer, however, the first sentence makes it perfectly clear that Douglass is referring to his *upcoming* escape.

(C) is incorrect. The change in Douglass's status as a slave comes after his "contemplated start."

(D) is incorrect. The passage never mentions any job that Douglass may have worked at.

15. **D is correct.** All the answer choices provided are possible reasons why Douglass might be hesitant to leave Baltimore. However, the directions tell you to select the *best* answer. In lines 56–60, Douglass says, "The thought of leaving my friends was decidedly the most painful thought with which I had to contend. The love of them was my tender point, and shook my decision more than all things else."

(A), (B), (C), and (E) are incorrect because they are either mentioned only briefly or not at all.

16. **A is correct.** In lines 60–62, Douglass states, "Besides the pain of separation the dread and apprehension of a failure exceeded what I had experienced at my first attempt." In this statement, Douglass indicates that he had failed to escape before and a second failure "would seal my fate as a slave forever."

(B), (C), (D), and (E) are incorrect. Although Douglass may have been fearful of the occurrence of each of these, they are not mentioned in the referenced lines.

17. **D is correct.** Both Stowe and Douglass wrote about their struggles with the pain they suffered. However, the question asks you to identify a pain that Mrs. Stowe suffered that Douglass did not. Stowe's letter specifically states that she lost a son, and the passage by Douglass contains no reference to children or death.

(A) is incorrect. Neither author discusses a struggle to write.

(B) is incorrect. Although the statement is true, it is not specific enough to be the correct answer. Stowe's letter specifically states that she lost a son.

(C) is incorrect. The years of research Stowe completed might have been burdensome, but she implies that she sees the writing of her second book as key to proving the descriptions and events that appear in her novel.

(E) is incorrect. Although it may be true, Stowe never mentions suffering from the *uncertainty* of getting either of her books published.

18. **C is correct.** Although Stowe wrote about the horrors of slavery, she never experienced slavery as Douglass did.

(A) and (B) are incorrect. Neither passage mentions the author's mother or father.

(D) is incorrect. Neither passage makes reference to gaining friends; only Douglass mentions the loss of friends.

(E) is incorrect. Stowe discusses the loss of family, but Douglass does not.

19. **B is correct.** Both Stowe and Douglass discuss the wretchedness of slavery.

(A) is incorrect. Stowe doesn't really discuss life in the South except to make a passing remark. Douglass clearly discusses his life as a slave, but he was a slave in the border state of Maryland, not a southern state.

(C) is incorrect because, although Stowe mentions her pain in writing, Douglass does not.

(D) is incorrect. Stowe discusses her loss of a child, but Douglass never does.

(E) is incorrect. Douglass never mentions any attempt to persuade others to support the idea that slavery was wrong.

GLOSSARY

BUILD YOUR SAT VOCABULARY

The following is a list of vocabulary words that have appeared in reading comprehension passages on recent versions of the SAT I. Since reading comprehension is such an important part of the test, studying this list can help you get a higher score.

DEVELOP A STUDY PLAN

Learning new vocabulary words doesn't have to be difficult as long as you develop a good study plan. Often just writing down a word and its definition will help you retain the meaning. You may want to use the word list to create flash cards that you can take with you anywhere to study when you have some free time. Using something like 3″ × 5″ cards, write an unfamiliar word on one side and its definition on the other. Then review the words in groups of 20. Review a new group every day. Review during your spare time. Review before you go to sleep at night. Review with your parents. Review with your friends. Review with a study group. Review in whatever way is most convenient and efficient for you. Stay focused. Stay on track. And remember that knowing these words will help you long after you have taken the SAT I!

A

abase
  v to degrade or lower in position

aberrant
  adj markedly different from an accepted norm

aberration
  n deviation from a right, customary, or prescribed course

abduction
  n the carrying away of someone illegally

abet
  v to aid, promote, or encourage the commission of (an offense)

abeyance
  n a state of suspension or temporary inaction

abjure
  v to recant, renounce, repudiate under oath

ablution
  n a washing or cleansing, especially of the body

abomination
  n a hateful or detestable action

abrogate
  v to abolish, repeal

abscond
  v to depart suddenly and secretly, as for the purpose of escaping arrest

abstemious
  adj characterized by self-denial or abstinence, as in the use of drink or food

abstruse
  adj dealing with matters difficult to be understood

abut
  v to touch at the end or boundary line

accede
  v to agree

acquiesce
  v to comply; submit

acrid
  adj harshly pungent or bitter

acrimony
  n sharp, bitter speech

acumen
 n quickness of intellectual insight, or discernment; keenness of discrimination

adage
 n an old saying

adamant
 n any substance of exceeding hardness or impenetrability

addendum
 n something added

admonition
 n gentle reproof

adumbrate
 v to represent beforehand in outline or by emblem

affable
 adj easy to approach

aggrandize
 v to make appear greater; to exalt

aggravate
 v to make heavier, worse, or more burdensome

aggregate
 adj total

agile
 adj able to move or act quickly, physically, or mentally

agog
 adj in eager desire

alacrity
 n cheerful willingness

alcove
 n a covered recess connected with or at the side of a larger room

alleviate
 v to make less burdensome or less hard to bear

aloof
 adj not in sympathy with or desiring to associate with others

altercate
 v to argue angrily

amalgamate
 v to mix or blend together in a homogeneous body

ambidextrous
 adj having the ability of using both hands with equal skill or ease

ambiguous
 adj having a double meaning

ambivalent
 adj characterized by a mixture of opposite feelings or attitudes

ameliorate
 v to relieve, as from pain or hardship

anathema
 n anything forbidden, as by social usage

animadversion
 n the utterance of criticism or censure

animosity
 n hatred

antediluvian
 adj of or pertaining to the times, things, events before the great flood in the days of Noah; hence antiquated or old fashioned

antidote
 n anything that will counteract or remove the effects of poison, disease, or the like

aplomb
 n confidence; coolness

apocryphal
 adj of doubtful authority or authenticity

apogee
 n the climax

apostate
 adj false
 n one who denies his faith

apotheosis
 n deification

apparition
 n ghost

appease
 v to soothe by quieting anger or indignation

apposite
 adj appropriate

apprise
 v to give notice to; to inform

approbation
 n sanction

appropriating
v taking possession of or using

aqueous
adj containing water

arbitrary
adj based on preference, bias, or convenience rather than on reason or fact

arboreal
adj of or pertaining to a tree or trees

ardor
n intensity of passion or affection

argot
n a specialized vocabulary peculiar to a particular group

arrant
adj notoriously bad

ascent
n rising; advancement

ascetic
adj given to severe self-denial and practicing excessive abstinence and devotion

ascribe
v to assign as a quality or attribute

asperity
n harshness or roughness of temper

aspire
v to desire something not yet attained

assailant
n one who attacks another

assiduous
adj unceasing, persistent

assuage
v to cause to be less harsh, violent, or severe, as excitement, appetite, pain, or disease

astringent
adj harsh in disposition or character

astute
adj keen in discernment

atonement
n amends, reparation, or expiation made from wrong or injury

attainable
adj reachable

audacious
adj fearless

augury
n omen

auspicious
adj favorable omen

austere
adj severely simple, unadorned

autocrat
n anyone who claims or wields unrestricted or undisputed authority or influence

auxiliary
n one who or that which aids or helps, especially when regarded as subsidiary or accessory

avarice
n passion for getting and keeping riches

aver
v to avouch, justify, or prove

aversion
n a mental condition of fixed opposition to or dislike of some particular thing

avow
v to declare openly

azure
adj blue, sky-like color

B

bailiff
n an officer of the court

baleful
adj malignant

banal
adj commonplace

banished
v driven away, banned, or expelled

bask
v to make warm by genial heat

beatify
v to make supremely happy

bedaub
v to smear over, as with something oily or sticky

beguiling
adj misleading by pleasant or alluring methods

bellicose
adj warlike

belligerent
adj manifesting a warlike spirit

benefactor
n a doer of kindly and charitable acts

benevolence
n any act of kindness or well-doing

benign
adj good and kind of heart

berate
v to scold severely

bewilder
v to confuse the perceptions or judgment of

blandishment
n flattery intended to persuade

blatant
adj noisily or offensively loud or clamorous

blithe
adj joyous

boisterous
adj with unchecked merriment or animal spirits

bolster
v to support, as something wrong

bombast
n inflated or extravagant language, especially on unimportant subjects

boorish
adj rude

breach
n the violation of official duty, lawful right, or a legal obligation

brevity
n briefness; terseness

brittle
adj fragile

broach
v to mention, for the first time

bumptious
adj full of offensive and aggressive self-conceit

buoyant
adj having the power or tendency to float or keep afloat

burnish
v to make brilliant or shining

buttress
n a support or prop

C

cabal
n a number of persons secretly united for effecting by intrigue some private purpose

cacophony
n a disagreeable, harsh, or discordant sound or combination of sounds or tones

cadence
n rhythmical flow or movement

cajole
v to impose on or dupe by flattering speech

callow
adj without experience of the world

calumny
n a false statement made maliciously to injure another's reputation

camaraderie
n good will and rapport among friends

candid
adj straightforward

cant
v to talk in a singsong, preaching tone with affected solemnity

capacious
adj roomy

capitulate
v to surrender or stipulate terms

captious
adj hypercritical

castigate
v to punish

cataract
n opacity of the lens of the eye resulting in complete or partial blindness, or large waterfall over a precipice

caustic
adj sarcastic and severe

censure
v to criticize severely; also, an expression of disapproval

centurion
n a captain of a company of one hundred infantry in the ancient Roman army

chagrin
  n keen vexation, annoyance, or mortification, as at one's failures or errors

chary
  adj careful; wary; cautious

chastised
  v punished; severely criticized

chicanery
  n the use of trickery to deceive

circumlocution
  n indirect or roundabout expression

clandestine
  adj kept or done in secret

coagulated
  v congealed or turned into a soft or semi-solid mass

coalesced
  v came together to form a whole; united

coddle
  v to treat as a baby or an invalid

coerce
  v to force

coeval
  adj existing during the same period of time; also, a contemporary

cogent
  adj appealing strongly to the reason or conscience

cogitate
  v consider carefully and deeply; ponder

cognizant
  adj taking notice

colloquial
  adj pertaining or peculiar to common speech as distinguished from literary

collusion
  n a secret agreement for a wrongful purpose

comestible
  adj fit to be eaten

commemorate
  v to serve as a remembrance of

compelled
  v forced

complaisance
  n politeness

complement
  v to make complete

comply
  v to act in accordance with someone's rules; to follow or abide by

comport
  v to conduct or behave (oneself)

compunction
  n remorseful feeling

comprehensive
  adj including all or everything

conceded
  v acknowledged reluctantly

conceit
  n self-flattering opinion

conciliatory
  adj tending to reconcile

concord
  n harmony

concur
  v to agree

condense
  v to abridge

conflagration
  n a great fire, as of many buildings, a forest, or the like

confluence
  n the place where streams or rivers meet

congeal
  v to coagulate

conjoin
  v to unite

connoisseur
  n a critical judge of art, especially one with thorough knowledge and sound judgment of art

console
  v to comfort

conspicuous
  adj clearly visible

consternation
  n panic

constrict
  v to bind

consummate
  v to bring to completion

contiguous
adj touching or joining at the edge or boundary

contrite
adj broken in spirit because of a sense of sin

controversial
adj of, producing, or marked by controversy or dispute

contumacious
adj rebellious

copious
adj plentiful

cornucopia
n the horn of plenty, symbolizing peace and prosperity

corporeal
adj of a material nature; physical

correlate
v to put in some relation of connection or correspondence

corroboration
n confirmation

counterfeit
adj made to resemble something else

countervail
v to offset

covert
adj concealed, especially for an evil purpose

cower
v to crouch down tremblingly, as through fear or shame

crass
adj coarse or thick in nature or structure, as opposed to thin or fine

credulous
adj easily deceived

cupidity
n avarice

cursory
adj rapid and superficial

curtail
v to cut off or cut short

cynicism
n contempt for others' opinions or beliefs

cynosure
n that to which general interest or attention is directed

D

dauntless
adj fearless

dearth
n scarcity, as of something customary, essential, or desirable

decapitate
v to behead

decimate
v to destroy a large portion; to destroy a tenth of a population by disease or warfare

defer
v to delay or put off to some other time

deft
adj skillful and adroit

deign
v to deem worthy of notice or account

deleterious
adj hurtful, morally or physically

delineate
v to represent by sketch or diagram

deluge
v to overwhelm with a flood of water

demagogue
n an unprincipled politician

demolish
v to completely destroy, annihilate

denizen
n inhabitant

denouement
n that part of a play or story in which the mystery is cleared up

deplete
v to reduce or lessen, as by use, exhaustion, or waste

deposition
n testimony legally taken on interrogatories and reduced to writing, for use as evidence in court

deprave
v to render bad, especially morally bad

deprecate
v to express disapproval or regret for, with hope for the opposite

deride
v to ridicule

derision
  n ridicule

derivative
  adj coming or acquired from some origin

descry
  v to discern

desiccant
  n any remedy which, when applied externally, dries up or absorbs moisture, as that of wounds

designate
  v to select or appoint by authority

desuetude
  n a state of disuse or inactivity

desultory
  adj not connected with what precedes

deter
  v to frighten away

detriment
  n something causing damage or loss

devoured
  v ate greedily or took in eagerly

dexterity
  n readiness, precision, efficiency, and ease in any physical activity or in any mechanical work

diaphanous
  adj transparent

diatribe
  n a bitter or malicious criticism

didactic
  adj pertaining to teaching

diffidence
  n self-distrust

diffident
  adj affected or possessed with self-distrust

dilapidated
  adj broken-down; ramshackle

dilate
  v to enlarge in all directions

dilatory
  adj tending to cause delay

disallow
  v to withhold permission or sanction

discernible
  adj perceptible by the senses or intellect

discomfit
  v to put to confusion

disconcert
  v to disturb the composure of

disconsolate
  adj hopelessly sad; also, saddening; cheerless

discountenance
  v to look upon with disfavor

discredit
  v to injure the reputation of

discreet
  adj judicious

discrete
  adj separate from others; distinct

disheveled
  adj disordered, disorderly, untidy

disparage
  v to belittle or to speak of in a disrespectful way

dissect
  v to cut apart

dissemble
  v to hide by pretending something different

disseminate
  v to sow or scatter abroad, as seed is sown

dissent
  n disagreement

dissolution
  n a breaking up of a union of persons

distraught
  adj bewildered

divert
  v to turn away from a steady course of action

divulge
  v to tell or make known, as something previously private or secret

dogmatic
  adj making statements without argument or evidence

dormant
  adj being in a state of or resembling sleep

dubious
  adj doubtful

duplicity
  n double-dealing

dwindle
  v to diminish or become less

E

earnest
adj sincere in spirit

earthenware
n anything made of clay and baked in a kiln or dried in the sun

ebullient
adj showing enthusiasm or exhilaration of feeling

eccentric
adj peculiar

edacious
adj given to eating

edible
adj suitable to be eaten

edify
v to strengthen, especially one's beliefs

educe
v to draw out

effervescent
adj bubbly

effete
adj exhausted, as having performed its functions; nonvirile

efficacy
n the power to produce an intended effect as shown in the production of it

effrontery
n unblushing impudence

effulgence
n splendor

egregious
adj extremely and conspicuously bad, flagrant

egress
n any place of exit

elegy
n a lyric poem lamenting the dead

elicit
v to educe or extract gradually or without violence

elucidate
v to bring out more clearly the facts concerning

emaciate
v to waste away in flesh

emancipate
v to set free from bondage

embellish
v to make beautiful or elegant by adding attractive or ornamental features

embezzle
v to misappropriate secretly and criminally

emblazon
v to set forth publicly or in glowing terms

eminent
adj outstanding

emulate
v to strive to equal or excel, especially by imitating

encomium
n a formal or discriminating expression of praise

encumbrance
n a burdensome and troublesome load

endemic
adj peculiar to some specified country or people

enervate
v to render ineffective or inoperative

engender
v to produce

engrave
v to cut or carve in or upon some surface

engross
v to occupy completely

enigma
n a riddle

enmity
n hatred

ensconced
v settled securely or comfortably

ensnare
v to trap

entangle
v to involve in difficulties, confusion, or complications

enticing
adj highly attractive or alluring

entreat
v to ask for or request earnestly

epicurean
adj indulging, ministering, or pertaining to daintiness of appetite

epithet
 n word used adjectivally to describe some quality or attribute of its objects, as in "Father Aeneas"

epitome
 n a simplified representation

equable
 adj equal and uniform; also, serene

equanimity
 n evenness of mind or temper or calmness, composure

equilibrium
 n a state of balance

equivalent
 adj equal to something else

equivocal
 adj ambiguous

equivocate
 v to use words of double meaning

eradicate
 v to destroy thoroughly

errant
 adj roving or wandering, as in search of adventure or opportunity for gallant deeds

erratic
 adj irregular

erroneous
 adj incorrect

erudite
 adj very learned

eschew
 v to keep clear of

espy
 v to keep close watch; to catch sight of, discern

estuary
 n wide lower part of a river

eulogy
 n a spoken or written laudation of a person's life or character

euphemism
 n a less offensive figure of speech

euphonious
 adj characterized by agreeableness of sound

evade
 v to avoid

evanescent
 adj fleeting

evince
 v to make manifest or evident

evoke
 v to call or summon forth

exacerbate
 v to make more sharp, severe, or virulent

excoriating
 adj censuring strongly; denouncing harshly

exculpate
 v to relieve of blame

exhaustive
 adj thorough and complete in execution

exigency
 n a critical period or condition

exonerated
 v freed from all blame

exorbitant
 adj going beyond usual and proper limits

expatiate
 v to speak or write at some length

expedient
 adj contributing to personal advantage

expiate
 v to make satisfaction or amends for

explicate
 v to clear from involvement

expostulate
 v to discuss

expropriate
 v to deprive of possession; also, to transfer (another's property) to oneself

expurgate
 v to remove erroneous or objectionable material

extant
 adj still existing and known

extempore
 adj without studied or special preparation

extenuate
 v to diminish the gravity or importance of

extinct
 adj being no longer in existence

extinguish
 v to render extinct

extirpate
 v to root out; to eradicate

extol
v to praise in the highest terms

extort
v to obtain by violence, threats, compulsion, or the subjection of another to some necessity

extraneous
adj having no essential relation to a subject

extricate
v to disengage or release from an entanglement or difficulty

exuberant
adj characterized by a rich supply or abundance

F

fabricate
v to invent falsely, lie

facetious
adj amusing

facile
adj not difficult to do

facilitate
v to make easier

factious
adj divisive or promoting dissension

fallacious
adj illogical

fallible
adj capable of making errors

farcical
adj ludicrous; clumsy; absurd

fastidious
adj difficult to please

fatuous
adj idiotic

fawn
n a young deer

fealty
n loyalty

feint
n any sham, pretense, or deceptive movement

felon
n a criminal or depraved person

ferocity
n savageness

fervid
adj intense

fervor
n ardor or intensity of feeling

festive
adj merry

fidelity
n loyalty

finesse
n subtle contrivance used to gain a point

flamboyant
adj characterized by extravagance and in general by want of good taste

fledgling
n a young bird

flippant
adj having a light, pert, trifling disposition

florid
adj flushed with red

flout
v to treat with contempt

flux
n state of constant change or movement

foible
n a personal weakness or failing

foment
v to nurse to life or activity; to encourage

foppish
adj characteristic of one who is unduly devoted to dress and the niceties of manners

forbearance
n patient endurance or toleration of offenses

forfeit
v to lose possession of through failure to fulfill some obligation

forgery
n counterfeiting

formidable
adj arousing fear; inspiring awe

forswear
v to renounce upon oath

fortify
v to provide with defensive support

fortuitous
adj happening by accident or chance

fragile
 adj easily broken

frantic
 adj frenzied

fraudulent
 adj counterfeit

frigid
 adj extremely cold

frivolous
 adj trivial

frugal
 adj economical

fugacious
 adj fleeting

fulminate
 v to cause to explode

fulsome
 adj offensive from excess of praise or commendation

furtive
 adj sly or stealthy

G

gainsay
 v to contradict; to deny

gait
 n carriage of the body while walking

gallant
 adj brave or chivalrous

gamut
 n the whole range or sequence

garrulous
 adj given to constant trivial talking

germane
 adj relevant

gesticulate
 v to make gestures or motions, as in speaking, or in place of speech

glimmer
 n a faint, wavering, unsteady light

gnash
 v to grind one's teeth, usually in anger

gossamer
 adj flimsy

gourmand
 n a connoisseur in the delicacies of the table

grandiloquent
 adj speaking in or characterized by a pompous or bombastic style

gregarious
 adj sociable, outgoing

grievous
 adj creating affliction

guile
 n duplicity

gullible
 adj easily deceived or duped

gyrate
 v revolve

H

habitable
 v capable of being lived in

haggard
 adj tired or worn in appearance

halcyon
 adj calm

harangue
 n a tirade

harbinger
 n one who or that which foreruns and announces the coming of any person or thing

havoc
 n devastation

heinous
 adj odiously sinful

heresy
 n an opinion or doctrine subversive of settled beliefs or accepted principles

heterogeneous
 adj consisting of dissimilar elements or ingredients of different kinds

hillock
 n a small hill or mound

hirsute
 adj having a hairy covering

homage
 n worshipful regard for another

hoodwink
 v to deceive

hospitable
 adj disposed to treat strangers or guests with generous kindness

humanize
v to make refined or gentle

hydrous
adj watery

hypocrisy
n extreme insincerity

hypodermic
adj related to the area under the skin

I

icon
n an image or likeness

iconoclast
n an image-breaker

idiosyncrasy
n a mental quality or habit peculiar to an individual

ignoble
adj low in character or purpose

ignominious
adj shameful

illicit
adj unlawful

imbibe
v to drink

imbroglio
n a misunderstanding attended by ill feeling, perplexity, or strife

imbue
v to dye; to instill profoundly

immaculate
adj without spot or blemish

imminent
adj dangerous and close at hand

immutable
adj unchangeable

impair
v to cause to become less or worse

impassive
adj unmoved by or not exhibiting feeling

impeccable
adj having no flaws; perfect

impecunious
adj having no money

impede
v to be an obstacle or to place obstacles in the way of

imperative
adj obligatory

imperious
adj insisting on obedience

imperturbable
adj calm

impervious
adj impenetrable

impetuous
adj impulsive

impiety
n irreverence toward God

implacable
adj incapable of being pacified

implicate
v to show or prove to be involved in or concerned

implicit
adj implied

importunate
adj urgent in character, request, or demand

importune
v to harass with persistent demands or entreaties

impress
v to affect strongly

impromptu
adj anything done or said on the impulse of the moment

improvident
adj lacking foresight or thrift

impugn
v to assail with arguments, insinuations, or accusations

impute
v to attribute

inadvertent
adj accidental

inane
adj silly

incandescent
adj glowing with heat

incessant
adj unceasing

inchoate
   adj incipient

incinerate
   v to burn to ashes

incipient
   adj initial

incite
   v to rouse to a particular action

incongruous
   adj unsuitable for the time, place, or occasion

inculcate
   v to teach by frequent repetitions

indelible
   adj impossible to erase or remove; memorable

indigence
   n poverty

indigenous
   adj native

indistinct
   adj vague

indolence
   n laziness

indolent
   adj habitually inactive or idle

indomitable
   adj unconquerable

indulgent
   adj yielding to the desires or humor of oneself or those under one's care

ineffable
   adj unutterable

ineluctable
   adj impossible to avoid

inept
   adj not fit or suitable

inestimable
   adj above value

inexorable
   adj unrelenting

infallible
   adj incapable of making errors

infuse
   v to instill, introduce, or inculcate, as principles or qualities

ingenuous
   adj candid, frank, or open in character or quality

inimical
   adj adverse

innocuous
   adj harmless

inscrutable
   adj impenetrably mysterious or profound

insensible
   adj imperceptible

insinuate
   v to imply

insipid
   adj tasteless

insouciant
   adj nonchalant

insurmountable
   adj impossible to overcome

insurrection
   n the state of being in active resistance to authority

intercede
   v to mediate between persons

interdict
   n authoritative act of prohibition

interim
   n time between acts or periods

interminably
   adv all the time, endlessly

intransigent
   adj not capable of being swayed or diverted from a course

intrepid
   adj fearless and bold

intrinsic
   adj inherent

introspection
   n the act of observing and analyzing one's own thoughts and feelings

inundate
   v to fill with an overflowing abundance

inure
   v to harden or toughen by use, exercise, or exposure

invalid
   n one who is disabled by illness or injury

invective
n an utterance intended to cast censure, or reproach

inveigh
v to utter vehement censure or invective

inveterate
adj habitual

invidious
adj showing or feeling envy

invincible
adj not to be conquered, subdued, or overcome

iota
n a small or insignificant mark or part

irascible
adj prone to anger

irate
adj moved to anger

ire
n wrath

irksome
adj wearisome

irrevocable
adj impossible to retract

itinerant
adj wandering

itinerate
v to wander from place to place

J

jargon
n technical speech usually related to a profession, confusing speech

jeopardize
v to imperil or put in danger

jocular
adj inclined to joke

jovial
adj merry

judicious
adj prudent

jugular
adj related to the throat

junta
n a council or assembly that deliberates in secret upon the affairs of government

juxtapose
v to place near each other

K

kernal
n a grain or seed

kiln
n a furnace or oven for making industrial products

knavery
n deceitfulness

L

laborious
adj involving tiresome work

labyrinth
n maze

lachrymose
adj given to shedding tears

lackadaisical
adj listless

laggard
adj falling behind

languid
adj relaxed

lassitude
n lack of vitality or energy

latent
adj dormant

laudable
adj praiseworthy

laudatory
adj pertaining to, expressing, or containing praise

legacy
n a bequest

legible
adj easily readable

levee
n an embankment beside a river or stream or an arm of the sea, to prevent overflow

levity
n frivolity

lexicon
n a dictionary

libel
 n defamation

licentious
 adj wanton

lien
 n a legal claim or hold on property, as security for a debt or charge

liquify
 v to turn into a liquid

listless
 adj inattentive

lithe
 adj supple

litigious
 adj quarrelsome

loquacious
 adj talkative

lugubrious
 adj indicating sorrow, often ridiculously

luminary
 n one of the heavenly bodies as a source of light

lustrous
 adj shining

luxuriant
 adj extraordinary or excessive growth

M

magisterial
 adj having an air of authority

magnitude
 n importance

malady
 n illness

malaise
 n a condition of uneasiness or ill-being

malcontent
 n one who is dissatisfied with the existing state of affairs

malediction
 n calling down of a curse

maleficent
 adj mischievous

malevolence
 n ill will

malign
 v to speak evil of, especially to do so falsely and severely

malleable
 adj pliant

mantle
 n cloak

masquerade
 n a masked costume party

massacre
 n the unnecessary and indiscriminate killing of human beings

maudlin
 adj foolishly and tearfully affectionate

mawkish
 adj sickening or insipid

maxim
 n a principle accepted as true and acted upon

mediocre
 adj ordinary

mellifluous
 adj sweetly or smoothly flowing

mendacious
 adj untrue

mendicant
 n a beggar

meretricious
 adj alluring by false or gaudy show

mesmerize
 v to hypnotize

meticulous
 adj over-cautious

mettle
 n courage

mettlesome
 adj having courage or spirit

microcosm
 n the world or universe on a small scale

mien
 n the external appearance or manner of a person

migrant
 adj wandering

mischievous
 adj fond of tricks

miscreant
 n a villain

miser
 n a person given to saving and hoarding unduly

misnomer
 n a name wrongly or mistakenly applied

moat
 n a ditch outside a fortress wall, often filled with water

moderation
 n temperance

modicum
 n a small or token amount

modulate
 v to vary in tone, pitch, or inflection

mollify
 v to soothe

molt
 v to cast off, as hair, feathers, etc.

monomania
 n the unreasonable pursuit of one idea

morbid
 adj caused by or denoting a diseased or unsound condition of body or mind

mordant
 adj biting

moribund
 adj on the point of dying

morose
 adj gloomy

motley
 adj composed of incongruous elements

multifarious
 adj having great diversity or variety

mundane
 adj worldly, as opposed to spiritual or celestial

munificent
 adj extraordinarily generous

myriad
 n a vast indefinite number

mystification
 n the act of confusing someone else

N

nadir
 n the lowest point

natal
 adj related to birth

nauseate
 v to cause to loathe

necessitate
 v to make indispensable

nefarious
 adj wicked in the extreme

negligent
 adj likely to omit what ought to be done

neophyte
 n having the character of a beginner

noisome
 adj very offensive, particularly to the sense of smell

nomad
 adj without a permanent home

nostrum
 n any scheme or recipe of a charlatan character

noxious
 adj hurtful

nugatory
 adj having no power or force

nuptial
 adj related to marriage, especially the marriage ceremony

nutriment
 n something that nourishes

O

obdurate
 adj impassive to feelings of humanity or pity

obesity
 n excessive body weight

obfuscate
 v to darken, to obscure

obituary
 n a published notice of death

oblique
 adj slanting

obliterate
 v to cause to disappear

obsequious
 adj showing a servile readiness to fall in with the wishes or will of another

obstreperous
adj boisterous

obtrude
v to be pushed or to push oneself into undue prominence

obtrusive
adj tending to be pushed or to push oneself into undue prominence

obviate
v to clear away or provide for, as an objection or difficulty

occult
adj existing but not capable of being perceived

odious
adj hateful

odium
n a feeling of extreme repugnance, or of dislike and disgust

officious
adj meddling with what is not one's concern

ominous
adj portentous

omiscience
n infinite knowledge

onerous
adj burdensome or oppressive

onus
n a burden or responsibility

opaque
adj incapable of passing light through the surface

opportune
adj occurring at the best possible moment

opprobrium
n the state of being scornfully reproached or accused of evil

optimum
adj most favorable or advantageous

opulent
adj characterized by rich abundance, luxuriant

ossify
v to convert into bone

ostentation
n a display dictated by vanity and intended to invite applause or flattery

ostracism
n exclusion from intercourse or favor, as in society or politics

ostracize
v to exclude from public or private favor

outlandish
adj crude or uncouth

overshadow
v to make insignificant

P

pacify
v to bring into a peaceful state

pagan
n someone who worships false gods

palate
n the roof of the mouth

palatial
adj magnificent

pallor
n extreme or unnatural paleness

palpable
adj perceptible by feeling or touch

panacea
n a remedy or medicine proposed for or professing to cure all diseases

panegyric
n a formal and elaborate eulogy, written or spoken, of a person or of an act

panoply
n a full set of armor

paragon
n a model of excellence

paramount
adj of supreme authority

pariah
n a member of a degraded class, a social outcast

parlance
n a way of speaking

paroxysm
n a sudden outburst of any kind of activity

parsimonious
adj unduly sparing in the use or expenditure of money

partisan
adj characterized by or exhibiting undue or unreasoning devotion to a party

pathos
n the quality in any form of representation that arouses emotion or sympathy

paucity
n fewness

peccadillo
n a small breach of propriety or principle

pecuniary
adj related to money

pedestrian
n one who journeys on foot

pellucid
adj translucent

penchant
n a bias in favor of something

penetrable
adj capable of being pierced

penitence
n sorrow for sin

penultimate
adj next to last

penurious
adj excessively sparing in the use of money

penury
n indigence

peregrination
n a wandering

peremptory
adj precluding question or appeal

perfidy
n treachery

perforate
v to make a hole or holes

perfunctory
adj half-hearted

peripatetic
adj walking or moving about

perjury
n a solemn assertion of a falsity

permeate
v to pervade

pernicious
adj tending to kill or hurt

persiflage
n banter

perspicacity
adj acuteness or discernment

perturbation
n mental excitement or confusion

petrify
v to convert into a substance of stony hardness and character

petulant
adj displaying impatience

phlegmatic
adj not easily roused to feeling or action

phosphorescence
n the property of emitting light

physiognomy
n the external appearance merely

pious
adj religious

pique
v to excite a slight degree of anger in

pittance
n a small portion or allowance

placate
v to bring from a state of angry or hostile feeling to one of patience or friendliness

platitude
n a written or spoken statement that is flat, dull, or commonplace

plea
n an argument to obtain some desired action

plebian
adj common

plenary
adj entire

plethora
n excess, superabundance

plumb
n a weight suspended by a line to test the verticality of something

plummet
v to fall straight down; to decline suddenly and steeply

pneumatic
adj related to or consisting of air or gas

poignant
 adj severely painful or acute to the spirit

polyglot
 adj expressed in several languages

ponderous
 adj unusually weighty or forcible

portend
 v to indicate as being about to happen, especially by previous signs

portent
 n anything that indicates what is to happen

pragmatist
 n one who takes a practical approach to problems

prattle
 v to speak in a childish way

precarious
 adj perilous

precedence
 n priority in rank, place, or time

preclude
 v to prevent

precocious
 adj having the mental faculties prematurely developed

predominate
 v to be chief in importance, quantity, or degree

premature
 adj coming too soon

presage
 v to foretell

prescience
 n knowledge of events before they take place

presumption
 n that which may be logically assumed to be true until disproved

preternatural
 adj extraordinary

prevalent
 adj of wide extent or frequent occurrence

prevaricate
 v to use ambiguous or evasive language for the purpose of deceiving or diverting attention

prim
 adj stiffly proper

pristine
 adj primitive

privity
 n knowledge shared with another about a private matter

probity
 n virtue or integrity tested and confirmed

proclivity
 n a natural inclination

procrastination
 n delay

prodigal
 n someone that is wasteful or extravagant, especially in the use of money or property

prodigious
 adj immense

prolific
 adj productive

profligacy
 n shameless viciousness

profligate
 adj recklessly wasteful

profuse
 adj produced or displayed in overabundance

prolix
 adj verbose

promote
 v to advance or help establish

propensity
 n a natural inclination or tendency

propinquity
 n nearness

propitious
 adj kindly disposed

prosaic
 adj unimaginative

proscribe
 v to reject, as a teaching or a practice, with condemnation or denunciation

protuberant
 adj bulging

provident
 adj anticipating and making ready for future wants or emergencies

provincial
 adj uncultured in manners and knowledge

prudence
  n caution

published
  n prepared and issued for public distribution

puerile
  adj childish

pugnacious
  adj quarrelsome

punctilious
  adj strictly observant of the rules or forms prescribed by law or custom

pungency
  n the quality of affecting the sense of smell

pusillanimous
  adj without spirit or bravery

purloin
  v to steal

pyre
  n a heap of combustibles arranged for burning a dead body

pyromania
  n a propensity to set things on fire

Q

qualm
  n a fit of nausea

quandary
  n a puzzling predicament

querulous
  adj related to constant complaining

quibble
  n a trivial distinction or objection

quiescent
  adj being in a state of repose or inaction

quintessence
  n the most essential part

quixotic
  adj chivalrous or romantic to a ridiculous or extravagant degree

quotidian
  adj of an everyday character, ordinary

R

raconteur
  n a person skilled in telling stories

radiance
  n brilliant, sparkling luster

ramify
  v to divide or subdivide into branches or subdivisions

rapacious
  adj seized by force, avaricious

ratify
  v to approve or confirm

raucous
  adj harsh

ravenous
  adj extremely hungry

ravine
  n a deep gorge, usually caused by the flow of water

reactionary
  adj pertaining to, of the nature of, causing, or favoring reaction

rebuff
  n a peremptory or unexpected rejection of advances or approaches

recalcitrant
  adj marked by stubborn resistance

recant
  v to withdraw formally a former belief

recede
  v to back away

reciprocity
  n equal mutual rights and benefits granted and enjoyed

recluse
  n one who lives in retirement or seclusion

recondite
  adj incomprehensible to one of ordinary understanding

recrudescent
  adj becoming raw or sore again

recuperate
  v to recover

redoubtable
  adj formidable

redress
  v to set right, as a wrong by compensation or the punishment of the wrongdoer

redundant
  adj superfluous or more than is needed

refractory
adj not amenable to control

regale
v to give unusual pleasure

regicide
n the killing of a king or sovereign

reiterate
v to say or do again and again

relapse
v to suffer a return of a disease after partial recovery

remonstrate
v to present a verbal or written protest to those who have power to right or prevent a wrong

renovate
v to restore after deterioration, as a building

repast
n a meal, figuratively, any refreshment

repel
v to force or keep back in a manner, physically or mentally

repine
v to indulge in fretfulness and faultfinding

repository
n a place where goods are stored

reprisal
n an act of retaliation on an enemy

reprobate
n one abandoned to depravity and sin

repudiate
v to refuse to have anything to do with

repulsive
adj grossly offensive

requisite
adj necessary

requite
v to repay either good or evil to, as to a person

rescind
v to make void, as an act, by the enacting authority or a superior authority

resilience
n the power of springing back to a former position

resolute
adj determined, unwavering

resonance
n reinforcement of sound by sympathetic vibrations

respite
n interval of rest

restive
adj resisting control

retinue
n the group of people who accompany an important person during travels

revere
v to regard with worshipful veneration

reverent
adj humble

ribald
adj indulging in or manifesting coarse indecency or obscenity

risible
adj capable of eliciting laughter

rotund
adj round from fullness or plumpness

rue
v to regret extremely

ruffian
n a lawless or recklessly brutal fellow

ruinous
adj extremely harmful

ruminate
v to chew over again, as food previously swallowed and regurgitated

rupture
v to separate parts of something violently

S

sacrificial
adj related to an offering for forgiveness of sin

sagacious
adj able to discern and distinguish with wise perception

salacious
adj having strong sexual desires

salient
adj standing out prominently

salubrious
adj healthful, promoting health

salutary
adj beneficial

sanction
v to approve authoritatively

sanguine
adj cheerfully confident, optimistic

sardonic
adj scornfully or bitterly sarcastic

satiate
v to satisfy fully the appetite or desire of

savor
v to perceive by taste or smell

scabbard
n the sheath of a sword or similar bladed weapon

scintilla
n the faintest ray

scoundrel
n a person without principle

scribble
n hasty, careless writing

sedulous
adj persevering in effort or endeavor

senile
adj related to weakness from old age

sequence
n the order in which a number or persons, things, or events follow one another in space or time

sequester
v to cause to withdraw, especially from society or daily living

serendipitous
adj being lucky in making an unexpected discovery

severance
n separation

shrewd
adj characterized by skill at understanding and profiting by circumstances

sinecure
n any position having emoluments with few or no duties

sinuous
adj curving in and out

skeptic
n one who doubts

skiff
n a small light boat propelled by oars

sluggard
n a person habitually lazy or idle

sober
adj subdued, serious

solace
n comfort in grief, trouble, or calamity

solvent
adj having sufficient funds to pay all debts

somniferous
adj tending to produce sleep

somnolent
adj sleepy

sonorous
adj resonant

sophistry
n reasoning sound in appearance only

soporific
adj causing sleep, also, something that causes sleep

specious
adj plausible, deceptively beautiful

spurious
adj not genuine

squalid
adj having a dirty, mean, poverty-stricken appearance

stagnant
adj not flowing, especially water

stanch
v to stop the flowing of, to check

stigma
n a mark of infamy or token of disgrace attaching to a person as the result of evil-doing

stingy
adj cheap, unwilling to spend money

stolid
adj expressing no power of feeling or perceiving

stringency
n strictness

sublime
adj majestic, impressive

submerge
v to place or plunge under water

subsidize
v to assist or support with financial aid

substantial
 adj having substance, of good quality

subterfuge
 n evasion

subvert
 v to destroy completely, to overthrow

succinct
 adj concise

succumbed
 v submitted or gave up to an overwhelming desire

sumptuous
 adj rich and costly

supercilious
 adj exhibiting haughty and careless contempt

superfluous
 adj being more than is needed

supernumerary
 adj superfluous

supersede
 v to displace

supine
 adj lying on the back

supplicate
 v to beg

suppress
 v to prevent from being disclosed or punished

surcharge
 n an additional amount charged

surfeit
 v to feed to fullness or to satiety

susceptibility
 n a specific capability of feeling or emotion

swarthy
 adj having a dark complexion

sybarite
 n a luxurious person

sycophant
 n a servile flatterer, especially of those in authority or influence

synopsis
 n a syllabus or summary

T

tacit
 adj understood

taciturn
 adj disinclined to conversation

tangible
 adj capable of being perceived by touch

taut
 adj stretched tight

teemed
 v abounded, swarmed

temerity
 n foolhardy disregard of danger, recklessness

tempestuous
 adj tumultuous, stormy

tenuous
 adj slender, flimsy

terse
 adj pithy

timorous
 adj lacking courage

tolerable
 adj modestly good

tolerant
 adj indulgent

torpid
 adj dull, sluggish, inactive

torrid
 adj excessively hot

tortuous
 adj abounding in irregular bends or turns

tractable
 adj easily led or controlled

tranquil
 adj calm or free from anxiety or tension

transgress
 v to break a law

transient
 n one who or that which is only of temporary existence

transitory
 adj existing for a short time only

transmute
 v to change the form or substance of something

travail
 n hard or agonizing labor

travesty
 n a grotesque imitation

trenchant
adj cutting deeply and quickly

trepidation
n nervous uncertainty of feeling

trite
adj made commonplace by frequent repetition

truculence
n ferocity

truculent
adj having the character or the spirit of a savage

tumescent
adj somewhat swollen

turbid
adj in a state of turmoil, muddled

turgid
adj swollen

turpitude
n depravity

tutelage
n the act of training or the state of being under instruction

tyranny
n absolute power unjustly administered

tyro
n one slightly skilled in or acquainted with any trade or profession

U

ubiquitous
adj being present everywhere

ulterior
adj not so pertinent as something else to the matter spoken of

ultimatum
n a final proposal of terms or conditions

umbrage
n a sense of injury

unctuous
adj oily

undermine
v to subvert in an underhanded way

undulate
v to move like a wave or in waves

untoward
adj causing annoyance or hindrance

upbraid
v to reproach as deserving blame

usury
n the lending of money at excessive interest rates

utmost
adj the greatest possible extent

utter
adj complete, absolute, entire

V

vacate
v to leave

vacillating
v swaying from one side to another

vagary
n a sudden desire or action

vagrant
n an idle wanderer

vainglory
n excessive, pretentious, and demonstrative vanity

valid
adj based on truth

valorous
adj courageous

vapid
adj having lost sparkling quality and flavor

variegated
adj having marks or patches of different colors, varied

vehement
adj very eager or urgent

venal
adj mercenary, corrupt

veneer
n outside show or elegance

venerable
adj commanding respect by virtue of age or position

venial
adj capable of being pardoned or forgiven, a forgivable sin

veracious
adj habitually disposed to speak the truth

veracity
n truthfulness

verbiage
  n use of many words without necessity

verbose
  adj wordy

verdant
  adj green with vegetation

veritable
  adj real, true, genuine

vestige
  n a visible trace, mark, or impression, of something absent, lost, or gone

vicissitude
  n a change, especially a complete change, of condition or circumstances, as of fortune

vigilant
  adj being on the alert to discover and ward off danger or ensure safety

virago
  n loud talkative woman, strong woman

virile
  adj masculine

visage
  n the face, countenance, or look of a person

vitiate
  v to contaminate

vituperate
  v to overwhelm with wordy abuse

vivify
  v to imbue with life

vociferous
  adj making a loud outcry

volatile
  adj changeable

voluble
  adj having great fluency in speaking

vulnerable
  adj capable of receiving injuries

W

waif
  n a homeless wanderer, especially a child

wean
  v to transform the young from dependence on mother's milk to another type of nourishment

whimsical
  adj capricious

whine
  v to utter in a complaining tone

winsome
  adj attractive

wizen
  v to cause to dry or wither

woefully
  adv sadly or deplorably

wrangle
  v to maintain by noisy argument

wreak
  v to inflict a punishment

wrest
  v to pull or force away, especially violent twisting

writhe
  v to twist the face, body, or limbs

Y

yammer
  v to complain persistently

yearn
  v to have a since desire for something

yelp
  n a shrill cry or bark

yokel
  n a simple country person

yore
  n time long past

Z

zealot
  n a person who excessively promotes a cause

zeitgeist
  n the intellectual and moral tendencies that characterize any age or epoch

zenith
  n the high point of prosperity or authority

zephyr
  n a gentle breeze

zoological
  adj having to do with animals